Seduction

Seduction

Men, Masculinity and Mediated Intimacy

RACHEL O'NEILL

polity

First published in 2018 by Polity Press

Polity Press
65 Bridge Street
Cambridge CB2 1UR, UK

Polity Press
101 Station Landing
Suite 300
Medford, MA 02155, USA

ISBN-13: 978-1-5095-2155-5
ISBN-13: 978-1-5095-2156-2 (pb)

A catalogue record for this book is available from the British Library.

Library of Congress Cataloging-in-Publication Data

Names: O'Neill, Rachel, author.
Title: Seduction : men, masculinity, and mediated intimacy / Rachel O'Neill.
Description: Medford, MA : Polity, 2018. | Includes bibliographical
  references and index. |
Identifiers: LCCN 2017050360 (print) | LCCN 2017061782 (ebook) | ISBN
  9781509521593 (Epub) | ISBN 9781509521555 (hardback) | ISBN 9781509521562
  (paperback)
Subjects: LCSH: Sex. | Flirting. | Masculinity. | Feminism. | BISAC: SOCIAL
  SCIENCE / Media Studies.
Classification: LCC HQ21 (ebook) | LCC HQ21 .O58 2018 (print) | DDC
  306.73--dc23
LC record available at https://lccn.loc.gov/2017050360

Typeset in 11.25/13 Dante by Servis Filmsetting Limited, Stockport, Cheshire
Printed and bound in the UK by CPI Group (UK) Ltd, Croydon

For further information on Polity, visit our website:politybooks.com

Contents

Acknowledgements

Thanks first and foremost to Rosalind Gill, who has supported the project from its earliest stages. Her dedication as an advisor is nothing short of extraordinary, and I am privileged to benefit from her intellectual generosity and scholarly acumen. As well as being a trusted mentor, she is a dear friend.

Funding for this research was provided by the King's College London Graduate School. Sara De Benedictis and Simidele Dosekun were steadfast companions in the protracted endeavour that is completing a PhD. I have discussed many of the ideas elaborated in this book with them at length, and both have read and commented on individual chapters at various stages of development. The wider community of gender and cultural studies scholars at King's sustained and enhanced my work. Thanks to Ana Sofia Elias, Bridget Conor, Christina Scharff, Hannah Hamad, Laura Harvey, Laura Speers, Natalie Wreyford and Toby Bennett.

Diane Negra and Andrea Cornwall were generous examiners, providing insightful commentary on the arguments presented in my thesis and stoking my ambitions for this book with their praise. Diane has an uncanny ability to recommend readings that give definite shape to ideas I am merely grasping at.

Living in London for the past decade has afforded many pleasures, not least of which has been the opportunity to participate in a variety of feminist collectivities. Jo Littler is owed thanks for organising more than her fair share of events, providing a space for discussion and debate that is always illuminating. Meg-John Barker deserves special mention for their work with the Critical Sexology network, a crucial forum for examining contemporary currents in sexual culture and imagining ways to relate otherwise. Pam Alldred, Róisín Ryan-Flood and Sumi Madhok each invited me to discuss my research with their students, whose insightful questions and perceptive observations have sharpened my thinking.

Alison Winch and Jamie Hakim have become valued interlocutors on all things mediated intimacy. I am particularly grateful to Jamie for gamely agreeing to spend three days together in the south of France. The conversations we had while walking around the city and meandering through galleries fortified my resolve as I began drafting the conclusion to this book. Long-distance as well as face-to-face discussions with Frank Karioris, Gareth Terry, Michael Flood and Sam de Boise have renewed my faith in the intellectual and political project of men and masculinity studies.

The Department of Sociology at the University of York has proved an exceptional environment in which to complete this book and also begin a new project. Nik Brown, who I imagine doesn't much like to think of himself as a line manager, has performed the role with aplomb. Dave Beer has championed my work at every opportunity, offering encouragement as well as intellectual sustenance through his sheer love of ideas. Kasia Narkowicz welcomed me immediately and became a fast friend. Xiaodong Lin has often gone out of his way to brighten my day. Joanna Latimer, Maggie O'Neill, Sarah Nettleton and Victoria Robinson all model the kind of feminist collegiality I aspire to, producing brilliant scholarship while conducting themselves with grace, candour and no small amount of humour. Clare Bielby has made the commute altogether more enjoyable.

The team at Polity have been an absolute pleasure to work with – my thanks to Ellen MacDonald-Kramer, Emma Longstaff, Mary Savigar and Rachel Moore. Thanks also to Caroline Richmond for her meticulous copy-editing.

My mother Janet is a continual inspiration to me, both for her immense personal fortitude and unwavering commitment to fighting injustice on many fronts. I am deeply appreciative of the close relationship we share. My father Michael has contributed to my intellectual development and academic career in innumerable ways, making profound sacrifices so that I would be free of the constraints that patterned his own life. The knowledge that he would support and be proud of me no matter what route I took ensured I could carve my own path. Each of my siblings, in their own way, inspires and motivates my work. I am especially grateful to my eldest sister Kate for the innumerable hours we have spent discussing the vagaries of gender, intimacy and sexuality.

London friends – Anne, Eric, Jon, Isaac, Natasha, Melissa, Sam – have provided welcome respite from work with food, drink, dancing and games. I relish the fact that, while some of you are also academics, this is largely incidental to our relationships. The absence of Farah – who died too young, when she was filled with life – is the cause of unbearable sadness. Occasionally her image flashes up before me, appearing momentarily in the gestures and expressions of a stranger who bears some passing resemblance to her, and my heart bursts for all that was and all that would have been.

It seems impossible to adequately express the love and gratitude I feel for my partner Chris, friend, lover, comrade. The scrawling notes he provided on each and every draft of each and every chapter of this book and the thesis that went before it were both entertaining and insightful, challenging me to nuance my thinking while at the same time affirming my most deeply held convictions. For this, and much more, I am so very grateful to you.

I am forever indebted to all those who participated in this project. I can only hope that this book does justice to the complex realities of your lives and experiences.

This book draws from and expands on material previously published in the following places: 'The work of seduction: intimacy and subjectivity in the London "seduction community"', *Sociological Research Online* 20/4 (2015); 'The aesthetics of sexual discontent: notes from the London "seduction community"', in *Aesthetic Labour: Beauty Politics in Neoliberalism*, ed. Ana Sofia Elias, Rosalind Gill and Christina Scharff, London: Palgrave Macmillan (2016), pp. 333–49; and 'Homosociality and heterosex: patterns of intimacy and relationality among men in the London "seduction community"', in *Masculinities under Neoliberalism*, ed. Andrea Cornwall, Frank G. Karioris and Nancy Lindisfarne, London: Zed Books (2016), pp 261–76.

Introduction

Standing at the front of a nondescript conference room in a hotel in central London, one of the lead trainers welcomes everyone to the event. After passing out some complementary notepads and pens, he introduces himself and describes how he became involved in the seduction industry. Aged twenty-one, he found himself single for the first time in his adult life, having been in a relationship with the same woman since he was a teenager. He was working long hours in an office job and becoming increasingly frustrated with the monotony of his daily routine. On top of this, most of his friends from home were now at university, so he had no one to go out with at the weekends. In short, he explained: 'I found myself in a situation where I didn't really know what to do.' It was then that, quite by chance, he saw a documentary about pickup on TV. He spent the next morning looking for information online and by lunchtime had signed up for a bootcamp the following weekend. Recalling the experience while pointing to a chair in the front row, he says: 'I sat right there. I didn't know anything about pickup, I didn't know the terminology, I didn't know who was teaching – I just wanted to learn to get women.'

A few hours later we set out for the first in-field session. It's a particularly busy weekend and the streets are crowded, despite the heavy rain. On the pavement outside the hotel each trainer is assigned two students. We peel off into groups and walk towards Covent Garden. Once we reach the market, the trainer I'm shadowing waves his hand around vaguely and says: 'If you see something, please go.' He is distracted, looking at his phone continually, and after twenty minutes spent walking around aimlessly the students begin to look doubtful. Eventually the trainer puts his phone away and leads his students down to the market's sunken courtyard, where he tells them to approach two women sitting outside a café. After a few minutes of stilted conversation, the women begin gathering their things. Seeing this, the trainer walks towards the group – smiling widely, his arms outstretched – as though rejoining friends. Soon the women are laughing and chatting amiably with the trainer. He leaves a few minutes later – evidently trying to give the students another chance – but the women depart shortly after he does. Nevertheless, the two men bound back towards us and flank the trainer on either side as we cross the courtyard, marvelling at his easy demeanour and cool confidence.

Later that afternoon, a different trainer sets up a flip chart at the front of the room for a session on conversation skills. Commenting on the downpour we've just escaped from, he jokes that Fifty Shades of Grey *is responsible for 'the wettest summer on record'. Almost as an afterthought, he turns and asks if anyone has read the book. Faced with a sea of blank expressions, he says: 'Right. Write this down.* Fifty Shades of Grey. *It's an erotic novel. It's what girls will be talking about, and it also allows you to introduce sexual themes very quickly.' The trainer begins writing on the flip chart, assuring students as he does so that developing conversation skills is not about memorising routines: 'I'm not going to tell you what to say. I'm going to tell you topics you can talk about and a way you can talk about them. Your own content should be exactly that – your own content.' The students scribble in their notepads as the lesson gets under way, attempting to commit to paper the diagrams the trainer somewhat haphazardly produces as visual aids. A key takeaway is the importance of listening, with the trainer explaining that women's most common complaint about men is that they don't listen. This, he says, is a missed opportunity: 'Girls will tell you everything you need to seduce them.'*

After a quick meal in a dimly lit Mexican restaurant, the bootcamp cohort arrives en masse at a club near Regent Street for the night-game session. The trainer in charge stations himself near the doorway of the club: from here, he can commandeer trainers as they shepherd students between the pulsing environs of the dance floor and the cool reprieve of the smoking area. I join him there, and for the next two hours we maintain this post, receiving occasional updates on milestones achieved. When this trainer leaves to make a phone call – one of the trainers scheduled to teach tomorrow has cancelled, and now a replacement has to be found – another sidles towards me. Earlier that evening, over dinner, he had been loudly complaining about how tired he was. With an exaggerated yawn, he leans toward me now and says: 'I didn't get any sleep last night.' Still I refuse to take the bait. He leans closer again, and I can feel his breath on my face as he grins lasciviously and says: 'The energy of eighteen-year-olds is just incredible.'

The next morning, back in the conference room, I sit towards the back and look over my notes. There's a jocular atmosphere as the students arrive, exchanging stories about the night before. The session begins with a trainer asking everyone how they're feeling now that they've completed the first half of the course. One student jumps to his feet, eager to respond. He explains that, while he was initially sceptical – to the point of suspecting the course might even be a scam, a remark that earns him a sarcastic 'Thanks!' from the trainer – it had already exceeded his expectations: 'I didn't think any of this would work. But by the end of the day, I was like, fuck, this works. This really works. I was just amazed. It's just like, my God, this is the Holy Grail.' A whoop goes up from the audience and soon everyone is cheering and clapping. As we go around the room so that each student can share his experience, I notice that a few are missing. They turn up later in the afternoon, looking rumpled and sleepless. One tells me he was out until 3 a.m. with a trainer who took him to the VIP lounge of a high-end nightclub. 'It was crazy,' he says. 'He was just picking out the girls.'

The above notes recall scenes from the first seduction 'bootcamp' I attended. During the year-long ethnographic study on which this book is based, I went to many more training events like this one, spending weekends moving between conference rooms and nightclubs, going to seminars held on university campuses and in pub basements, observing one-to-one coaching sessions that traversed parks, cafés, shopping centres, train stations. I interviewed many of the people I met during my fieldwork, ranging from those who were new to the practice through to others who had spent years honing their skills and teaching them to other men. I undertook extensive media analysis, examining the mass of autobiographical books and blogs as well as instructional videos that promise to guide men through their interactions with women. Throughout this process, my central concern has been to understand what makes seduction so compelling for those drawn to participate in this sphere. What leads men to seek out this particular form of expertise? What motivates them to read up on the topic, join forums and take courses, often at considerable expense? What is it that they hope to realise or achieve?

While seduction has a long and variegated history, within the cultural formation known as the 'seduction community' it refers to a very particular set of knowledge-practices organised around the belief that the ability to meet and attract women is a skill heterosexual men can cultivate through practical training and personal development. Though many of its key tenets are informed by or drawn from fields such as business management and evolutionary psychology, those who establish themselves as experts in this sphere lay claim to a distinct form of expertise variously denoted as 'seduction', 'pickup' or 'game'. Having originally taken shape in the 1990s in the United States, this cultural formation now manifests in urban centres across the world, from Stockholm to Mumbai, from Sydney to Shanghai, from Houston to Tel Aviv. Though the language of 'community' persists, it is a decidedly commercial enterprise, a kind of community-industry hybrid. Likewise, while those involved in this sphere often refer to themselves and are elsewhere referred to as 'pickup artists', or 'PUAs', there is a good deal of ambivalence around these terms – for reasons that will become clear below – such that many seek, at least nominally, to distance themselves from them.

The spectacle of seduction

The seduction community has been an object of media fascination for over a decade. When it first came to public attention in the anglophone world in the mid-2000s, many news publications deployed intrepid male journalists to discover this clandestine world by attending seduction seminars and other events, on which they duly reported in mildly disapproving yet begrudgingly admiring tones. An array of documentaries soon followed: Channel 4's *The Rules of Seduction* (2007) tapped into cultural anxieties about masculinity in 'crisis' and explored issues of social isolation among men, while more recently Amazon's *Attract Any Woman Anywhere* (2017) invoked a familiar 'battle of the sexes' narrative, emphasising the manipulative tactics deployed by both women and men in contemporary dating culture. Long before these features, the documentarian Louis Theroux interviewed the self-proclaimed 'godfather of the seduction community' Ross Jeffries as part of his *Weird Weekends* series (2000), which set out 'to discover the genuinely odd in the most ordinary setting'.

The figure of the serial seducer has been subject to numerous portrayals on the silver screen, some of which acknowledge the existence of a wider community-industry, while others obscure this by focusing on individual womanisers. In an early forerunner, Robert Downey Junior plays Casanova to Molly Ringwald in brat-pack rom-com *The Pick-Up Artist* (1987), using a tightly scripted deck of lines and routines. Later, the ensemble film *Magnolia* (1999) sees Tom Cruise as the maniacal Frank T. J. Mackey preaching his particularly noxious brand of seduction – 'Respect the cock, tame the cunt' – to large audiences in packed-out convention centres. Subsequent Hollywood incarnations offered more sympathetic readings, framing seduction coaching as an almost benevolent enterprise whereby certified studs help 'nerds' and 'losers' meet women. In *Hitch* (2005), the eponymous 'date doctor' – played by the famously congenial Will Smith – coaches a select group of eminently well-intentioned clients while refusing to work with those who seek to prey on women. In the box-office smash *Crazy, Stupid, Love* (2011), the newly minted male feminist icon Ryan Gosling plays charming Jacob, who helps the hapless Cal (Steve Carrell) sleep with a bevy of women after Cal's wife leaves him. Jacob's motivation is not financial – no money appears to change hands and he is not shown teaching other men. Rather, he takes pity on Cal, who reminds him of his own once similarly emasculated and now sadly deceased father.

Staked as it is around the promise of personal transformation, the system of expertise elaborated within the seduction industry proved readily adaptable to the dramatic conventions of reality television. Leading the trend, Vh1's *The Pickup Artist* (2007–8), saw a predictably 'geeky' cohort of participants placed under the tutelage of skilled seducers and put through a series of increasingly outlandish challenges. The format introduced large audiences to a colourful cast of real-life industry personalities, some of whom became minor celebrities and were subsequently wheeled out for tabloid talk shows such as *Dr Phil* (2008) and *Tyra Banks* (2009). Elsewhere, the journalist turned seduction guru Neil Strauss attempted to seduce the actress Jessica Alba on *Jimmy Kimmel Live!* (2005). The nomenclature of seduction has seeped into other popular entertainment forums, with stock characters in shows such as *How I Met Your Mother* (2005–14) and *The Big Bang Theory* (2007–) dabbling in seduction theory in order to parlay their friendships with women into sexual encounters. Seduction logics are also more subtly manifest in shows such as Aziz Ansari's *Master of None* (2015–), where Dev employs a highly formulaic approach to online dating and uses the same open-ended message to start conversations with every woman in whom he is interested.

In a darker turn, the 'White Christmas' (2014) episode of the speculative fiction series *Black Mirror* sees Jon Hamm – famed for his portrayal of the advertising executive Don Draper in the acclaimed series *Mad Men* (2007–15) – as a once highly skilled seduction coach now consigned to a remote outpost. Through a series of flashbacks, we learn that Hamm's character, Matt, used to teach other men how to meet and sleep with women using the augmented reality device 'Z-Eye', which allowed him to see through their eyes while providing verbal instruction via a two-way voice communication system. One night, hunched over a laptop in his home office, Matt remotely guides a student named Harry as he gate-crashes a Christmas office party, eventually going home with a woman he meets there – much to the excitement of the group of men following the proceedings via a live-streaming 'watcher's club'. However, Harry's would-be conquest has misunderstood why he appears to be talking to himself. Believing that, like her, he wants to kill himself, she poisons them both in a gruesome murder-suicide. Seeing this, Matt immediately disconnects and attempts to destroy the evidence of what he has been doing, only to wake his sleeping wife, who uses the Z-Eye to 'block' him from her life entirely. By the end of the episode, Matt has been registered as a sex offender and 'blocked' by all, meaning that he will never again be able to communicate with anyone.

Promising men 'mastery' with women, the seduction industry has unsurprisingly attracted a good deal of feminist commentary and criticism, much of it stemming from the transnational but US-dominated feminist blogosphere. The American feminist news and lifestyle site *Jezebel* has long reported on the seduction industry: it has examined the underlying assumptions and possible implications of the techniques promoted here and catalogued the exploits of key figures within the industry. Other high-traffic feminist websites such as *xoJane* and *Feministing*, as well as aggregator sites such as *Buzzfeed*, routinely feature articles on seduction; many of these are highly critical, with titles such as 'Do pickup artist techniques lead to sexual assault?' (North 2012) and 'Are pickup artists contributing to rape culture?' (Smith 2012). Elsewhere, the writer David Futrelle (2017) maintains a website dedicated to tracking what he terms 'the new misogyny' elaborated online via the 'manosphere', a conglomeration within which he includes PUAs alongside MRAs (Men's Rights Activists) and MGTOWs (Men Going Their Own Way). Some feminists have taken a more equivocal stance towards seduction, with the blogger Clarisse Thorn exploring the industry and incorporating some of the advice administered here into her own 'sex-positive' feminism in *Confessions of a Pickup Artist Chaser* (2012). Elsewhere, the pro-feminist site *The Good Men Project* has run articles criticising some of the more obviously egregious elements of seduction while seeking to retain many of its core themes under the auspices of 'ethical pickup' (O'Malley 2014).

Public debate over and attention to the seduction industry reached new heights in November 2014, when a series of campaigns were launched to ban the seduction instructor Julien Blanc – an employee of the American company Real Social Dynamics (RSD) – from countries including Brazil, Canada, Germany, Japan and Singapore, where he had been scheduled to lead training events as part of a world tour. Blanc drew particular criticism for the sexist and racist content of his teachings, which appeared to endorse sexual violence as a seduction tactic and to advocate a kind of sexual neo-imperialism. In a video on his *YouTube* channel – entitled 'White male fucks Asian women in Tokyo (and the beautiful methods to it)' – Blanc boasted about roaming the city streets and grabbing women in order to force their heads towards his groin. On Twitter, he posted an image of the 'Power and Control Wheel' commonly used in domestic violence intervention programmes to help women identify abusive behaviours, captioning this with the statement 'May as well be a checklist . . . #HowToMakeHerStay'.

What began with a Twitter hashtag started by an Asian-American woman named Jennifer Li, #TakeDownJulienBlanc, quickly developed into a loosely coordinated global initiative. In the UK, a petition calling on the then home secretary, Theresa May, to deny Blanc a visa quickly attracted widespread public support and extraordinary levels of media attention. Politicians from across the political spectrum lined up to denounce Blanc publicly and lobby May to exercise 'sensible border control' (quoted in Watt and Mason 2014). Articles and opinion pieces discussing the controversy appeared in the *Daily Mail, The Telegraph, The Independent,* and the *New Statesman.* On Saturday 15 November, the story made the front page of *The Guardian,* which printed a large image of Blanc accompanied by the headline 'The pickup artist. Should he be banned from Britain?'. A few days later, it was announced that Blanc's visa application had been rejected by the Home Office. As multiple news outlets reported at the time, it was the first known instance of a person being denied entry to the UK on the grounds of sexism. Within a matter of weeks, Blanc had become a figure of international opprobrium, encapsulated in the *Time* magazine headline 'Is this the most hated man in the world?' (Gibson 2014).

Though the media event that engulfed Blanc was unprecedented in terms of the level of scrutiny he attracted, it continued a well-established pattern whereby the deviance of pickup artists was affirmed and reified. In doing so, this cultural figure – temporarily embodied by Blanc – became knowable as an individuated problem that could be safely contained through recourse to state intervention. Blanc himself was subject to a variety of armchair diagnoses which saw him branded as a narcissist and sociopath. Commentary about the kinds of men who attend his and other seduction events also proliferated, much of it simultaneously derisive and dismissive. Hadley Freeman, a prominent feminist voice in the UK, penned an article detailing her encounters with men employing seduction tactics and counselling: 'Women, beware this PUA army of sleazebags, saddos, and weirdos' (2014).

This book complicates the narrative through which those who participate in the seduction community have become sedimented in the public imaginary as by turns pathetic, pathological or perverse. It does so by locating this community-industry firmly within the broader cultural moment of which it is part and interrogating the economic, social and political arrangements that animate this moment. It is a specifically feminist analysis, one that is critical of the seduction industry but which resists the temptation to isolate this formation from wider cultural currents. Rather than pointing the finger and apportioning blame, or resorting to mockery and ridicule, I want to move towards a more difficult conversation which recognises the seduction industry not as a *deviation* or *departure* from current social conventions but as an *extension* and *acceleration* of existing cultural norms.

This, then, is a study that refuses to partake in spectacle and insists instead on taking the seduction community seriously – without assuming that this means accepting it on its own terms. It charts one among the myriad ways in which the twin rationalities of neoliberalism and postfeminism are remaking every aspect of contemporary life, including its most intimate dimensions.

Researching the seduction industry in London

London represents a major hub within the transnational seduction industry and a popular destination for seduction training in Europe. The industry has had a presence in Britain for at least ten years, with the first UK-based training company, PUA Training, established in 2007 by Richard La Ruina. Today, a panoply of private companies as well as independent trainers offer fee-based seduction training services that include one-to-one coaching, weekend 'bootcamp' courses and live-in 'residential' programmes, the cost of which ranges from several hundred to thousands of pounds. Blogs and online forums provide spaces for men to document their activities, discuss techniques and give advice to one another. Those with established profiles as trainers often host channels on social media sites such as *YouTube*, where their videos can garner hundreds of thousands or even millions of views. The industry has developed its own dedicated lexicon, comprising a range of jargon terms and acronyms which serve to designate various conceptual premises and technical manoeuvres. Where these words appear in this book, they are placed in inverted commas to designate their origins within the industry. Though in many cases their meaning is readily apparent, explanations are provided where necessary.

Aside from the small number of company headquarters registered to private apartments in the city centre – where trainers often live together and host clients – the seduction industry is spatially and temporally discontinuous. Adhering in no fixed place, it instead continually consolidates and disaggregates in the capital's streets, cafés, bars and nightclubs. Nevertheless, its urban geography is well known to those who participate in this sphere, running down Tottenham Court Road via Oxford Street and Bond Street, taking in Soho, Piccadilly Circus, Leicester Square and Covent Garden. The Strand and the South Bank are also popular haunts on account of the many public spaces and tourist attractions in these areas, while Knightsbridge and Kensington represent more upmarket destinations. Seduction seminars regularly take place on London university premises, their central locations making these venues practical while additionally lending the industry academic gravitas.

Participating in the seduction industry can be a costly undertaking, with a weekend 'bootcamp' at an established company currently retailing for anywhere between £500 and £900. Week-long live-in 'residential' programmes can cost £3,000 to £5,000. Instructors working with private clients on a one-to-one basis generally charge upwards of £100 per hour, with some commanding considerably more than this. Commercially, it is a highly competitive industry, with low barriers to entry and minimal over-heads. While the tabloid press occasionally run articles exclaiming over the vast sums of money made by coaches (Spencer 2016) and estimates elsewhere suggest it is a $100 million industry (Samra 2017), many of those I spoke to presented seduction training as a precarious enterprise. One trainer explained: 'It's a lot of smoke and mirrors. These companies might look big, even things like Venusian Arts, RSD, Daygame, PUA Training – but I know all of those guys, and they're all kind of run in people's bed-rooms.' Publicly available financial records seem to corroborate this, with many UK-based seduction training companies operating at a relatively low turnover, at least on declared earnings.

Because of the costs involved, participation at live events in London is concentrated among middle-class men with professional occupations such as teaching, engineering, business and finance. The majority are in their twenties and thirties, though some are considerably older. While most of those involved in the industry are white, typically comprising between half and three-quarters of participants at events I attended, this is generally considered unremarkable and goes unremarked upon. By contrast, it is the relative overrepresentation of British Asian men vis-à-vis the general population that most often draws commentary, a discourse informed by the positioning of South Asian British men as either effeminate or hypermasculine (Kalra 2009) alongside the coding of British Muslim men as sexually predacious (Tufall 2015). Meanwhile, white seduction trainers routinely appropriate aspects of rap and hip-hop culture to bolster their own masculine repertoire, variously fashioning themselves as 'hustlers', 'players' and 'pimps' in displays of what Nancy Leong (2013) terms 'racial capitalism'.[1]

Gaining access to the seduction industry in London as a researcher proved difficult. Many established companies as well as freelance trainers ignored or refused my requests for meetings. Some of those I met with vetted me extensively, asking about my research questions, intended methods and publication plans. Some offered conditional access on terms to which I could not agree, such as the trainer who said he would allow me to observe his teaching only if he could use any recordings I produced for commercial purposes. The difficulties involved in researching the seduction industry stem, in part, from its taciturn character. Those with a commercial stake in the industry are often wary of receiving negative publicity but know also that publicity of any kind is likely to bring them new students and increase revenue. The difficulties I faced were also partially related to my positioning as a woman, which marked me out not simply as an outsider but also as a potential target. As one trainer put it to me: 'They're trying to get you. So they can't let you see what they're going to get you with, you know?' At the same time, it was often suggested that, as a woman, I could use myself as a kind of bait to source participants, as when the same trainer later said: 'You just need to go to Tiger Tiger [a nightclub] on a Saturday night and they'll come and talk to you.' I discuss how such dynamics shaped my experience of researching the seduction community at length in the Postscript: Power and Politics in Feminist Fieldwork.

In the end, the bulk of my fieldwork was enabled by a small number of individuals whose approval not only granted me access to the spaces they administered but also provided inroads to those overseen by their friends, colleagues and business associates. I attended a number of bootcamp programmes, where teams of trainers teach groups of students how to choreograph their interactions with women through a combination of seminar presentations, live demonstrations and practical exercises. I also sat in on individual training sessions and attended a variety of talks, meet-ups and promotional events. Observing these proceedings proved crucial to understanding the discursive patternings, relational dynamics and affective rhythms that animate the seduction industry. In some cases, I was additionally provided with access to company training materials and student profiles, information which further enhanced my understanding of the industry's pedagogic remit and client base. While undertaking fieldwork I was very often able to make detailed notes in situ, my own jottings rendered inconspicuous by virtue of the fact that many of those around me were also writing. Where this was not possible, I recorded key words and phrases, later using these to write up more extensive reports. By the end of my fieldwork, I had filled four 200-page diaries with hand-written notes, extracts of which appear throughout this book.

Through my fieldwork I recruited a total of thirty-two interview participants, the majority of whom I met with individually in the identikit environs of the coffee-shop chains that populate central London. Where, in a small number of cases, distances involved did not allow us to meet in person, interviews were held over the phone or by Skype. In almost all instances, I had already met and spent time with participants and was able to talk to them about events we had both attended, the people we had met there, and so forth. When recruiting participants I sought to include a broad cross-section of those involved in the London seduction community, from bootcamp students and private coaching clients, freelance trainers and company employees, event managers and CEOs. Though the majority of these participants were men – reflecting the overwhelmingly gendered composition of the industry – I also interviewed a small number of women who work in the industry, whose gendered exceptionality is continually highlighted by themselves and others via their designation as 'female trainers' and 'wing girls'. Short biographical notes for all participants, each of whom has been given a pseudonym, are in the Appendices. Collated demographic information – encompassing age, education, occupation, 'race' and ethnicity, disability and mental health – is also included. On average, interviews lasted two hours, though some went as long as four or five. Some participants were, at their own request, interviewed on a second occasion. Others kept in touch via email, periodically sending me updates about their activities as well as links to or copies of materials they felt would be relevant to the research. Once compiled for analysis, transcripts totalled almost 600,000 words, or just over seven times the length of this book.

Long before beginning my fieldwork I kept tabs on the huge array of media produced by this industry, and I have continued to do so since completing it. For the past eight years I have subscribed to the mailing lists of a number of British and American seduction training companies and have received an average of fifteen to twenty promotional emails per week, the continual flow of which has allowed me to stay apace of new products and decipher industry trends. I have amassed a virtual library of seduction texts, read innumerable blog posts and forum discussions, and watched countless hours of video content, all of which provide insight into what it is the industry markets to men. I have given special attention to autobiographical books and blogs where trainers document their own personal transformation, gesturing to a past in which they were lonely and unpopular while showcasing a present in which they enjoy near constant access to beautiful women as part of a more generally enviable lifestyle of world travel, financial independence and male camaraderie. Examining these texts provides insight not only into the working lives of these men but also into the psychic investments of those who look to them as masculine exemplars, and for whom these texts function variously as blueprints for living, fantastic escapism, sexualised entertainment and erotic kindling.

I have followed English-language reporting on the seduction industry the world over and compiled what now amounts to hundreds of news articles from countries including the UK, the US, Australia, China, France, Germany, India and Israel.

Instructional videos posted on sites such as *YouTube* represent an especially important media source, as many participants cited these videos as their primary mode of engagement with seduction expertise. To this end, I have followed the *YouTube* channels of a number of key figures within the industry over the duration of the project, watching the videos they produce and reading the discussion threads these generate. By far the most popular genre is the 'in-field' video, whereby trainers covertly film their interactions with women and later add 'how-to' commentary via voice-overs or explanatory subtitles. Indeed, in recent years in-field footage has become such an important marker of expertise that now any trainer who does not offer this kind of content is liable to find their legitimacy called into question. Richard La Ruina, for example, one of the few British seduction trainers without a public playbook or commercial catalogue of in-field videos, routinely faces demands for evidence of his expertise in below-the-line comments on his *YouTube* channel.[2]

In analysing the various materials this research produced, my process was both inductive and recursive, with lines of enquiry developed by reading across interview transcripts to examine common patterns and then putting these into dialogue with fieldwork observations and media analyses. Consistent with feminist poststructuralist approaches, analysis was orientated towards 'understanding the cultural conditions of possibility for being in the world' (Gavey 2011: 186). Thus, in addressing the question of why involvement in the seduction industry is compelling to many men, I train attention not only towards psychological processes and interpersonal dynamics but to the relationship between culture and subjectivity at a more fundamental level. To this end, it is important to state that, while I am interested in how claims to expertise are made – a theme taken up at greatest length in chapter 3 – this book does not attempt to address the commonly asked question of whether or not seduction techniques actually 'work'. Research of this kind, utilising surveys and psychological measures, is available elsewhere (Hall and Canterberry 2011). Neither do I attempt to inventory the full range of seduction methods available or provide an organisational history of the industry. Instead, the focus throughout is on how this cultural formation variously reflects, reproduces and reanimates broader social patterns.

In the dedicated Postscript at the end of this book, I discuss my experiences undertaking this research at some length. However, it is worth flagging two interrelated methodological issues regarding my research practice from the outset. First, in researching the seduction community I did not take up the knowledge-practices elaborated in this sphere by approaching strangers and attempting to convert these encounters into further meetings or relationships. Elsewhere, the British artist Alex Brew has done precisely this, spending a week meeting men using techniques outlined in a popular seduction handbook for a project entitled 'femme-takingliberties' (2011). Of this experience, she writes:

> Attempting to perform the ways of interacting described in the book was depressing in some ways and led to incredibly surprising and human interactions in others. For a start, I was originally going to follow the suggestion of 100 approaches in a day but it was too much. That's gruelling. You can't be human at all approaching that many people in a day. You're bringing the capitalist productivity model into your personal life. Maybe I'll try it some time but it's a horrible prospect. Then there's the problem that you can't really just be open to a person. You have to stay in control of your game. Everything is about your performance, your pick-up . . . I felt a bit of a dishonest shit at times. (Brew 2011)

Yet, while I did not apply myself to the hard graft of seduction, over time I nevertheless took on aspects of the seduction mindset. Even without realising what I was doing, while observing training sessions I found myself scanning crowds in much the way trainers do, observing interactions with the same appraising eye, calculating odds on eventual outcomes. However, I also maintained a different perspective from trainers and students, one more closely attuned to the variety of repertoires women use to negotiate unwanted advances in public settings.

Second, in researching this community-industry I have been unable to address directly women's experiences of being 'seduced'. While to do so would clearly throw up a host of ethical as well as practical questions, the decision not to seek out women's voices has been a continual source of concern for me as a feminist researcher. After all, women have long been positioned as the proper 'object' of feminist study, such that projects without women at their centre are liable to have their feminist credentials called into question (Wiegman 2001). And yet, while creating knowledge about women's lives and experiences is undoubtedly an important goal of feminist research, 'if our concern is to understand women's oppression we need to target our attention on the ways it is structured and reproduced . . . Studying women's lives as a feminist means that male dominance, masculinity and men are always part of the research' (Kelly et al. 1994: 33). Women's experiences of seduction have, however, been examined elsewhere in the work of the American artist Angela Washko. After reading a series of seduction handbooks produced by the infamous US-based pickup artist Roosh V – whose titles include *Bang* ([2007] 2010), *Bang Ukraine* (2012) and *Don't Bang Denmark* (2011) – Washko decided to curate an online project called *Banged*. She posted a series of calls asking women who had slept with Roosh V to be interviewed, stating: 'If you have been with this man, he has made a very public assessment of you but hasn't given you a voice . . . I can promise you anonymity, respect, and an opportunity to critique the experience. There is plenty out there online about this guy's sexual conquests . . . but nothing about [women's] experiences' (Washko 2015). The project later expanded to include women who have had encounters with any man using seduction techniques, the result of which is an archive of stories by turns comical, exasperating, unnerving, enraging and devastating.

Seduction as mediated intimacy

This book approaches the seduction community as a site of 'mediated intimacy', a concept originating in the work of the social and cultural theorist Rosalind Gill. In a study of women's magazines (2009), Gill examines how the sex and relationship advice these texts provide frames intimate subjectivity as a site of labour. Her analysis identifies a series of representational patterns or discursive repertoires. The first of these is 'intimate entrepreneurship', whereby sex and relationships are to be meticulously planned for, continually evaluated and actively managed. Second, these texts elaborate a kind of 'men-ology', explaining what men are like and giving women detailed instruction in how to please and appease them. Third is what Gill terms 'transforming the self', as women are called upon to remodel how they think and feel about their bodies, desires, sexual practices and relationships. Taken together, these repertoires exhort women to *work* on their sexual selves and *invest* in an intimate skill set: 'to self-monitor and monitor others, to work on and transform the intimate self, to regulate every aspect of their conduct, and to present every action – however constrained or normatively demanded – as the outcome of individual choice and a deliberative personal biography' (Gill 2009: 366).

More recent work undertaken by Gill in collaboration with Meg-John Barker and Laura Harvey argues that intimate life is shaped by a large variety of media, far beyond texts that are explicitly advice-orientated:

'we live in a world *suffused and saturated with representations of intimate relationships*; our understandings about love and sex are not bounded by advice that announces itself with "how-to" guides' (Barker et al. 2018: 24). Thus even media that are not of an obviously instructive character set out certain expectations, producing collective – though contested – conventions about what is normal and desirable in sexual and intimate relationships. Moreover, advisory discourses originating in the self-help genre percolate through a range of other media, such that each informs and inflects the other. To give but one example of this, the book (Behrendt and Tuccillo 2004) and, later, the film (2009) *He's Just Not That into You* – which, as the title suggests, purports to decipher men's otherwise unfathomable romantic cues for women liable to read them in an overly positive light – was inspired by an episode of *Sex and the City* (2003), where Carrie's new boyfriend gives Miranda insight into what is presented as a universal and immutable male psychology.

To talk about intimacy as *mediated*, then, is to talk about how intimate life is patterned by media representations which churn all around us and cycle through our lives. Narrating and aestheticising the interpersonal dynamics of attraction and desire, sex and romance, lust and love, media provide unspoken guidelines for the organisation of feeling. And, while intimacy is always mediated in some sense – most obviously through language but also through affect, bodies, technologies (Attwood et al. 2017) – media have become a key source of knowledge and information about sex and relationships, not least as the influence of religious dictum and other traditional forms of authority wane (Plummer 1995). Directed by commercial imperatives, the most widely consumed forms of media exploit readily recognisable and easily consumable tropes, thereby reproducing highly conventional ideas about what relationships should look and feel like. Popular media distils and dramatises the 'regulatory fictions' (Butler [1990] 2011) of gender and sexuality, providing 'supplied states of being' (Lorde 1984) which we are encouraged to align ourselves with and measure ourselves against. Even if, as individuals, we were never to read a sex advice column or consult a relationship self-help book, the ideas promoted here nevertheless seep into our lives and shape everyday forms of being and relating. Media provide the backdrop against which we understand and articulate our desires. Ideas borrowed from the media inform how we feel about a one-night stand or marriage proposal. Their iconography enters into the very moment at which a relationship is consolidated or breaks down. Idealised imagery sets a yardstick against which actually existing relationships are evaluated. While the social arrangements produced as a result of these continual interchanges are certainly not determined by media representations, our intimate lives are nevertheless indelibly impressed by and patterned with their influences.

Through its emphasis on the dynamic interplay between culture and subjectivity, the concept of mediated intimacy directs attention towards the shaping of intimate life by wider cultural rationalities, most especially those of neoliberalism and postfeminism. While as an economic system neoliberalism is centred around minimising welfare provision, privatising public assets and maximising corporate profits (Harvey 2005), it necessarily gives rise to particular modes of sociality and subjectivity (Gilbert 2013; Hall 2011). As a mode of governance, neoliberalism 'normatively constructs and interpellates individuals as entrepreneurial actors in every sphere of life' (Brown 2005: 42). While foregrounding the market, it is 'not only or even primarily focussed on the economy' but, rather, involves 'extending and disseminating market values to all institutions and social action, even as the market itself remains a distinctive player' (ibid.: 39–40). Closely related to neoliberalism, postfeminism describes a social landscape or cultural sensibility wherein feminism is both 'taken into account' and 'undone' (McRobbie 2009). Elements of feminism are incorporated into social and political life, such that the wide variety of movements coalescing under this banner are deemed unnecessary. Postfeminism 'positively draws on and invokes feminism as that which can be taken into account, to suggest that equality has been achieved, in order to install a whole repertoire of new meanings which emphasise that it is no longer needed, it is a spent force' (ibid.: 12). By co-opting the language of feminism, postfeminism converts 'empowerment' and 'choice' into consumer activities that substitute for political engagement and collective action. Where women are constructed as the 'beneficiaries' of social change, any remaining inequality can be understood only through a grammar of individualism. Thus 'postfeminism proclaims for gender what neoliberalism advocates in a broader sense: both assert that the individual bears ultimate responsibility for their social status' (Negra and Tasker 2013: 348).

In approaching the seduction community as a site of mediated intimacy, I want to push against interpretations offered elsewhere, which characterise this formation as either a subculture (Baker 2013) or a self-help movement (Hendriks 2012). Though it has some of the trappings of a subculture – the jargon, the secrecy – it is nowhere near as bounded or alternative as this framework implies. Similarly, while it is suffused with logics of self-betterment and individual uplift, to label the seduction industry as a self-help movement fails to address the specifically *gendered* and *sexual* character of the system of expertise enumerated here, the result of which is that issues of power and inequality are downplayed or disregarded altogether. In addition, both these framings overlook the financial interests at play in this so-called community, the very language of which lends it a sense of authenticity and inclusivity that is commercially beneficial.

In the main, however, recognising the seduction community as a site of mediated intimacy means attending to the ways in which the form of expertise elaborated here is not *distinct from* but, rather, *continuous with* much sex and relationship advice administered elsewhere. To this end, it is worth noting that those who work in the seduction industry routinely contribute columns to, write features for, and are profiled by major magazines such as *Cosmopolitan* and *Men's Health*. Many additionally dispense advice to large audiences via popular online sites such as *AskMen*, where they rebrand themselves as 'dating experts' and 'lifestyle coaches'. The industry borrows from and is informed by many of the same knowledge formations that undergird heterosexual sex and relationship advice more generally, most particularly that of evolutionary psychology, a major purveyor of the 'two sexes, two cultures' paradigm (Potts 1998) and one that has come to enjoy outsized authority amid a more general 'psychologisation' of everyday life (Rose 1998). Principles and techniques elaborated in the seduction community frequently manifest elsewhere, such that 'negging' – a much discussed seduction tactic that involves making negative statements about someone so as to undermine their confidence – has been inaugurated by journalists as a 'dating trend' (Bradshaw 2012; Woolf 2012). Because the seduction community is so widely dispersed and disaggregated, its logics find many ways of entering into heterosexual intimacies.

In pursuing an analysis of the seduction community as a site of mediated intimacy, I also hope to extend the concept's theoretical purchase in three ways. First, through ethnographic research I seek to go beyond a concern with textual representations in order to examine how mediated intimacy is lived and experienced. To this end, I examine how men take up and try on the advice elaborated in this setting, adopting certain seduction axioms while bypassing others. At the same time, and recognising the ways in which media technologies have entered into the relational fabric of intimate life, I consider how men in this setting use media to work on their sexual selves. The arguments developed in this book thus work with the notion of 'mediated' while de-centring 'media'.

Relatedly, and this is my second theoretical concern, in utilising the language of mediated intimacy I want to think about how that which *goes* between *gets* between. This line of enquiry is born of a recognition that sex and relationship advice frequently corrals us to inhabit categories to which we have been assigned rather than chosen, and to follow scripts we have inherited rather than authored. We are told, in a whole variety of ways, that by occupying these categories and taking up these scripts we are aligning ourselves with happiness (Ahmed 2010b). And yet this is not to say that happiness is what we will get by adhering to prevailing wisdom or newfangled expertise. Thus, while in general usage 'mediate' refers to the process whereby things are brought together – in the sense of arbitrate, liaise, conciliate – one of the ambitions of this book is to use the term to think about interceptions and impediments. Indeed, the Latin root 'mediatus' – which means 'placed in the middle' – directs us to explore precisely this predicament, whereby that which promises to enable intimacy may actually serve to occlude it.

Third, and most substantially, this book centres questions of men and masculinity. While the majority of sex and relationship advice is implicitly or explicitly directed towards heterosexual women – a trend reflected in existing analyses – the system of expertise enumerated in the seduction industry is overwhelmingly produced by and for heterosexual men. Recognising it as a site of mediated intimacy prompts a consideration of how neoliberalism shapes the intimate subjectivities of men, while also demanding attention be paid to the ways in which men navigate the terrain of postfeminism in the context of their intimate relationships. These issues have been largely overlooked in existing scholarship within feminist cultural studies and sociological masculinity studies.

To begin with, where masculinities scholars attend to the workings of neoliberalism, it is generally with an understanding of neoliberalism as an economic programme rather than a cultural rationality. As a result, we have a good deal of research on what might be thought of as the henchmen of neoliberalism – corporate managers and finance executives (Connell and Wood 2005; Griffin 2013) – but rather less on those who may be called upon to model themselves on the version of masculinity these men propagate. Indeed, scholarship that engages this kind of analysis is often more likely to be found beyond the conventional purview of masculinity studies, in areas such as anthropology (Cornwall et al. 2016) and cultural analysis (Gilroy 2013), both of which I engage with.[3] Informed by the interventions by poststructuralist scholars in masculinity studies (Cornwall and Lindisfarne 1994; Frosh et al. 2001; Wetherell and Edley 1999), and deliberately bypassing entrenched debates about hegemonic masculinity (Beasley 2008; Connell and Messerschmidt 2005; Messerschmidt 2012), I am concerned to examine how neoliberal rationalities centred on management and entrepreneurship shape the intimate subjectivities of heterosexual men. In doing so, I am interested less in arguing that neoliberal capitalism is fashioning a new hegemonic variant of masculinity than in examining how the logics of neoliberalism get under men's skin.

In relation to postfeminism, scholarship in this area overwhelmingly privileges subjects that are middle class (Ringrose and Walkerdine 2008), white (Butler 2013) and Western (Dosekun 2015), all of whom are almost invariably *women*. As well as foreclosing a consideration of the ways in which postfeminism addresses working-class women and women of colour and circulates in contexts far beyond the US and the UK, this has meant that men are almost wholly overlooked in discussions of postfeminism, save for the work of film and media studies scholars on 'postfeminist masculinities' (Gwynne and Muller 2013; Hamad 2014; Negra and Tasker 2013). In an illuminating comment that points to possible reasons for this oversight, Angela McRobbie argues that the reluctance among many feminist scholars to deal in the language of 'patriarchy' and 'male power' has resulted in an 'empty space of antagonism to male dominance' (2015: 17). On the other side of this equation, scholarship on postfeminism has been all but ignored within masculinity studies, an inattention that reflects a more general failure to keep pace with contemporary currents in feminist scholarship (Beasley 2013) and that has given rise to variants of masculinities theorising which all but dispense with questions of sexual politics (O'Neill 2015, 2016a). Addressing the 'feminist theory deficit' in masculinity studies (Berggren 2014), and taking up the 'man question' left outstanding in feminist scholarship on postfeminism (Howe 2012), I consider how men are located within and seek to negotiate this terrain. Recognising postfeminism as a site for the retrenchment of gender inequality, I interrogate the role men play in this and examine how intimate life becomes a proxy through which to address social grievances.

Though the seduction industry has long been an object of spectacle and its participants the subject of sensationalist media portraiture, the men represented in this book are very ordinary. If their desires and discontents strike us as being anomalous or aberrant, then we need to look much more closely at the context in which they have been formed. This book does so by centring the question of why seduction – as a system of expertise, collection of knowledge-practices and homosocial sphere – is compelling for many heterosexual men at this particular conjuncture. It argues for a conception of the seduction industry not as a discrete subculture or self-help movement but as a site of mediated intimacy, intricately connected with the broader media churn that privileges certain patterns of being and relating while foreclosing others. It engages the analysis of masculinity, but without mobilising this as an explanatory device, as though there were no wider context to the formation of masculine subjectivities and the organisation of men's practices. To develop this mode of analysis is not to abnegate critique – far from it – but is instead to insist on the necessity of asking difficult questions and having uncomfortable conversations. It is only too easy to condemn singular figures and caricature those who follow them, but politically this strategy does not take us very far. Examining the seduction industry as the product of a wider reorganisation of intimate life – one in which we are all implicated – is at once a much more complicated, and much more urgent, endeavour.

1

The Work of Seduction

I arrive at Oxford Circus a little before the appointed 12 p.m. meeting time. By ten past, all the students and trainers are there, and together we set off to a nearby café for a briefing session. I fall into step with the lead instructor, who jokes that, by the end of the weekend, I'll have learned enough about seduction not to fall prey to it myself. He goes on to muse that perhaps all women should attend a course like this 'for their own self-defence'. When we arrive at the café, he is greeted by two men sitting at a corner table. He walks over to where they are sitting, shakes each of them by the hand, and asks what they're doing here. Having themselves taken the bootcamp just a few months previously, the pair have come to London for the day to hone their skills and have arranged a double date that night with women they met on their last excursion. Wishing them good luck, the lead instructor rejoins the present bootcamp cohort where they have gathered, coffees in hand, at another table towards the back of the café.

After each student has introduced himself, the lead instructor goes over the schedule for the weekend and asks if everyone has studied the online course to which they have been given access ahead of the bootcamp. He spends a few minutes summarising the key principles and core techniques students will be learning, reminding them to 'give girls that movie moment'. Satisfied that they have a basic understanding of the central tenets they will spend the rest of the weekend refining, another trainer pulls out a backpack and spills its contents on the table. A tangle of wires lie in front of us, and he explains that each student will wear a small hidden microphone throughout the weekend so that their interactions with women can be more closely evaluated. Once everyone has been fitted out, we leave the café, the instructor saying: 'Try to do five before lunch.'

Later that afternoon, I stand with two trainers outside the flagship Topshop store at Oxford Circus while waiting for the bootcamp collective to assemble again. One points towards the enormous billboard that towers over us and tells the other that he had approached the model on the street a few days previously. I look up at the image. The woman is white, young and slim. She leans against a worn-out dresser, her long blonde hair falling over her shoulders, the scarlet dress she is wearing slit to the thigh. She is everything advertising tells women to be – and has the billboard in central London to prove it. The other trainer scarcely glances up before pronouncing: 'She's not that hot.' The first trainer seems taken aback by this response, but only for a moment. Quickly recovering his composure, he nods in agreement and says: 'She's not great and definitely not as good in real life.'

In *Undoing the Demos*, the political theorist Wendy Brown (2015) examines how the relentless economisation of social life taking place over the past four decades in the US has fundamentally undermined the country's social institutions. Brown is clear in arguing that, while it involves the market, economisation is not the same as or reducible to commercialisation or commodification. Rather, 'neoliberal rationality disseminates the model of the market to all domains and activities – even where money is not at issue – and configures human beings exhaustively as market actors, always, only, and everywhere as *homo oeconomicus*' (Brown 2015: 31). While Brown is concerned primarily with institutions such as government and education, she makes some suggestive comments about how neoliberal rationalities might enter into and repattern intimate relationships, for example noting that, within neoliberal contexts, 'one might approach one's dating life in the mode of an entrepreneur or investor', attempting to maximise 'return on investment of affect, not only time and money' (ibid.).

This chapter examines how logics of management and enterprise organ-ise the intimate subjectivities of men who participate in the seduction community. I discuss how those involved in this sphere attempt to 'sort out' their intimate lives by approaching their relationships with women in much the same way as they do other endeavours such as work or study. I examine how men spoke about their past relationships and attempt to make sense of the pervasive dissatisfaction which patterned these narra-tives. I also look at how an aspirational ethos shapes the embodied impulses of desire, as female beauty is held up as an index of masculine worth. I argue that the entrepreneurial logic that characterises men's engagements with seduction generally is literalised among professional seducers or career pickup artists – those who make a living in the seduction industry – for whom the accumulation of sexual experience functions as a means not only to acquire masculine status but to generate economic capital. I conclude by examining practices of sexual self-branding – whereby trainers document their intimate lives and open these out for public consumption – demonstrating that, within the seduction community, already tenuous distinctions between life and work under neoliberalism are decidedly collapsed.

Cultivating a sexual work ethic

In 2012 the erotic novel *Fifty Shades of Grey* (James 2012) created a transnational phenomenon, with 70 million copies sold worldwide. The book centres on the relationship between a young woman graduate and a powerful male business magnate – the eponymous Grey – and was considered notable for its BDSM themes and imagery. Accounting for the book's tremendous popularity, Eva Illouz (2014) argues that though conventionally viewed as a romantic fantasy, *Fifty Shades* is better understood as a kind of self-help text. She describes the threefold movement charted by the book's main narrative, which 'encodes the aporias of heterosexual relationships, offers a fantasy for overcoming these aporias, and functions as a self-help sexual manual' (ibid.: 30). Outlining the broader cultural trajectory of which *Fifty Shades* is part, Illouz cites the best-sellers *Men are from Mars, Women are from Venus* (Gray 1992) and *The Rules* (Fein and Schneider 1995) as forerunners. For Illouz, each of these texts has achieved wide cultural resonance because it taps into collective anxieties and shared preoccupations about sex and relationships, while framing these in an explanatory way by providing instruction in the successful management of intimate life (Illouz 2014: 23).

Published in the interim between these titles is Neil Strauss's *The Game* (2005), an autobiographical self-help guide in which the author chronicles his engagements with the then burgeoning seduction community in the United States and his eventual transformation into a full-fledged pickup artist. Strauss introduces himself by cataloguing his physical shortcomings and underlining his undesirability:

> I am far from attractive. My nose is too large for my face and, while not hooked, has a bump in the ridge. Though I am not bald, to say that my hair is thinning would be an understatement . . . I am shorter than I'd like and so skinny that I look malnourished to most people, no matter how much I eat. When I look down at my pale, slouched body, I wonder why any woman would want to embrace it. So, for me, meeting girls takes work. (2005: 4)

Over the course of 500 pages, Strauss details his rise within the seduction community and regales readers with a seemingly countless number of sexual exploits. The book predictably culminates, two years later, with Strauss becoming involved in a relationship with a woman who does not easily submit to his cultivated charms, but who eventually comes to love him for who he really is. After this, he supposedly leaves seduction behind, claiming: 'To win the game is to leave it' (2005: 473).[1]

The Game topped the *New York Times* best-seller list for two months in 2005, and it remains a best-seller across a range of categories on sites such as Amazon more than a decade after its initial publication. Yet where the relational programmatics proscribed by books such as *Mars and Venus*, *The Rules* and *Fifty Shades of Grey* are more or less explicitly addressed to heterosexual women, the advice elaborated in *The Game* is unambiguously directed towards heterosexual men. Within the seduction community, *The Game* functions as a kind of Urtext. Virtually everyone I spoke to had read or was at least familiar with the book, and many men referenced the text as a means to explain or make sense of their own engagement with the industry. Describing why he had first begun attending seduction training events some months previously, Ali said:

> Well, I guess it's an area of my life that I've never felt like I really . . . handled that well. I feel like I did well academically and creatively, and I've always been fine socially, but when it comes to the relationship side of things I feel like I'm never – I guess, similar to what Neil Strauss says in *The Game*, he felt like – I think he says he felt like that was an area of his life that he never really felt he had any control over. And I feel like . . . I feel the same. I never had much control. I was always waiting for something to happen, or stuff was acting upon me. And this kind of seems like a way to gain control in that area of my life.

As a popular best-seller that has amassed a large general readership – the UK paperback edition boasting endorsements from *GQ*, *The Guardian* and *Elle* magazine – *The Game* provides a form of social recognition for heterosexual men who feel they lack control and agency in their intimate lives. At the same time, it serves to legitimate discursively and reproduce performatively the perception that men *should* exercise control in their relationships with women and premises that this can be achieved by utilising the knowledge-practices elaborated therein. In this way, *The Game* follows the same threefold movement as *Fifty Shades* and other best-selling sexual self-help guides: it stages the aporias of heterosexual relations by demonstrating the author's inability to attract women, provides a symbolic resolution to this by showcasing his transformation into a successful seducer, and offers readers a compendium of practical resources with which to manage their own intimate lives as Strauss exhaustively details the tactics and techniques he employed over hundreds of sexual encounters.

For many of the men I spoke with and interviewed, discovering seduction as a distinct system of expertise – often through reading *The Game*, but also through encounters with the wide range of seduction guides, TV programmes, DVD series and online materials that have since become available – was accompanied by profound feelings of relief and reassurance. When we met, Moe was attending his second seduction bootcamp, having flown to the UK from Sweden to take the two-day course with a London-based company. He described the sense of optimism that taking these courses had inspired in him: 'It actually gave me a feeling that there is hope, I can do something about this. I can change, really. It's not only for those who . . . it's nothing you're born with – you can learn it, you can change.' Similarly, Ali explained how he felt after attending a seduction seminar:

> Probably more a sense of . . . I think calmness almost. I feel like I'm working towards something, so things . . . I will get better. And there's like a peace that I know as long as I keep doing this I will have this area of my life sorted. It just feels better, in a way, knowing that you can do something. And there's . . . it's like another skill.

Statements such as these readily illustrate the strong affective dynamics that engagement with this community-industry can generate among men who feel they lack control in their intimate lives. The particular form of expertise on offer here contravenes the pervasive assumption that success with women and dating is a matter of inheritance or good fortune. Instead, sexual and intimate relationality is understood as a skill or competency that can be cultivated through practical training and personal development. Seduction thus enjoins heterosexual men to cultivate a 'sexual work ethic', whereupon 'the domain of intimate relationships is treated as analogous to the domain of employment' (Rogers 2005: 186).

Where an equivalency is drawn between the world of work and the world of sex, the competencies required to run a successful business can be deemed analogous to those necessary to become successful with women. When I asked Ryan, whom I had met at a weekend seduction training programme, how he had decided to take the course, he described having shopped around online comparing various options. He decided to enrol on this particular course after being impressed by the sales technique of the trainer featured in the company's promotional video: 'I thought, well, this guy can definitely sell. So if he can sell me the product, I think he is good with girls also. And I thought, I can learn from him. Because of the way he talked, very confident. If he can convince me, then he probably can convince girls.' Competency in negotiating sexual relationships is thus assumed to be synonymous with business prowess, as Ryan reasons that, if a trainer can convince him to pay £700 for a weekend course, he can probably also convince women to sleep with him. At the same time, Ryan implicitly positions himself as more discerning in his consumer choices than women are in their sexual choices, supposing that it is likely to be easier for the trainer to entice women into bed than it is for him to entice men such as Ryan onto a costly seduction training programme. Notably, heterosexual sex is understood as a matter of inducement: just as the salesman persuades customers to buy his products, so the seducer convinces women to sleep with him.

The framing of intimate relationality as a skill that can be honed and developed draws on and redeploys the logic of meritocracy, which in its current iteration works to marketise the idea of equality by combining an essentialised notion of talent with a belief in social mobility (Littler 2013). Adam, a trainer who has worked in the seduction industry for a number of years, explained: 'I think what game does, it kind of gives power back to those who are not the biggest, strongest, most athletic. It's a set of skills that can actually be learnt by different people, which makes it quite accessible to all.' Through an appeal to equal opportunities – the contention that these skills are available to everyone – it is premised that any man can achieve greater control in his relationships with women, provided he is willing to make the necessary effort to do so. As a configuration of sexual practice, seduction channels the meritocratic feeling of neoliberal culture at large by facilitating an ethos of competitive individualism within the domain of intimate relationships. There is, however, a kind of compulsion embedded within this promise of control, as those who take up these knowledge-practices become wholly responsible for the relative success or failure of their sexual relationships. This sense of responsibility functioned as a constant exhortation to work more and try harder; as Antonio related: 'If you don't do anything, nothing happens. As with everything in life, if you don't work, if you don't . . . you're just responsible for your own luck, that's it.' Similarly, Emmanuel described: 'How I see it now is you're responsible for yourself. You're responsible for where you're going in life.' While appealing to equality, the ultimate effect of meritocracy is to resecure hierarchy and inequality. After all, meritocracy 'endorses a competitive, linear, hierarchical system in which by definition people must be left behind. The top cannot exist without the bottom. Not everyone can "rise"' (Littler 2013: 54).

Anxious attachments

Inevitably, not all of those who seek out the forms of expertise made available within the seduction community actually realise the kinds of sexual relationships to which they aspire. Yet, although a number of participants admitted that investment in seduction training had not enabled them to realise their intimate ambitions, this was almost invariably framed as their own personal failing. Indeed, this was the case even when use of seduction techniques had resolutely negative implications for their relationships with women. Anwar described losing a much valued relationship some weeks after attending a pickup training course: 'She just said I'd changed and she said that she didn't know me anymore. And I think the fact that I – I mean, I have really deep feelings on this, in the sense that, I mean, she was the reason I took the course, because I wanted her. She was the only thing I really cared about.' When I asked Anwar how this made him feel about seduction training, he said:

> I'm mad and angry. But not at pickup, I'm angry at me. Because it's my fault. I mean, it's not game's fault, okay? It's not game's fault, it's my fault. If I'd done . . . because I . . . as I said, it's a bit like you give me a set of tools and if I didn't know how to use those tools properly, I'm going to make a mistake. So it's not game's fault. It's my fault for not having the skills and using them properly. And so, I'm not bitter, for game. It's my fault.

Having undertaken a weekend bootcamp with the sole intention of using the skills he would learn there to further this relationship, Anwar's change of demeanour following the course – hastened by trainers who encouraged him to become more commanding and less agreeable, saying he was too much of a 'nice guy' – quickly brought the relationship to an end. As he himself said: 'It's because of PUA she's gone.' Unwilling to criticise the efficacy of seduction knowledge-practices, Anwar insistently blames himself for being unable to master the 'tools' seduction provides. In doing so, he accedes to the prevailing cultural mandate wherein the 'neoliberal subject is required to bear full responsibility for their life biography' (Gill 2008a: 436). And yet it is only by locating the fault with himself that Anwar is able to sustain the fantasy that seduction will eventually, and with sufficient effort on his part, enable him to realise the kind relationship he desires. His attachment to seduction can thus be seen as a form of 'cruel optimism', a relation in which 'something you desire is actually an obstacle to your flourishing' such that 'the object that draws your attachment actively impedes the aim that brought you to it initially' (Berlant 2011: 1).

While a number of those I interviewed reported not yet having realised the benefits seduction promises in their personal lives – though they expected to do so in the future – many claimed that undertaking seduction training had yielded dividends in their professional lives. Such claims were made irrespective of the kind of employment participants held, with university students, school teachers, scientists, financial consultants, engineers and bankers all reporting that engagement with these knowledge-practices had accorded them various advantages in the workplace or when seeking employment. In our interview I asked Ravi, who works as a researcher, whether or not he had experienced any changes in his life since undertaking seduction training. In response he told me:

> In my professional life I have drastically and visibly seen the difference. Because now I'm more confident presenting something in front of an audience – before I was not. I can talk more confidently, more decisively, with my manager, with my boss. Before I was not like that. So these are some of the visible changes I got. I explicitly owe it to game, this side of things.

Noting that he had neglected to mention anything about dating or relationships, I asked Ravi if he had seen any changes in his interactions with women. He explained: 'The other side I have still to work on many things. But I'm seeing the results, so I know if I put more hard work into it, if I'm more determined, then down the line I'll definitely get results on the sexual part, the actual pickup part of it.' Impressing that what is needed is greater dedication and further investment, Ravi demonstrates how, by reimagining success with women along entrepreneurial and meritocratic lines, the seduction industry gainfully exploits the neoliberal fantasy that 'anything can be achieved if the correct disposition has been adopted' (Gilroy 2013: 26).

The work-centric modes of sociality and subjectivity made available within neoliberalism are entirely naturalised within the seduction industry, such that the idea that undertaking a seduction training programme would confer professional benefits was almost wholly unremarkable to participants. Despite the negative implications that the training had for his personal life, Anwar continued to believe that this could be of enormous professional value: 'It's clearly geared towards sex, okay, but the skills are transferable . . . It's about social interaction, understanding and connecting with people. I mean, that's worth the money on its own. As a business man, I would pay to put my people on that course.' Elsewhere, Derek described how the skills he had gained through seduction training enabled him to beat out candidates with more prestigious educational qualifications when interviewing for a high-profile job. He recalled being momentarily disheartened when, upon arriving for the interview, he discovered that he was the only candidate not to have attended either Oxford or Cambridge: 'I'm just like, "I've got nothing on these guys." But I do. I've got everything on them. Because they may be very smart, but can they string a few words together? Not really.'

For Derek, the skills he has acquired through seduction training afford him a form of cultural capital equivalent to or, indeed, greater than that of an elite Oxbridge education, commonly regarded as the express route to power in British society. However, when he later mentioned that it was a woman who conducted the interview, another set of relational dynamics came into focus: 'I'm in this interview, with a *woman*, and I'm thinking to myself, "You're nothing on the shit I've been through this week. You're literally nothing."' It was not simply Derek's enhanced communication skills that enabled him to outperform other candidates but, rather, his ability psychologically to resist the gendered power dynamics of the interview situation, where a woman held authority over him as a potential employer. That Derek achieved this by ascribing a position of powerlessness to the woman interviewing him demonstrates that seduction training provides men with more than just 'soft skills' with which to sharpen their advantage in the supposedly feminised world of white-collar labour. Rather, skilful interaction with women itself becomes a means to triumph professionally, a dynamic also described by Tiantian Zheng in a study of Chinese hostess clubs: 'Women became a testing ground for male entrepreneurial ability. In this competitive world, it was the skill of men in charming women and keeping them under control that came to define their success' (2009: 10).

The framing of intimate relationality as a competency to be acquired can lock those who seek to realise this skill set into a pattern of perpetual training. In describing their engagement with seduction, participants often invoked exercise as a metaphor, explaining that practising seduction is akin to going to the gym: in order to build muscle tone, it is necessary to work out on a regular basis, as the well-muscled body requires constant conditioning simply to retain its existing state. Many men described concerns about losing the skills they had already acquired. For Elijah, this was such a serious concern that it led him continually to sabotage and eventually end a six-month relationship with a woman he cared for a great deal. Despite these strong feelings, throughout the relationship he constantly worried that his seduction skills were deteriorating and, in order to prevent this from happening, was often unfaithful. Elijah broke up with his girlfriend after a friend told him he was losing his edge, a conversation he recounted as follows: 'He was like, "You're slowing down man, what happened to you?" And I was like, "I don't know, it's this girl man." He was like, "You have to break up with her." I said, "I know, man, but I like her, she's so perfect." Then I was like, fuck, I have to choose. It took me like a month, then I just broke it up.' For Elijah the necessity of this choice was clear: 'I decided to break up with her because I wanted to keep my game.'

While anxieties about losing seduction skills were commonplace, the kind of compulsive quality this can engender was most acutely illustrated by Derek, who had been practising seduction for just over a year when we met. In our interview he explained how this engagement had changed over that time:

> The whole thing is with this, I've constantly been trying to fix some problem that is only ever replaced by another problem – you know what I mean, like? These sorts of things are just constant. You know, like, you get better at one thing, and then something else isn't quite right. And, yeah, so it's – it's quite hard. Now, I'm just like . . . I was out last night, and I'm just walking around the streets at, like, I don't know, at like eleven o'clock at night, on my own, and I'm just like, 'What the fuck am I doing out here?' Just asking myself, genuinely, 'What are you doing out here now?' And I'm just, like, 'I don't know.' It started out with some real motivation, desire to be good at this, but now it's almost fear of losing this ability. Like, I go out and slog – even though I know I can get . . . it doesn't faze me in the slightest. You can pick out any girl, and I'll be over there, in a heartbeat, I'll be over there. And I know that I've got a very good chance of getting her number, going out on a date with her and sleeping with her – that's not an issue. But, it's a case of . . . I don't know, like, sometimes *I don't want to*, you know, *I just don't want to*, but I'm still out here. Like, to be honest, like, today, I didn't really feel like it, but I was like, 'Fuck it', you know, 'You've gotta do this, cause if you don't, you could be back to where you were.' And, like, it happens, trust me, it happens. It doesn't matter how good you are – if you stop doing it, you will go back.

For Derek, the need to maintain the skill set he has worked so hard to develop – having undertaken multiple training courses at a cost of several thousand pounds – has become an end in and of itself, such that the act of seducing women has become entirely dissociated from any kind of embodied desire for sex or intimacy.

Derek's fixation exemplifies the unhappy hallmarks of the entrepreneurial subject who is continually in progress and never complete. In this he exhibits symptoms of what Mark Fisher terms 'depressive hedonia'; noting that depression is usually characterised by anhedonia, an inability to experience pleasure, Fisher describes depressive hedonia as 'an inability to do anything except pursue pleasure' (2009: 22). As an affective and somatic condition, depressive hedonia is produced by or symptomatic of the profound insecurity neoliberalism fosters across a range of sites, including sexual and intimate relations. The supreme irony in Derek's case is that, while seduction training has apparently enabled him to exercise greater control in his relationships with women – he claims probable odds on sleeping with any woman he approaches – he now finds himself locked into an obsessive cycle of trying to maintain this skill set by sleeping with women in the absence of any desire to do so.

Through these kinds of anxious attachments, the promise of control which seduction extends to men can bind those who become involved in the industry to this system of expertise in insidious ways. Trainers in the industry are all too familiar with this dynamic, having often fallen prey to it themselves. Jack described cautioning the men he coaches by saying: 'Know when you're going to leave the game. Know when you're going to get out of it. It's very important to be able to do. Come in, learn the skills, find out your goal, reach your goal, get out.' For Adam, however, this was not such a clear-cut issue, as he described the self-perpetuating dynamic the industry sets up through its promises of mastery with women: 'It's an industry that feeds itself. The more people are exposed to it, the more people want it.' Later he elaborated on this point:

> It's almost seen as like a sport: you improve your game. There's no – what's the end of that? So it sets up something which is destined to fail in many ways. If your friends are fellow pickup artists, and all you talk about is the girls that you've gone out and slept with and the things you're doing sexually, and every time you see a girl you know you can go and speak to her – there's no end. And the thing is those challenges – that rush that you get – normalises. And what happens when something normalises? You have to then take bigger and bigger leaps. Things have to become more and more drastic. So people, you know, get addicted to approach and they get addicted to going out and doing it. I'll have people say, you know, 'I've slept with a hundred women', but I'll go, 'Yes, but a hundred women have also left you.' That's the reality of it. Game is a very good patch, but it's not a solution. It's like a fad diet, I suppose. Yes, it's very good for a short term, but you can't live like that.

The expertise made available within the seduction community is compelling to many men because it appears to acknowledge the difficulties and frustrations they experience in their intimate lives while at the same time promising a means to overcome such predicaments. The industry packages intimacy as a competency that can be acquired through practical training and personal development, such that the pursuit of sex and sexual relationships becomes a form of work: the work of seduction. While analogies to exercise and sport are common, and seduction is often referred to as not simply a game but *the* game, this is not a recreational pastime or diversion but a form of labour that requires ongoing investment, often at considerable cost. The entrepreneurial subjectivity these men embody makes it possible to see – indeed, makes it impossible to ignore – the ways in which neoliberalism enters into the very fabric of intimate life. This, in turn, has implications for the kinds of relationships men have and want to have with women, as market logics orientate desire in some ways and not others.

Desire and discontent

When talking about how and why they had first become interested in seduction, men I spoke to invariably made reference to their past sexual and intimate relationships or described a relative lack thereof. For some, this was a topic they arrived at after some time and were evidently hesitant to discuss in any detail. For others, it was a central locus of their self-narrative. While the kinds of relationships they recounted varied widely – including live-in girlfriends and long-distance partnerships; marriages accompanied by separation or divorce; one-night stands and casual affairs; no-strings-attached and friends-with-benefits arrangements – participants were, without exception, dissatisfied with their sexual and intimate lives. On the one hand, this is hardly surprising: the seduction industry, after all, promises men greater control in their relationships with women and is, as such, likely to be populated by those who feel they lack this. Yet these narratives also point towards a broader problematic, wherein intimacy and sexuality have become sites of more persistent forms of discontent.

This issue is explored at length by Eva Illouz in *Why Love Hurts* (2012). Illouz departs from the more optimistic analyses of love and sex in late modernity put forward by scholars such as Anthony Giddens (1992) and Ulrich Beck and Elisabeth Beck-Gernsheim (1995), analyses which have already been contested on empirical grounds for overstating the extent of such transformations and ignoring continuing inequalities between women and men (Jamieson 1999). Illouz, however, charts a different analytic trajectory. Her particular concern is the manner through which romantic disappointment and suffering – generally perceived as intensely personal and uniquely individual experiences – are culturally produced and commercially managed. She highlights how desire patterns disaffection, arguing that 'culturally induced desires . . . create ordinary forms of suffering, such as chronic dissatisfaction, disappointment, and perpetual longing' (Illouz 2012: 207). This insight suggests that, in order to understand the pervasive sense of dissatisfaction among men who become involved in seduction, it is necessary to examine what it is that feeds their disappointment at a cultural level. That is, to understand what brings some men to this industry, we must not only recognise the irrevocably social dimensions of heterosexuality (Jackson 1996) but attend to its contemporary 'structure of feeling' (Williams 1977). My interest, then, is to examine how the embodied impulses of desire are formed in and through wider cultural currents, producing distinct patterns of eros and eroticism.

Men who seek out sex and relationship advice generally do so because they want greater control in their intimate lives. Of course, what this means to individual men varies considerably, though commonalities can nevertheless be found. While trainers I spoke with frequently impressed that many, if not most, of their clients are pursuing monogamous relationships – thereby staking a claim to operate within the 'charmed circle' of sexuality (Rubin 1984) – the majority of men I interviewed described being motivated largely by a desire for casual sex, at least in the immediate term. Discussing his decision to undertake a weekend training programme, at a cost of several hundred pounds, Doug said simply: 'I just wanted more casual sex.' Similarly, Kalim explained: 'For me, it's mainly dissatisfaction with my sex life. Doing this is mainly to get laid more.'

Even among those for whom the primary motivation was not casual sex, this often came to be seen as a necessary prerequisite to achieving other goals. Antonio explained that, although he was not particularly interested in having one-night stands, doing so might prove useful in allowing him to decipher his own wishes: 'I'm also willing to get a little bit of experience to know what I really like, what I really want.' Similarly, George described becoming more open to the idea of casual sex since first learning about seduction: 'Now I think maybe I can just try some less serious relationships and see how things go. But in the past I would never think that.' David, the only man I interviewed who stated that he had become involved in seduction specifically because he wanted to get married, described coming to the conclusion that he would have to spend a period of time modelling trainers by pursuing casual sex in order to reach his actual goal of meeting his future wife: '[Marriage] is what I'm looking for, but if it means that on the way what I need to do is to be with the wrong people, to do all the things that these guys are doing, then that's what I'm going to have to do.'

While the majority of participants described themselves as currently seeking casual sex, most assumed that they would eventually become involved in some kind of committed relationship. For some, this was something they actively looked forward to. Gavin, for example, spoke about the kinds of things he hopes to do with a future girlfriend, such as sharing a romantic meal on Valentine's Day. For others, however, commitment was simply an eventuality they would reconcile themselves to when the pursuit of casual sex became untenable. This latter tendency was exemplified by Mark, who posed the rhetorical question: 'Because what are you going to do when you're forty, or even when you're fifty? Still walk around Trafalgar Square opening sets?'[2] In general, men I interviewed subscribed to a kind of 'two-phase' masculinity (Eck 2014; also Terry and Braun 2009) where the pursuit of casual sex is supposed to give way eventually to a monogamous relationship as a sign of heterosexual maturity. Thus, despite the emphasis placed on casual sex, the form of expertise elaborated within the seduction industry does not fundamentally challenge or undermine heteronormative and mononormative relationship structures (see also Farvid and Braun 2013a).

Those who described themselves as pursuing casual sex tended to assume the desirability of such encounters was self-evident. Such assumptions are in keeping with the exigencies of the 'male sexual drive' discourse (Hollway 1984), whereby men are positioned and position themselves as always wanting and needing sex. Doug for example, quoted above, did not immediately elaborate why he 'just wanted' more casual sex. Yet, when I asked him to detail more precisely what it was that appealed to him about having casual sex, his explanation was notably lacking any explicit sense of carnality. Instead, it suggested a transactional view of sex in which men are consumers and women providers. Doug outlined the financial rationale underpinning his decision to undertake a seduction training course, saying that, by comparison with other investments he makes in casual sex – such as fashion and body work – acquiring seduction skills is likely to offer him a better return: 'It seemed like the investment would be worth it. You know, I spend time in the gym and I was trying to figure out, what's the payout from that? I buy nice clothes, what's the payout from that? What's the expected payout from this? Almost certainly higher than either of those two.' His reasoning is based on a commonly held understanding of sex as a commodity controlled by women and to which men seek to gain access using certain kinds of incentives or interactions, such as buying drinks or providing emotional support (Mooney-Somers and Ussher 2010). Doug calculates the relative cost of casual sex by tallying the various amounts of money he spends towards this end in order to provide a sound financial justification for undertaking a costly seduction programme. With heterosexual sex understood as a commodity controlled primarily by women, seduction is simply a means for men to ensure access to this resource, replacing what are regarded as less effective means of sexual procurement. As Doug later explained, his central reason for taking the programme was that he wanted to ensure ready access to casual encounters: 'I would want to know that, if I wanted to have casual sex, I could walk into a bar and it wouldn't be a problem for me.' Seduction thus enables heterosexual men – or at least promises to enable them – to act as sexual consumers without having to resort to paying for sex. In this way, the seduction industry extends a market ethos to non-commercial sexual encounters and relationships.[3]

When I asked participants who described seeking out casual sex what they enjoyed or found appealing about these interactions, few spoke about the pleasure of encountering others' bodies or the excitement of forging fleeting connections. Rather, they described the sense of achievement these encounters would furnish them with, especially when looking back on them in later life. Doug explained: 'I'll regret it if I'm old and married – which I probably will be – and thinking I should have chased more women when I was younger. I don't want to look back and regret not doing that when I was in my twenties.' In a related manner, Derek described wanting to sleep with as many women as possible now so that he could later enjoy these memories: 'I want to look back at this time, when I'm old, and think, fucking hell, you absolutely killed it! You know, you had a good time, you did what most people would never do. Because it takes a lot of balls to do this.' Like many other men I spoke to, Doug and Derek relate a desire for casual encounters that are valuable not so much as experiences in and of themselves but as experiences that can later be reflected upon. The prospective and anticipatory relation these formulations express is unambiguous, as even before having such encounters they each imagine themselves *looking back* on them from the perspective of a distant future in ways that bolster their sense of masculinity. This framing exemplifies the operation of the extended present in which 'the future is always-already within the present; measured, planned for, determined, chosen in the present' (Coleman 2010: 273). Sexual desire comes to be marked by the logic of capitalist labour organisation, with casual sex valued not so much for the physical sensation and interpersonal connection this may offer as for enabling 'the creation of potential' (Adkins 2008: 194, cited in Coleman 2010: 280).

Intimate ambitions

Many of those I interviewed felt it was important to accrue a certain number of sexual partners before becoming involved in a committed relationship. Though it has become commonplace today, the idea that sexuality represents a unique realm of accumulation is a relatively recent invention (Illouz 2012), one that illustrates the increasing centrality of sexual acts and practices to identity formations (Plummer 1995). Having ended his last sustained relationship in order to maintain his skills as a seducer, Elijah had resolved to become involved in a serious relationship only once he had fulfilled an as yet undetermined sexual aggregate, saying that, while he wanted a girlfriend in the future, he would defer this 'Until I'm satisfied with everything, with the women I've been with.' When I asked how he would know he had reached this point, he said: 'It depends when I'm satisfied, innit? It's when I'm satisfied. It probably would be like . . . you know what, really it could come down to twenty, or thirty. It could come down to around that number, you never know.' Another participant, a trainer with many years of experience, described having already reached his personal benchmark after sleeping with a hundred women: 'It's irrelevant whether I get to a hundred and fifty, or two hundred, or if I sleep with a supermodel. It's like I've ticked off that part of my life. Like, women – it's not a problem for me any more. Women is not one of my problems.' Having amassed what he believes is a sufficient number of sexual partners, he no longer feels the need to add to this figure or make special acquisitions in the form of high-status women. Indexing the outer-directed sense of achievement he experienced on reaching this benchmark, the trainer added: 'You can say you've done it, you know.'

While some participants quantified their intimate ambitions in precise numerical terms, others described wanting to reach a more diffuse 'level' of sexual experience. As Moe explained: 'I want to have great experiences with girls. And eventually, someday, I will get married as well. But I've promised myself that I won't get into a relationship, a serious one, until I feel that I've arrived at a level I'm very pleased with.' Moe's commitment to persevere in pursuing casual encounters represents a form of sexual apprenticeship, allowing him to gain experience so that he can forge a successful relationship career in the longer term. It is 'aspirational labour' in the sense of being 'forward-looking, carefully orchestrated, and entrepreneurial' (Duffy 2015: 446), though without financial incentive. Moe went on to explain that becoming a skilled seducer would be important in order to secure future relationships against possible risks: 'I don't want to meet my dream girl and then make her disappointed, or lose her to some cooler guy.' Acquiring sexual experience thus becomes a way of future-proofing relationships, insuring against possible betrayal and relationship break-down. Evincing a similar logic, Rahul claimed that it is crucial to 'work on yourself and your life, get it to a competent level' in order to ward off competition from other men: 'Especially if you're going to go for the really hot ones [women]. You're going to compete with their boyfriends or you're going to compete with other guys that are going to go after them.' In an intensely competitive romantic field in which the 'entrepreneur of himself has only competitors' (Donzelot 2008: 129–30, cited in McNay 2009: 58), acquiring seduction skills and amassing sexual experience seemingly provides a means for some men to gain advantage over others.

Many participants felt that seduction training had given them an upper hand vis-à-vis other men, with Antonio telling me: 'Just from this bootcamp I feel like I've gone from disadvantaged to totally advantaged.' Moreover, the advantage they believed they had already acquired or would eventually acquire through seduction training not only pertained to their relationships with other men – cast as competitors in the sexual marketplace – but also extended to the relationships they envisioned having with women in the future. Derek, for example, said:

> I need to go out there, and do a lot of stuff, before I can commit to anybody. Because I want her to know that I chose her out of thousands, you know. I want her to know that, actually, there was something about her. She wasn't the first thing that I ever got my hands on, you know. She wasn't the first person I ever was with, that I thought, wow, you know. I want her to know, definitely, that I had options. I could have had anybody. But I chose her.

For Derek, having relationships with many different women now is a means to gain leverage in an imagined future relationship. Borrowing a phrasing used by prominent figures within the UK seduction industry,[4] he suggests that his eventual partner will be both impressed and intimidated by his wealth of sexual experience and will be made to know she is not the first woman to win his attentions and need not necessarily be the last. This same sensibility was elsewhere in evidence when Danny described the advantages of meeting women in person as opposed to online. Recalling how a brief stint on a dating website left him feeling 'like such a pussy', he explained:

> When you start the girl on the street, as long as you've done it well, it creates a much better and stronger impression. And it can actually

> resonate for the rest of the relationship also. Because the girl knows, okay, this guy met me by approaching me, so . . . he's got game. Generally girls respect you more. So it resonates for the rest of the relationship and girls are actually less likely then to take the piss by treating you badly. Because they know that you're a man with options.

For both Derek and Danny, becoming a 'man with options' is a means to carry an advantage into their future relationships with women, relationships that are inscribed with an almost adversarial dynamic. Far from the democratic bargaining and mutual exchange of the 'pure relationship' envisioned by Anthony Giddens (1992) as the contemporary ideal, here intimate relationships are given over to a much more competitive ethos of self-interested individualism, such that every aspect of coupledom becomes a matter of tactic and strategy. Nevertheless, the contractual character of heterosexual intimacy outlined by Giddens remains, and indeed is now taken to an extreme conclusion, as prospective partners vie to secure the best deal for themselves *against* each other rather than open themselves out *to* one another.

Alongside this desire to achieve greater control over the *kinds of relationships* they have with women, men I interviewed routinely described a desire for greater choice over the *kinds of women* with whom they have relationships. Specifically, they wanted to be able to access a higher 'quality' or 'calibre' of women than would otherwise be within their reach, often on the basis that the attractiveness of a man's sexual partners is a direct indicator of his social value and personal worth. It was not uncommon for participants to describe women in terms of a one to ten 'scale' of sexual attractiveness, calculations made largely on the basis of aesthetic criteria, judgements about which are intimately bound up with structures of class and 'race' (Dabiri 2013; Gebrial 2017). In many cases, participants described their past sexual partners as having been insufficiently attractive. Talking about his past relationships – consisting primarily of one-night stands with women he met in bars and clubs – Gavin said:

> The women I went for in the past, okay, these would be women in the nightclubs who were somewhat common, I'd say. I didn't go for the girls that I was really attracted to, I just went for the girls that I thought I could get really. That was basically what my past was. I just went for what I thought I could get. So I was picking off easy targets, pretty much.

With a cynicism to which he himself appeared oblivious, Gavin invokes a classed insult to claim that the women he used to sleep with were of low standing. In doing so, he implicitly positions himself as aspiring to date women who are not only more attractive physically but also of a higher socio-economic status. In an interesting reworking of long-standing cultural conventions linking masculine status with access to beautiful women, he indicates that his pursuit of women to whom he was not attracted had been an indicator of poor self-esteem. The predatory dynamic that characterised these encounters is acknowledged straightforwardly and without any apparent unease, as Gavin describes himself as 'picking off easy targets.'

While Gavin made these comments when discussing casual sexual encounters – women with whom, by his own admission, he did not have particularly meaningful relationships – other participants described a comparable sense of discontent when talking about women with whom they had been in serious relationships. Jay, for example, described his ex-girlfriend, whom he had been with for over four years, as 'quite attractive, but not like . . . my ideal'. He went on to explain the difficulty this posed as their relationship progressed: 'I mean, when she woke up in the morning, without make-up, it wasn't . . . I didn't . . . I liked her better with make-up on, so . . . so, yeah. More than . . . more than other people, you know. I think she needed a little bit of make-up on, at least.' Explaining why he eventually ended the relationship, Jay noted: 'If I'm going to be waking up next to her, like, every day, that would be a problem in the long term.' Reproducing a commonplace logic through which women's bodies are figured as deficient and in need of modification or adornment, Jay complains that his ex-girlfriend was simply not attractive enough unless she performed certain kinds of aesthetic modification. The breakdown of their relationship is thereby attributed to the inadequacy of her unmade-up face rather than the unrealistic standards of beauty to which women are held in society at large and which Jay himself has evidently internalised. Elsewhere, Moe described his ex-girlfriend as 'not that attractive' and repeatedly invoked the spectre of feminine excess by labelling her as 'big'. Explaining why the relationship lasted almost two years despite his unhappiness, Moe admitted: 'In my mind it was the best I could get, if I could get any at all.' Here again a connection is drawn between male self-worth and female attractiveness. The overwhelming sense of disgust that permeated Moe's memory of this relationship was palpable, as he asserted: 'I will never, *never*, go back to that again, *never*. I will even do whatever. I mean, I will even be single to never go back to that. It's what motivated me to get into all this, really.'

The readiness among men I interviewed to criticise the appearance of women, and especially that of their sexual partners, stands in stark contrast to the innocuous male gaze imagined in postfeminist media culture, wherein 'the male gaze is veiled as benign, and instead it is women who are represented as looking at other women's bodies' (Winch 2014: 5). Their commentary also challenges the common presumption among women that it is only or primarily *other women* who police and enforce feminine beauty ideals, as research elsewhere demonstrates (Stuart and Donaghue 2011). While postfeminism figures women as 'self-beautifying subjects, doing it for themselves and not at the behest of men' (McRobbie 2015: 10), many men nevertheless expect women to perform this labour. Such processes operate at an embodied rather than simply a discursive level as culturally produced and media-administered standards of female beauty circumscribe who and what can be desired.[5]

Aspirational bodies

In talking about the kinds of women they wanted and, indeed, planned to have relationships with, participants tended to place a great deal of emphasis on physical appearance. For many, it was only natural that as heterosexual men they would give primary importance to women's looks. At the same time, it was almost invariably assumed that women are comparatively unconcerned by the appearance of their male partners. James, for example, claimed: 'Men respond to, like, the visual. Like, we see attractive women. Whereas women respond to different things.' Gavin similarly contended that 'Women are more emotional rather than visual like we are.' In a more assertive tone, Brent posited: 'We are like visual 100 per cent of the way. Guys will talk about mentality – that might be in the second phase – but in the beginning it's all about the body. If they say [otherwise] they're total liars.' Ralph, in his late forties, commended women for being able to look beyond physical appearance: 'I genuinely do feel that women care less about looks than guys do. And, you know, I'd big women up for that. I think they do care more about what a person's like inside.' He went on to elaborate that, as an older man, this made him feel better about his own appearance: 'It's just good to know that women are deep enough to see more in you than just the . . . just the sort of . . . the exterior.' While some men were not entirely comfortable with the emphasis they themselves put on women's physical appearance, this was nevertheless presented as somehow unavoidable, an inextricable fact of male sexuality. Having detailed his own aesthetic preferences, Anwar related: 'I know I sound shallow, and I hate myself for saying it . . . but then sexually, at a sexual level, it matters.' Others, however, seemed to attach a certain pride to their exacting physical standards, as though this was a mark of discernment, with Ralph pronouncing himself 'incredibly fussy about women', while elsewhere Brent stated: 'I'm really picky. I mean, there's no other word for it. I really am.'

In interviews and during field work, men I spoke with regularly offered detailed specifications about the physical characteristics their desired partners should embody, including age, weight, height and body shape; skin, hair and eye colour; 'race', ethnicity and nationality. Some had refined these specifications through discussions with seduction trainers, who very often ask students to supply details of their preferred 'type'. While individual men routinely framed their preferences as unique and idiosyncratic, the overall uniformity of these descriptions was striking, as participants almost invariably described a feminine ideal closely resembling that which is exalted in contemporary advertising and celebrity culture: young, slim and able-bodied, normatively white or an exoticised 'Other', with conventionally attractive physical features such as large breasts, long hair and a slim waist. Harry provided an illustrative example:

> I like long legs, toned. Petite, short petite body. I don't really like girls that are a lot taller than me, so if she's the same height as me or shorter, that's what I like. I like a nice flat stomach. To me that is really, really sexy. And, you know, healthy soft good looks. Long hair I find really attractive. And, like I said before, I'm kind of veering towards more of, like, the Scandinavian look these days.

Notably, Harry's description of the physical characteristics his sexual partners should embody – alongside those given by many other men I interviewed – fails to reproduce the postfeminist logic whereby the objectification of women's bodies is routinely accompanied by a kind of ersatz sense of contrition or self-consciousness, as in contemporary 'lad lit' (Gill 2014). Rather, objectifying descriptions of women's bodies were for the most part offered freely and without any apparent discomfort, and participants seemed entirely comfortable dictating the aesthetic standards to which they expect women to conform. This was perhaps most explicit in injunctions for women to actively shape and maintain their physique, with a number of participants relating preferences for women who 'work out' and are 'in shape'. As Harry described: 'Something I'm really into is girls that take care of themselves and are quite fit. That's something I'm definitely attracted to.' Elsewhere Gavin stated: 'I like girls that work out. You know, someone who has a figure like a fitness model.'

National and racial typologies abounded in men's descriptions of their ideal intimate partners, with participants regularly citing preferences for women of a particular national or ethnic group. Again there was little discomfiture about this, a pattern that is itself indicative of the 'reorganized (and reorganizing) hierarchies of value' within neoliberalism which 'attempt to bleach "race" from the story but sustain its imposition and entrench its most pernicious effects' (Redclift 2014: 581). The most commonly mentioned preference overall was for white women, with many participants citing Eastern European and Russian women – imagined as uniformly fair and feminine – as their absolute ideal. A number of South Asian men cited an exclusive preference for white partners. Rahul, for example, announced: 'I like Eastern European women, definitely. I think they're the most stunning. I don't like Oriental girls pretty much at all, unless they're really, really good looking. And I don't like Indian girls. I don't really like Asian girls, I'm just not attracted to them. I like white skin . . . more.'

While for Rahul this preference was unproblematic, other South Asian men took a more politicised view of how their attraction to white women had been shaped. Javed, who grew up in India, said: 'It's almost like the entire Indian psyche is such, because of all the colonialism, being a third world country, is like saying, yeah, white is best, this is the best you can get, this is the thing to aspire to, and therefore that's like the gold standard.' Having staked out this critique, Javed almost immediately went on to position his own attraction to white women as a matter of happenstance: 'As it happens, I think, from all the day-game approaches I've done, I think I like Eastern European girls, I find them quite attractive. I find blondes quite attractive.' Elsewhere, Anwar cited media influence in explaining his attraction to white women: 'I find white girls more attractive than Asian girls, purely because when you grow up . . . when you're a teenager growing up, everything on TV is telling you Western girls are attractive. You see your first Page 3 girl, and she's English and she's baring her breasts.' Later he went on to invoke stereotypes of undifferentiated Asian and British Asian women as sexually repressed and culture bound: 'I've found that [white] English girls are generally honest about their affection and their attitudes and their opinions. Whereas Asian girls, it's always . . . because they have all these constraints, they're never open and honest about how they really feel . . . It's all the cultural issues that the girl brings.'

Where white men were interested in dating and having relationships with women of colour, this was often related as a desire to sample racial difference. James, for example, a white man from Northern Ireland, answered a question about the kinds of relationship he wants to have by saying:

> I like to use an analogy here. Like, do you know the Kellogg's variety
> cereal boxes you get? I just want to try every one, if you know what I
> mean. So, I think actually at the minute I like black girls, so I'm approach-
> ing a lot of black girls. I like Asian women, I like Middle Eastern. I haven't
> really been approaching any of them, but I do find them attractive.
> That's just personally me, because the dark skin appeals to me. It's just
> exotic.

The apparently practised analogy James uses here, likening women of
different ethnicities to foodstuffs, is an unambiguous instantiation of what
bell hooks (1992) describes as 'eating the Other' – or, as she notes in British
parlance, 'getting a bit of the Other'. Indexing a desire to 'try every one',
James reifies a view of racial difference as a commodity to be consumed,
ascribing sameness to the women who occupy the racialised categories
he names. This is not an anti-racist gesture but, rather, a form of sexual
adventurism whereby 'exploration into the world of difference, into the
body of the Other, will provide a greater, more intense pleasure than
any that exists in the ordinary world of one's familiar racial group' (ibid.:
24–5). Sexual encounters with non-white women provide 'an alternative
playground' for white men 'to affirm their power-over in intimate relations
with the Other' (ibid.: 24).

Overall, the exhaustive aesthetic specifications participants offered
regarding their desired sexual partners suggest that 'it is often not women
per se that men desire, but women's bodies' (Burkett and Hamilton 2012:
827). Yet what is most notable about these accounts is the relentlessly
aspirational ethos which permeated participants' descriptions of their ideal
sexual partners. Men I interviewed appeared thoroughly preoccupied with
attaining a higher 'calibre' of intimate partner, a pattern trainer Danny also
touched upon when explaining why men seek out his services:

> The reason why some guys – why a lot of guys – want to do game is so
> that they can attract higher value women. So they might be dating, say,
> fives and sixes, and they actually want to have a girl who's a ten in terms
> of looks. And so, in order to attract her and possibly try to keep her
> there, they have to work on themselves and learn game.

The market mentality underpinning this situation was not lost on Danny,
who himself acknowledged: 'It's an exchange of values – "What can I get
for what I'm offering?" It becomes very economical.' In a society in thrall to
market metrics, in which women's bodies are constantly held up to sexual
scrutiny, it is at once entirely lamentable and thoroughly predictable that
a logic of value exchange so completely pervades the way in which some

heterosexual men relate to their intimate partners, both real and imagined. The overwhelming concern to attain access to so-called high-value women – whose worth is calculated using aesthetic criteria that are deeply classed and racialised – demonstrates that the very architecture of desire is being remade by the economisation of social life within neoliberalism. This aspirational orientation can be read as an expression of the form desire takes in a culture 'enamoured with the upgrade' (Gregg 2013: 309), where sex is frequently regarded as 'a consumptive rather than a relational act' (Gilbert 2013: 13).

Yet while the seduction community systematises sexual value judgements to a greater extent than may be found elsewhere, its basic ethos is consistent with contemporary cultures of heterosexuality more broadly, wherein practices of rating and ranking abound in a kind of 'sexualised audit' (Phipps and Young 2014). Nevertheless, it seems likely that engagement with seduction bolsters men's sense of sexual entitlement, with a number of those I interviewed claiming to have become increasingly exacting on account of their involvement in this sphere. Having already stated that he is 'really picky' about women, Brent elaborated: 'Actually, through pickup it became even worse. Sometimes I can see a really nice girl, but if I don't think that I should go, my head just . . . that's why I say that it made me more picky – I just don't settle for less, I would say.' Elsewhere Elijah explained: 'Every time I go out with a woman I kind of get bored of them. Because I think I can do better.' These kinds of statements demonstrate that, rather than ameliorating the sense of dissatisfaction which leads heterosexual men to seek out seduction training, involvement in this sphere can actually exacerbate the sense of disaffection they experience. As such, seduction may well contribute to patterns of dissatisfaction and disappointment that seem to pervade the intimate realm. Far from the celebrated 'democratisation of desire' (McNair 1996), wherein sensuality becomes radically pluralised and de-hierarchised, the affective rhythms and embodied impulses of desire are being taken over by the machinations of an economic system that privileges capital acquisition over all else. Where sexuality becomes overdetermined by market logics, it produces a kind of circumscribed libidinousness that is entirely generic in its aims and ambitions. There is an emptying out of the subjective and the interpersonal, as a capitalist logic of value comes to undermine and obscure a more expansive appreciation of human values.

Intimate enterprise

The 'frequently asked questions' page of the popular London-based seduction training company Daygame includes the question 'How do I become an instructor for your company?'. The response states:

> We do not actively advertise for new instructors, but select from guys that we have seen in action – on the street and based on their results. These might be ex bootcamp students, or guys who we've heard about through word-of-mouth. Our instructor initiation process involves shadowing existing instructors until competency with teaching, as well as picking up girls, is achieved. Let us know if you think you've got what it takes and we'd be happy to see you in action. (Daygame 2015)

Rhetorically, this statement accomplishes a number of things. Becoming a Daygame instructor is encoded with a certain sense of exclusivity, as these jobs are not advertised and cannot be applied for directly. Those who aspire to work in the industry are informed that their performance 'on the street' will serve as the definitive criterion by which they are judged, and, as such, they are advised to approach their day-to-day interactions with women as a kind of preliminary audition or continuous interview. Undertaking training courses with Daygame is highlighted as the best route to becoming a company employee, with former students listed as the principal cohort from whom new instructors are drawn. Investment in a bootcamp course – at a cost of between £700 and £950, depending on location – is thus presented as a means for men not only to achieve greater control in their intimate lives but also to realise an elusive career in the seduction industry.

That a question about how to become an instructor appears on the FAQ page of a company such as Daygame – similar questions also feature on the webpages of other seduction training companies – is testament to the appeal that working in the industry holds for many who enter it as students or clients. Indeed, a number of men I interviewed – including those who were relatively new to seduction – described wanting to become trainers or set up their own business ventures. In his late forties, and having been engaged with seduction for less than six months at the time of our interview, Ralph declared:

> If I became good at this, you know, if I genuinely became good at it, then I could potentially run bootcamps for older guys. That's a gap in the market. So, you know – and I'm saying, if I was genuinely say fifty years old, and regularly pulling girls in their twenties, then . . . you know, when I sort of actually started to work out why it was happening and

what was working, and it felt like I could share that, there's a gap in the market there.

Despite his relative inexperience, Ralph envisions himself running seduction training events in the near future. His desire to become more proficient interacting with women is caught up with a desire to respond profitably to the business opportunity he believes he has identified. Intimate relationships are framed as a possible route to financial gain, as he seeks to capitalise on his positioning as an older man in an industry dominated by men in their twenties and thirties. Unlike some of the other men I spoke to who related commercial ambitions, Ralph does not work in business or finance: he is a schoolteacher.

This drive to entrepreneurialise – to create a business interest where one did not exist before – is consistent with a broader enterprise culture that encourages us all to mine the contents of our intimate lives in pursuit of possible profit (Bröckling 2015; du Gay 1991). Yet, while an entrepreneurial ethos structures men's engagement with seduction generally, it is among those who actually make a living from seduction that intimate life comes most clearly to 'replicate and facilitate work patterns' (Maddison 2013: 107). Although there are no formal requirements to working in this industry, there is a general expectation that seduction trainers should have and be prepared to demonstrate 'experiential authority', a concept developed by Celia Kitzinger (1994) to describe the authority she is very often granted by others when talking about lesbianism, simply by virtue of the fact that she herself is a lesbian. Within the seduction industry, experiential authority functions in a slightly different way, with trainers deemed knowledgeable and authoritative not simply because they are heterosexual men but, rather, because they are heterosexual men who have – or, at least, who claim to have – slept with significant numbers of women.

Having worked in the industry full-time for a number of years, William explained the basis for becoming an instructor:

> You have to have done it. I mean, it's a massive trend at the moment for guys setting up their own things and trying to bypass the harsh reality that you have to have done it *over* and *over* again. I would never train with someone who hasn't put in hours and hours of the work and has got, like, provable skill. I always say to guys, I mean, get some girls under your belt, you know. Literally, twenty, thirty girls. Get videos filmed of you in different scenarios. Get other people who are credible in the industry to watch you and to go out with you, because skill recognises skill, you know. I mean *YouTube* viewers don't really recognise skill, but

someone who's done it for years and years, if you go out with them and they say, 'Yeah, this guy, he's got balls, he can do it', then that's very validating.

Outlining the various criteria an aspiring trainer must fulfil in order to break into the industry, William highlights the importance of gaining recognition from those already established as experts. In doing so he indicates that, while having sex with women is a necessary precondition to gaining entry to the industry, it is ultimately recognition from other men that allows sexual capital to be translated into economic capital. Another trainer, Danny, further emphasised the need for prospective trainers to amass sexual experience:

> I think every coach and trainer, they're only good if they've actually gone out and have been successful themselves. And by success I definitely mean going out and getting laid. Not gone out and had dates. A good trainer needs to have gone out, dated and have gotten laid . . . I genuinely wouldn't take any trainer seriously unless he's . . . I don't know . . . had sex with . . . I don't know . . . forty or fifty women. And it's not just the numbers, it's also about the quality. So they would have needed to – he would have needed to have slept with quality women also. So not just unattractive women and low self-esteem women. Then I could say he might be qualified as a trainer. But there are guys out there that teach that are definitely not speaking from experience, they're speaking from textbooks. There are a lot of guys out there like that.

For seduction trainers, the accumulation of sexual experience not only functions as a means to acquire masculine status but serves as a kind of vocational training. While the precise number of women a would-be trainer needs to have slept with in order to be deemed credible is not agreed upon – William put the figure at twenty to thirty, while Danny raised this to forty or fifty – the need to accrue experience in order to legitimately claim expertise is absolute. Both criticise those who presume to teach others without having themselves acquired the necessary expertise – an expertise they attest can be achieved only by sleeping with the requisite number and calibre of women.[6]

That becoming authoritative on the subject of how to seduce women is understood and experienced as a form of work is highlighted in William's indictment of those who attempt to 'bypass the harsh reality that you have to have done it *over* and *over* again'. Yet while having sex with women is a prerequisite to becoming a trainer – or, at least, a prerequisite to becoming a trainer whose claims to expertise are recognised and endorsed by others in the industry – trainers are not paid to seduce women *per se*. Rather, they sell their knowledge about *how* to seduce women, knowledge that is produced by seducing women. As a mode of enterprise that involves having sex but not selling sex, their work exemplifies the profound entanglements of intimacy and commerce in contemporary capitalism (Bernstein 2010; Hochschild 2012).

Branding the sexual self

In her work on the 'branded self', Alison Hearn (2008, 2014) argues that the reflexive project of the self – widely regarded among sociologists as a characteristic feature of modernity – has more recently become a concerted form of labour. This mode of selfhood is marked by the visual codes of mainstream media culture and orientated towards the pursuit of cultural value and material profit. Its production involves 'creating a detachable, saleable image or narrative, which effectively circulates cultural meanings' and thereby 'either consciously positions itself, or is positioned by its context and use, as a site for the extraction of value' (Hearn 2008: 198–9). Charting the evolution of what she calls 'Me, Inc.' via management and marketing literature through to reality TV programming, Hearn argues that within contemporary culture the self is 'explicitly defined as a promotional vehicle designed to sell: one that anticipates the desires of a target market. The most important work *is* work on the self' (2008: 205). Noting the imbrication between the branded self and celebrity culture, she further contends that 'celebrity [not only] functions . . . as cultural resource in and through which individuals construct their identities, but becomes a generalizable model of profitable self-production for all individuals' (ibid.: 208).

Professional seducers or career pickup artists – those for whom seduction training is a sole or primary occupation – embody the logic of the branded self as they engage elaborate practices of self-promotion and package themselves as branded entities. Among the most successful sexual self-branders to emerge from the London seduction scene is Tom Torero, whose alias means 'bullfighter' in Spanish. With a 360 degree branding strategy and distinctive visual style – bull horns feature heavily – Torero exhaustively documents his activities through a wide range of media, spanning autobiographical books, a diary-style blog and multiple social media accounts. In 2012, he released his first book, a self-published work entitled *Daygame* (2012). It opens with an anecdote that serves to highlight the transformation Torero has achieved:

'Leave your drink but bring your bag' I grinned as I took her by the hand and led her from the candle-lit glow of the dark cocktail bar to the sobering light of the bathrooms. The few guests in the venue were oblivious to what was going on in front of them. It was early on a Tuesday evening and the trickle of customers were watching the jazz trio in the corner. An hour before I had met this stunning long-legged Asian girl on the busiest shopping street in Europe, and now I was about to fuck her in the toilets of a bar after kissing her on the sofas. *'This is crazy!'* she gasped as we shut the disabled toilet door and I pushed her up against the wall. *'Somebody will hear us!'* My head was spinning, not from alcohol or fear, but from the dizzy realisation of how far I'd come in the last few years, from an introverted Oxford geek to one of the best daytime seducers of women in the world. (2012: 3)

Set within this general narrative arc, over the next 450 pages Torero relays a seemingly endless procession of sexual exploits, boasting titles such as 'Brazilian from Coffee Shop', 'Polish Threesome', 'Strip Club Close and Lay' and '18 Year Old Swedish Girl'. The purpose of these stories is not simply to allow Torero to share his experiences but to do so in a way that demonstrates the efficacy of the seduction techniques he employs and thereby shore up his personal brand. Known within the industry as a pioneer of daytime seduction, Torero is keen to assert the potency of his methods:

> In the last three years I have slept with 100 attractive women, some of them extremely beautiful and 'well out of my league'. Not by meeting them in nightclubs or bars, not online or through my social circle, but by stopping them in the street in broad daylight, stone cold sober. Lawyers, dancers, doctors, nannies, models, air-hostesses, students, nurses, TV presenters, wives, writers, strippers, bankers, painters, musicians, from nearly forty different countries. I don't have classically good looks, a powerful job, a flash car or an expensive suit. What I do have is daygame. (Ibid.)

With this matter-of-fact preamble, Torero is effectively marketing himself to the widest possible audience. His approach is presented as one that enables men to meet virtually any kind of woman, even while dispensing with conventional markers of masculine status. Torero's own identity is amalgamated with the daygame method, presented as his unique possession, to which other men can gain access by paying for his products and services.

As well as writing about his sexual pursuits, Torero records many of his interactions with women, sharing a portion of the content freely online

while selling the rest via pay-to-access products. Referred to in the seduction community as 'in-field videos', these are essentially how-to guides
based on real interactions with women who do not know they are being
filmed. To create these videos, Torero – like many other trainers – covertly
records his interactions using hidden devices and later annotates the
content with details of the various techniques he has employed at every
stage. One such video, posted on Torero's *YouTube* channel in 2014 and
entitled *Bar-to-Bedroom: Full Date Infield!*, had been viewed over 120,000
times before being removed from the site. The audio-only recording begins
with Torero walking to meet his date and culminates with the sounds of a
woman moaning, apparently in sexual ecstasy. At the outset of the video,
he speaks directly to his audience: 'The plan is to do my dating model, do
a couple of venues, and then I'm going to do the one date model. So I'm
going to take her back to the house for the plausibly-deniable film and
run the train. I'll keep this recording so you can hear it all.' Like much of
the content on *YouTube* – a platform that enjoins its users to 'broadcast
yourself' – in-field recordings can be regarded as simultaneously public
and private performances. Private sexual encounters are recorded in the
knowledge that they will be made public. In this way, the private performance is always already mediated by the presence of an audience imagined
and anticipated in advance.

In December 2014, Torero became mired in scandal when it emerged
that he had paid an actress to appear in at least one of his supposedly candid
'kiss close' videos. This revelation prompted dozens of blog posts and
comment threads debating his credibility, and Torero eventually admitted
that the video had indeed been staged. Commenting on the fallout of this,
one of his colleagues decried 'the charlatans and fakes . . . who will either
lie, evade or use smoke'n'mirrors to convey a credibility to their customers
that they don't deserve', while defending Torero for having 'distinguished
himself as someone who *could* be trusted by virtue of his copious library of
infield recordings on the street, on dates, and even in the bedroom' (Krauser
2014b). Despite the controversy, the episode did not seem to damage the
Torero brand, and he has since gone on to publish a number of further
seduction guidebooks, maintain a popular blog and podcast series, and
release new in-field programmes. The most recent of these, entitled *Stealth
Seduction*, currently retails for US$199 and is billed as an 'up-close-and-per-
sonal infield daygame collection'. The advertisement for the product boasts:

- 16 successful seduction infields leading to a notch on the belt (4+
  hours of video, 11 hours of audio)

- 12 more infields of number closes, instant dates, failed dates and rejections (1.5 hours of video, 1 hour of audio)
- 16 nationalities of girls (including British, American, Canadian, Japanese, German, French, Polish, Singaporean, Moldovan, Spanish, Egyptian, Ukrainian, South African, Russian, Colombian and Iranian)
- Infield pickups in over 15 cities around the world from London to Las Vegas.

(Torero 2017)

By filming their encounters with women, seduction trainers extract value from their very selves, inviting others to participate vicariously in their sexual lives. At the same time, they extract value from the women who are unknowingly made to appear in these recordings, whose bodies and voices are pressed into service for the accrual of cultural and economic value in which they themselves do not share.

Flagrantly disregarding women's privacy, in-field videos readily exemplify the noxious combination that results from the intersection of ruthless self-interest and the kind of culturally ingrained misogyny that makes violating women's consent commonplace and acceptable. That the production, sharing and sale of in-field footage has become so pervasive in recent years demonstrates a disconcerting willingness among seduction trainers to betray the trust of their sexual partners in pursuit of financial gain. This kind of easy and unthinking exploitation is entirely in keeping with the logic of the branded self, 'one of the more cynical products of the era of the flexible personality: a form of self-presentation singularly focused on attracting attention and acquiring cultural and monetary value', which 'trades on the very stuff of lived experience in the service of promotion and possible profit' (Hearn 2008: 213).

Professional imperatives

Among those who work in the seduction industry, the distinction between work and life already made tenuous within neoliberal culture is frequently collapsed. Although many of the trainers I interviewed were reluctant to talk about their personal lives, and some evaded questions about their relationships with women, indicators of this blurring of boundaries nevertheless appeared in interviews. Danny, for example, admitted:

> I know one guy hired me specifically because he had seen me out with one of my girlfriends, he'd seen some of my pictures, so he thought, 'Yeah, okay, I can see that you've got a stunning girlfriend.' And he said

that the reason that he never went to this other coach was because he saw him and his girlfriend, and his girlfriend was like a six or something. So rationally he thought, 'What's the point going to him if he can only get a six?' He wanted to come to me to learn how to get the eights and nines.

For Danny, having an attractive girlfriend adds value to his brand by advertising his ability to access high-quality women to potential clients. This same logic is commonly evidenced in online review forums, where the skills and capacities of individual trainers are frequently evaluated by reference to their partners; trainers whose girlfriends or wives are deemed unattractive are frequently accused of fakery or delusion. When I later asked Danny if dating attractive women is therefore a professional imperative, he said: 'Yeah. I kind of like that, though. The reason I like that is because it encourages you not to . . . not to slack. It encourages you to date the women that you truly want to date anyway. Because I truly want to date very attractive women. So in a way it's good. It's like a reinforcing mechanism.' Here the regulatory force of the branded self comes more fully into view. As Hearn argues, branded selves are required to maintain control of their image at all times, even in private: 'Ultimately your personal brand is not only a pretty veneer; it is intended to be a rhetorically persuasive version of yourself' (2008: 206).

Danny readily admits that his career as a seduction trainer more or less dictates his choice of intimate partner. Yet, while he initially suggested that this is a positive force which serves simply to reaffirm his own desires, elsewhere he appeared somewhat more ambivalent about how such professional imperatives impact his personal life: 'It's a bit fucked up, though, because you can easily get into – find yourself in a trap of doing it for ego validation, doing it to feed the ego. So you're asking yourself, why am I actually sleeping with this girl? Is it to get my numbers up or is it because I genuinely want to have sex?' Danny's uncertainty here reflects the same sense of compulsion discussed in earlier sections of this chapter, whereby some of those who engage with seduction find themselves pursuing sexual encounters in the absence of any desire to do so. Yet, while for amateur seducers this kind of compulsion was usually underpinned by a fear of losing the skill set they had worked so hard to develop, for trainers such as Danny this was also caught up with the need continually to bolster his professional credentials and enhance his credibility within the industry. Here the potential loss of seduction skills – understood not as a decline in real terms but as a failure constantly to increase one's sexual aggregate –

acquires further regulatory force because of the potential material implications, namely loss of income.

Jenny provided further insight into these dynamics when she described the difficulties faced by her male colleagues in attempting to reconcile the demands of the jobs with the expectations of their intimate partners. Though I had actually asked Jenny about her experiences working in the industry as a woman, to which she initially responded by discussing how difficult it is to deflect the sexual attentions of her students, she quickly changed track to highlight the plight of male trainers:

> They have different issues, poor souls. Sometimes they have to . . . the student is gaming a girl who's really hot but her friend is not. And the trainer has to game the friend who's really not attractive. And they will . . . they will go quite far, in order to secure it with the other girl. They go really far. I'll leave it at that. That's a problem that women don't have to worry about.

Jenny later went on to explain how some of these same male colleagues manage the realities of their professional lives alongside their personal relationships by issuing ultimatums to their partners, while others resort to deception:

> I know that there are trainers who have said to their girlfriends, like, 'Look, you're my girlfriend, but this is what I do for a living, and this is how far I have to go sometimes, you know. I have to be open to approaching women, I have to be open to going out and sleeping with girls, I need to demonstrate for students and I need to live this lifestyle. If you want to be with me, you have to accept that.' And the girl, sometimes, has gone into an open relationship and accepted that as part of being in a relationship with him. Other trainers, I don't know what their girlfriends say. . . . I don't know if they know all about the situation or if they're being lied to – I have no idea. It's something that – I don't want to even approach the subject, I think it's a sensitive subject even for them. Because I think they do like their girlfriends a lot and they kind of . . . I don't judge, I don't judge if someone cheats on their girlfriend. It's not my issue, it's not my problem.

As Jenny indicates here, having sex is often regarded as part of the job description for male trainers, who are called upon to demonstrate seduction techniques at first hand and provide assistance to students. Moreover, trainers need to have – or at least be seen to have – a hedonistic sexual lifestyle involving multiple partners. After all, the branded self markets not a singular product but, rather, 'a whole way of life' (Hearn 2008: 205).

Many of the male trainers I spoke to related concerns about telling the women with whom they have relationships about their livelihoods. Jack described the tension this can create in relationships:

> I'm very selective about when I tell people. Usually I'm not going to tell somebody unless I've been seeing them for a while. And, even then, it has to be in the right way, because . . . I'm naturally a very private person anyway. Obviously you can't start saying it to everybody because not everybody's going to last, so I think it's only one of those things I'll say to somebody I view as a . . . prospect. But nobody's really kind of . . . lasted, as it were.

Given the extent of Jack's involvement in the industry, not telling the women he dates about his work involves a not insignificant amount of evasion. Andrew, who is also deeply engaged in this sphere, similarly lamented the difficulty of telling women about his work:

> Any way you explain it, without being very vague or lying, it doesn't sound good, it's not socially acceptable. On the other hand, if you were teaching women, then it's okay – there's many ways to make that sound okay. You know, 'I teach women how to find good guys, how to have better relationships', or something – it sounds fine. But 'I teach men how to meet women' – it's just disastrous, any way you say it.

Though frustrated by the negative responses that revealing the nature of their employ often elicits, Jack and Andrew had each developed strategies to broach the issue with women, drawing on available cultural resources to frame their work in the best possible light.[7]

The perceived impetus among male seduction trainers to hide their professional activities from intimate partners – and, for many, from friends and family also – both indicates and generates considerable ambivalence. Andrew further explained that, though he was frustrated by the negative connotations surrounding seduction, he would not actually want his partner to readily accept his status as a seduction trainer:

> You know, my ideal girl would not like what I do. Or wouldn't like the look of it. She wouldn't mind what I actually do, but she wouldn't like the look of it . . . I would think that she shouldn't like it. I wouldn't want her to like it. Like, if she was looking at the website, for example, I would want her to be repulsed. Not just by the website, but by . . . you know, the fact that she's with me and I'm the guy that's behind it.

Andrew's logic here is deeply contradictory. Although he expects partners ultimately to accept his work as a seduction trainer, he wants the women he dates first to express disapproval and, indeed, disgust at his activities. Such contradictory impulses may well reflect Andrew's own ambivalence about his work in the seduction industry. It is possible that he harbours a certain amount of shame or guilt and that, by displacing this onto his intimate partners – by demanding they express repugnance – he is able to ameliorate the cognitive dissonance his job engenders. Yet it is significant here that Andrew refers specifically to his 'ideal girl', indicating that he does not necessarily want every woman he dates to problematise his professional dealings. Rather, his 'ideal girl' is expected to prove herself morally worthy by initially challenging, before ultimately conceding, his status as a pickup trainer. Andrew's reasoning is thus not only hypocritical but deeply conservative, as he demands his partners conform to an ethical standard from which he himself is not only exempt but which he profitably contravenes.

The professional imperatives that organise work in the seduction industry exemplify a more general penetration of intimate life by the marketised and marketising logics of neoliberalism. The intimate lives of these men are thoroughly embedded in the marketplace, the sexual skill set they cultivate is transformed into a commodity, and their relationships with women are amalgamated into a brand identity. Trainers epitomise the mode of intimate subjectivity that characterises men's engagements with seduction generally: distinctly entrepreneurial, organised by logics of opportunity and outcome, centring on and facilitating work-centric patterns of social relations. Crucially, this form of selfhood is not particular to men who participate in this community-industry but is instead one manifestation of a cultural logic that routinely figures sex and intimacy as sites of labour and management. What is in some way distinct about the expertise on offer here is that it is almost exclusively elaborated by and directed towards heterosexual men. In chapter 2, I take up this issue by examining the seduction industry as a specifically homosocial formation.

2

Pedagogy and Profit

A trainer stands in the middle of the room, portable speaker in hand, telling students to get up and dance. He's running a session on 'state control', the intent of which is to teach students how to give themselves a boost so that they can feel confident and sociable whenever and wherever they need to. Turning the music up still louder, he opens the door at the back of the room and beckons everyone to follow. A disconnected conga line takes shape and snakes out into the foyer and through the dining room. Hotel guests look on bemused, but as the shuffling posse works its way around the room a security guard follows close behind and asks who's in charge. Another trainer stands up and suddenly launches himself at the guard. Pulling himself up to his full height in a vain attempt to match the other man's much larger frame, the trainer begins ridiculing the guard's employment and intelligence, proclaiming himself to be infinitely smarter and more successful. Within moments the other trainers intervene. One drags his colleague away, telling him to calm down. Another tries to placate the security guard, making promises, providing assurances. Later that day I ask them what could possibly have prompted the trainer to levy such an assault. One shrugs and looks away. The other sighs heavily and says: 'That's just how he is.'

At the end of the day – the event has been allowed to continue following negotiations with hotel management, though the instigator of the attack has been barred from the premises – the students collectively retreat to the bathroom to get ready for the night-game session. They return fifteen minutes later wearing fresh clothes, the smell of cologne heavy in the air. As they chat excitedly at the back of the room, a number of other men start to filter in, until the group has swelled to almost double its original size. Most, I soon learn, are either past students or former employees. One tells me that, though he stopped teaching with the company over a year ago, he still comes along most weekends for the night-game sessions: 'I like to help out with the teaching, you know, see the trainers, meet the new guys.' Later we get to talking about my research, and he asks if I've paid to attend this or any of the other events I've been going to. When I tell him I haven't, he rolls his eyes and says: 'Of course not. That's how it is – for girls.'

The club is a sprawling, multi-storey affair. One of the more senior trainers has been tasked with managing the night-game session, and I shadow him as he walks from room to room checking in on the others. His job, he explains, is to make sure that, amid the heady atmosphere, trainers teach and students get taught. Towards the end of the night, we are looking for a student–trainer duo that went missing early on in the evening and haven't checked in since. We walk through a series of themed rooms and a maze of corridors before eventually descending into a small subterranean bar. There we find them standing towards the back of the room, flooded in red light. The trainer leans against the wall, one arm draped casually over the shoulder of the woman he is with. Beside him stands the student, his arms wrapped around another woman's waist, pulling her body firmly against his. Satisfied with this, the night-game manager raises a hand in signal to them both. The trainer nods ever so slightly, while the student grins wildly in return. We head back upstairs to meet the others for the final debrief. It's approaching midnight, when the night-game session officially ends – though for some it will continue unofficially into the early hours of the morning.

Masculinities scholarship has long emphasised the centrality of sexuality in ordering hierarchies among men. Raewyn Connell – whose work virtually inaugurated the sociological study of men and masculinity – argues that, in contemporary Western societies, 'the most symbolically important distinction between masculinities is in terms of sexuality' (2000: 102). In keeping with the dictates of 'compulsory heterosexuality' (Rich 1980) and the workings of the 'heterosexual matrix' (Butler [1990] 2011), heterosexuality is a constitutive component to culturally authoritative constructions of masculinity,[1] even as masculine hierarchies are always shaped by structures of 'race', class, (dis)ability, nationality and religion. Importantly, however, it is not enough for men simply to lay claim to heterosexuality in any general sense. Rather, heterosexuality must be continually proven by demonstrating that one has the capacity to sexually access women's bodies.

Participants routinely highlighted this dynamic in interviews, with Ali explaining: 'It's something that's such a big part of male identity. Like, the worst way to insult a man's pride is to say you're a virgin, or something like that. Because it's completely negating everything about you as a man.' Likewise, Javed stated: 'Essentially, the context we all live in as men is that sexual inexperience means that you're worthless as a man. You're nothing.' The construction of masculinity as necessarily heterosexual is thus heavily imbricated with another critical marker of masculinity: the capacity to exert control and resist being controlled by others (Schrock and Schwalbe 2009). Bluntly put, for many men, 'to be masculine is to fuck women' (Connell 2000: 120).

This chapter explores the relational dynamics and affective textures that pattern the seduction industry as a homosocial formation. I take up the question, elsewhere addressed by scholars such as Michael Flood (2008) and Diane Richardson (2010), of how men's relationships with other men shape and give meaning to their relationships with women. I demonstrate that the desire among men to reconfigure their heterosexual relationships is very often caught up with a desire to reconfigure their homosocial relationships. Tracing the emotional contours of relationships forged among men in these settings, I examine how participation in the seduction community offers men access to forms of sociality that are otherwise unavailable and, at the same time, directs these relationships towards realising normative conventions of what it means to be a man. Finally, I consider what is bought and sold in the context of live training events and one-to-one coaching relationships, which offer men a space to work on their masculinity under the auspices of male camaraderie and friendship.

Men, sex, silence

When explaining why they had become involved in the seduction industry, men I interviewed generally cited a desire for greater choice and control with women. Yet, while their stated purpose was to become skilled in negotiating heterosexual relationships, their relationships with and among men were recurrent subjects of discussion. At the outset of our interview, in response to a question about why he had first attended a seduction event, Emmanuel described having been bullied when he was seventeen after admitting to some of his classmates that he was still a virgin. These events were still extremely painful for Emmanuel, now in his early twenties. Eyes downcast and speech halting, he explained:

> They had their stories about girls and then like . . . with me it was just like . . . they really, really, like – they just really brought my self-esteem really down. And every single day when I used to come into college I would always get it, people like that just bullying me. I just wish I didn't even open up to them. Because it was just like . . . they were just tormenting me a lot at the time.

That these experiences eventually spurred Emmanuel to seek out seduction training demonstrates how 'ridicule from one's peers serves as an instrument of control to ensure that the ideal of male heterosexuality is pursued' (Holland et al. 2004: 161). His reference to the boys who bullied him as having had an abundance of sexual stories highlights how heterosexual experience circulates as a form of currency among men and organises their relationships with one another (Flood 2008; Ringrose et al. 2013).

Emmanuel was one of a number of men who related experiences of bullying and harassment when accounting for their participation in this sphere, as other participants recounted similar scenarios involving male peers and family members. Still others described forms of marginalisation that did not involve direct censure or overt ridicule but were nevertheless hurtful and exclusionary. Anwar, for example, spoke about being unable to participate in rituals of sexual story-telling among his friends:

> They're all these amazing guys and they've all got lots of stories. And when we get together I'm normally the one that can't say anything, because I've only slept with six women, you know. And so I don't say anything. I just laugh and joke and try and, you know, try and join in, but I can't because . . . I have never been that guy. And they won't acknowledge it, and they just don't . . . they don't then ask me to give any stories. Because they kind of know in their heart of hearts I've never done it.

Anwar's description here highlights the importance of exchanging sexual stories to the composition and enactment of male homosociality, precisely because 'heterosexual confirmation must be diffracted somehow back through the patriarchal structure, then recognised and authorised by other men . . . the confirmation of a man's sexuality through a woman is imbricated in his need to be validated as masculine *by other men*' (Buchbinder 1998: 110). Importantly, it is not that Anwar lacks sexual stories entirely – as he says, he has slept with a number of women – but, rather, that he is unable to relate the *kinds* of sexual stories that carry value among his friendship group. As C. J. Pascoe (2007) contends, rituals of sexual story-telling among heterosexual men are not so much about communicating a desire *for* women as about demonstrating an ability to exercise mastery *over* women's bodies, both literally and figuratively. In relating such stories, men not only affirm their masculinity: 'They affirm subjecthood and personhood through sexualised interactions in which they indicate to themselves and others that they have the ability to work their will upon the world around them' (Pascoe 2007: 86). Because Anwar is unable to relate sexual stories that foreground masculine power, he forfeits masculine status.

Anwar's sense of being on the periphery of his friendship group – involved but not really included, participating but not really belonging – was evidently very distressing for him and constituted a significant focus of discussion during our interview. Relating this to his identity as a British Pakistani man, he described the difficulties of being 'stuck between two cultures': 'You sit in this cultural divide, where English people don't fully accept you because you're not technically fully the same, and the Asian people don't accept you because they think you're a coconut – brown on the outside, white on the inside.' Anwar further explained that, while his friends – all of whom are white – regularly set each other up with women, they had never done so for him. Expressing the hurt this caused him, he said: 'It makes me feel socially inadequate, and it makes me feel like I'm worthless. And I don't know whether it's a cultural thing, because I'm Asian, because I'm this person and they see me as being of less value.' Anwar's desire to become more skilled with women is thus indelibly bound up with a desire to disrupt the racialised and racialising logics that circumscribe his relationships with men, a sentiment shared by many of those for whom seduction represents a means to contravene received hierarchies of 'race' and class. Crucially, however, this is not about contesting inequality at a structural level but about learning to work within the parameters of these systems in order to gain access to a limited set of privileges. Individual self-work is thus proffered as the solution to structural inequalities, on the basis that 'the routine damage wrought by racial orders can be privately overcome' (Gilroy 2013: 34).

Across interviews and during many informal conversations I had during fieldwork, men I spoke to impressed that the seduction community provides a space to talk about subjects typically inadmissible among men. Derek explained: 'A lot of PUAs are offering each other somebody to talk to, about something that actually most people don't talk about. For guys – guys don't talk about this sort of stuff.' James similarly disclosed: 'Because this is the thing, like, in male circles guys don't talk about it with each other. And I think that's the good thing about the gaming [seduction] community, because you go down and you can talk about it.' With these kinds of comments, participants shed light on the 'privatising effects' (Richardson 2010) and 'necessary silences' (Karioris 2014) that frequently structure men's relationships with one another, such that it is not acceptable to admit uncertainty or express anxiety, particularly about sex and relationships. Attempting to explain why relationships among men also engaged with seduction are different from those he shares with men elsewhere, Ralph surmised: 'Guys don't normally talk with each other about how hard they find it. But in effect, there's almost . . . you're there to become better at something – so there's almost an implicit admission that you're not a stud.' Involvement in the seduction community thus functions as a kind of tacit concession to a lack of heterosexual prowess, therefore temporarily suspending the need for men to possess – or effect possession of – this critical marker of masculine status.

For many men, friendships forged through a shared interest in seduction provide a welcome source of support. James relayed a series of examples:

> Last week I went out after that bootcamp and had coffee and a bite to eat with one of the guys. And we had a really in-depth conversation and it was . . . just talking about it, you know – his experiences, my experiences – it was good, like, it was really good. And this week as well, another guy from the bootcamp texted me looking to go out. So it's like you get support from everywhere. It's really . . . it's essential. Men do need to team up, in a way, sort of to . . . to get through this.

Having had an exceptionally difficult year, during which his marriage had collapsed and his ex-wife moved abroad with their young son, James evidently felt buoyed by these encounters. Curious to know more about the content of these conversations, I asked if he discussed these recent travails with men he met through the seduction community, to which he responded:

> You can discuss your personal life, but it is more the mechanics, because again that's mechanics – men's brains are just naturally wired to think like that. You always talk about that there. You talk about everyday things as well, but it's definitely mostly the mechanics. Men like to fix things, so it is in a way like a project that goes on.

For James, the seduction community is not and does not need to be a space of emotional intimacy, as he asserts a view of men's relationships with other men as naturally and inevitably directed towards problem-solving and collective learning rather than problem-sharing and intimate disclosure. While allowing for a certain amount of emotional expressivity, these relationships retain a utilitarian quality, as the ultimate goal of interactions among men is to realise greater control and choice with women.

For many participants, the most significant difference between friendships born of a shared interest in seduction and those wrought elsewhere was that they enabled rather than impeded sexual encounters with women. Many men told stories about how they and their friends try to sabotage one another's sexual prospects by humiliating each other in front of women. These stories were recognisably 'laddish' – replete with ribald humour, brash language and boorish behaviour – an interactional style that has been described as a kind of 'template' masculinity for young British men (Dempster 2011). In one example of sexual sabotage, Jack recalled trying to introduce a friend from home to a woman he had met on a recent night out, only for the friend to pronounce to her: 'You know, my friend Jack here is a cunt.' Though he had been embarrassed by it at the time, Jack explained to me that his friend was 'having a bit of a laugh'. In an addendum that clearly indicates how laddishness serves to reinforce the primacy of men's homosocial relations over and above their relations with women, he added: 'See, he loves me really.' Jack went on to explain that this is not something that would happen if he was out with other trainers, describing how, instead, they support one another when meeting women: 'I'll say something nice about him, I'll say "He's such an awesome person." You know, you're nice about them. That sort of thing.'

Like Jack, Brent emphasised the cooperative character of his friendships with other men involved in the seduction community, describing how they support one another in their attempts to become more proficient seducers: 'We're constantly wondering how we can help each other improve, gaming wise. And basically we give each other honest feedback. It's like, "Okay, I think you fucked up when you did this," or "I think you should have done this better." We really get some honest feedback with each other.' These relationships are characterised by the provision of constructive criticism, with feedback mechanisms built into everyday interactions, as men collectively attempt to realise goals that are shared but ultimately individual. Derek further illustrated this dynamic when, in our interview, he related the events of the previous evening:

> Last night my friend sent me a text, like, 'I'm just on an instant date.' And I was, like, 'Oh wow, that's really good work,' you know. I was really pleased for him, that he was on an instant date. He ended up going back to – they ended up going back to his flat, and he ended up having sex with her. Now, when I saw him, I was just, like, 'Mate,' you know, like, 'Congratulations' and stuff, you know. Not because it's, like, 'Oh wow, you got laid,' you know, but, like, 'Wow, you're really moving in the right direction. You've really, you know, you've really improved a lot here.' So, you know, it's a lot of high-fiving, that kind of stuff, you know, guy stuff really. Really pleased for each other. And just being, like, 'Okay, so, how are you going to replicate that success, how are you going to do that again?' So it's all about learning.

Derek's description highlights the strong affective dynamics generated through the sharing of sexual stories among heterosexual men, as the moment is imbued with an almost indescribable high. Yet here the purpose of such story-telling is not simply to affirm masculinity but also to learn from one another. Derek emphasises the lack of rivalry between himself and his friend, noting that each is always happy for the other when they have sex with a woman. No sooner has Derek congratulated his friend than he exhorts him to think about how he will improve his performance and build on this success. After all, 'it's all about learning.' In this way, the work of seduction is socialised through friendship.

In her writing on 'postfeminist sisterhood', Alison Winch (2012, 2014) describes a modality of female sociality in which friendships between women become sites of mutual governance. This kind of girlfriendship is highly strategic, as neoliberal rationalities penetrate the bonds of interpersonal relationships through the socialisation of competitive individualism. Such relationships are specifically directed towards the achievement of normative femininity, to which the possession of an aspirational body – slim, toned, conventionally attractive – is central. Bonds between women thus become an investment in the self, on the basis that 'girlfriends are essential in enabling feminine normativity. Their intimate networks of comparison, feedback and motivation are necessary in controlling body image' (Winch 2014: 2). Through shared involvement in seduction, a similar dynamic is elaborated among men, albeit in inverted form. Where postfeminist sisterhood encourages women to engage reciprocal regimes of regulation as a means to *achieve* aspirational female bodies, in the context of the seduction community men engage similar forms of surveillance in order to *access* these aspirational female bodies. The seduction industry thus elaborates a kind of tactical fraternity among men. The coarse yet convivial dynamics of laddishness give way to something altogether more deliberate and calculating, as relationships between men become sites of reciprocal governance directed towards the realisation of a masculine ideal centred on heterosexual prowess. Like the postfeminist girlfriends of Winch's analysis, these masculine subjects are 'not content with being' and 'must always be becoming' (ibid.: 23).

Though involvement in the seduction community can enable men to circumvent the silences imposed by the ordinances of heterosexual masculinity, it almost invariably brings new silences into being. While some of those I spoke to suggested that seduction is effectively an open secret among heterosexual men, practically all of the men I interviewed were concealing their engagement with this sphere from friends and family. When we spoke, David had been involved in the industry on and off for a number of years and had recently taken twelve months out of work to focus on seduction full-time. When I asked if he had told any of his friends about this, he looked horrified and said:

> I can't tell my male friends anything about the pickup industry, it would be just be weird if I told them . . . No, never. No way, no way. No chance. No chance! It would just be weird, like to admit that I need to go to a pickup artist or something. It just should be natural, it's just what men should do, right? It's just what men are programmed to do.

For David, disclosing his involvement in this sphere would be tantamount to admitting that he is not a man. Elsewhere, Ralph explained that he too found it impossible to discuss with friends: 'I find that I can't actually talk about this with my own friends. I haven't told anybody else that I've done this, in my normal circle of friends.' He went on to recount how he had tried to broach the topic with members of his football team – believing that some of them would benefit from attending the events he had been to – but dropped the subject when it became apparent that it was not going to go over well:

> I tried to broach the idea, I said – I just mentioned, 'I've read about this [seduction event] on the web.' My mates were, like, 'That's stupid, that sounds ridiculous,' and 'What's wrong with these guys?' And I was, like, phew! Because I actually wanted to put it out there before sort of admitting to my football team that I'd done this. But the reaction I got was actually very negative.

The seduction industry does not dismantle but, rather, sustains and ultimately capitalises upon the 'privatising effects' (Richardson 2010) and 'necessary silences' (Karioris 2014) of male homosociality, as those who gather in this setting *work around* rather than throw off the injunction of silence. It upholds conventional understandings of what it means to be a man, as the centrality of heterosexual prowess – a competence or proficiency that frequently shades into dominance and ascendancy – remains absolute. Even as relationships forged in this setting can allow for a certain amount of emotional expressivity, these relationships are ultimately self-interested. In this way, we see how 'Men in their seeking for intimacy must disown intimacy itself and aim to find it through its explicit rejection' (Karioris 2014: 107).

Styling masculinity

Assembled in university seminar rooms or clustered around coffee-shop tables, at the outset of commercial training events students are asked to introduce themselves. Trainers running these events are not especially interested in their personal biographies – where they are from, what they do for a living, and so on. Instead, they want to know about their experience with women to date, their familiarity with seduction knowledge-practices, and what it is they want to achieve by taking the course. It is the kind of introductory exercise a teacher or lecturer might use at the beginning of a course – a means to quickly assess students' prior knowledge and objectives going forward, information which can then be used to refine the lesson plan and teaching objectives. At one such event I attended, the first student to introduce himself described having spent the past two years reading about seduction online. Frustrated by his inability to convert the wealth of knowledge he had accumulated into action, he had come on the course to gain in-field experience. His goal for the weekend was to become more confident in bars and nightclubs, where he often felt out of place and was too intimidated to approach women. By way of conclusion, he added: 'Obviously if I get laid that's a big bonus.' The next student began by boasting that he had cured himself of his 'approach anxiety' and could now approach any woman he wanted to; he claimed to have made more than three hundred approaches over the past two months. Evidently sceptical of the awkward-looking man who stood before him, the trainer leading the event interjected to ask: 'What kinds of results have you been getting? Have you got phone numbers, have you got make-outs?' The student shifted uncomfortably and began to explain that he wanted to practise starting conversations with women before attempting these greater feats. The trainer interrupted him again: 'Right, make-outs and phone numbers – write that down. You can't do three hundred approaches and not get that, okay.' With a quick reassuring smile, he then added: 'We're going to help you with that.'

A third student explained that, while he has had a number of long-term relationships, he lacks confidence on account of his short height. Asking him to stand up for a moment, another trainer looked him over and said: 'You're a hot guy, man, but you've got to believe in yourself. It's something we're going to work on.' The fourth student – who had flown to London just for the weekend – described having taken two previous bootcamps with other companies but still found himself unable to date the kinds of women he really wants to be with. The trainer leading the event nodded with recognition and took the opportunity to explain to the group as a whole: 'If you're getting with girls who are not at the level you want, you're settling. And settling is the worst thing you can do. Because every time you see a guy with a hotter girl, you think "I wish I was him."' Calling attention to the confessional style of these introductions, the next student introduced himself by joking about his drinking problem, an oblique reference to the first of the twelve steps that structure Alcoholics Anonymous meetings. As the laughter this comment provoked subsided, he explained that, like others, he was seeking greater confidence and also wanted to work on his conversation skills, as he finds it difficult to sustain interesting discussions with women. One of the last students to introduce himself stood up slowly and began to explain that he sees himself as a 'decent guy', when the trainer interrupted him, saying: 'The problem is, you're not the guy that's going to take them home and bend them over. We need to get you to be that guy.'

Through these introductory exercises, students are called upon to apprehend themselves as objects-of-knowledge and subjects-in-progress, so that trainers can begin the process of making them over. While they are conducted under an aegis of camaraderie, there is nevertheless an element of compulsion attendant on these exercises. Trainers are not averse to cajoling those reluctant to comply with their disciplinary gaze, as was demonstrated when the same trainer impelled one student to reveal his sexual inexperience to the entire bootcamp cohort. Evidently believing that this man had had few, if any, previous sexual encounters with women, the trainer asked: 'Have you had *any* relationships in the past? Be honest.' On occasion, men attending group training events may misread the affective subtext of these introductory sessions and offer too personal a testimony. Such outpourings are swiftly curtailed and redirected by trainers, with a certain amount of tact but little sympathy; while seduction enables and, indeed, often requires men to talk about their perceived sexual shortcomings, training events are not intended as forums for men to disclose their emotional travails or personal hardships.

Instruction in fashion and grooming represents a major component of many seduction training programmes, whether this takes the form of a weekend bootcamp, a week-long residential course or one-to-one coaching. While different companies have different strategies for precisely how they approach this – some offering general fashion advice to all students as part of their overall programme and others including individual consultations with dedicated style advisors – this is very often a requisite part of the course. As one trainer told me: 'It's not an optional session – you have to learn to dress well.' Opening one such session held as part of a bootcamp, the same trainer explained to the audience why it is so important for men to address their image if they want to become more successful with women:

> If you want to get girls that are average looking, then you can dress averagely, and it's fine. But if you really want to get high-quality, classy

girls, they put a lot of effort into themselves. They think about what they're going to wear. And if you're not doing the same, you're not going to be able to get that ten.

While taking an interest in fashion and grooming might seem to trouble conventional understandings of masculinity as 'the natural dividend of the male body' (Weber 2009: 183), consumer culture increasingly enjoins men to engage such practices in order to realise an iteration of manhood defined 'by a heterosexualised logic that situates the "real man" as the agent of desire' (ibid.: 202).

Having established the functionality of fashion for men – which is to be undertaken not for its own sake but as a means to gain access to a higher calibre of sexual partner – the trainer detailed some fashion dos and don'ts. Outlining the various high-street brands and designer labels students should wear, he explained that, while it is not necessary to spend a fortune on clothes, it is important to know where and how to shop for one's age and build. Enjoining students to look at the way he and the other trainers present themselves as a kind of guideline, he explained: 'We get a lot of attention for the way we look.' He then told students to line up at the front of the room and began making individual assessments. While some were assessed favourably and commended for having made appropriate fashion choices, others were disparaged for their lack of sartorial acumen. As with fashion advice directed to men in makeover culture more generally – from upmarket men's magazines such as *GQ* and *Esquire* to television shows such as *Queer Eye for the Straight Guy* (2003–7) – the emphasis throughout was on learning how to embody the 'economic markers of manhood' on the basis that 'the *appearance* of status and wealth can trump the actual possession of such qualities' (Davis et al. 2014: 265–6).[2] One student, casually dressed in jeans and a jumper, was told to compare himself to another more sharply turned-out student, the trainer admonishing: 'Who looks like he owns the yacht, and who looks like he cleans the yacht?'

Halfway through this session, the trainer called on Doug to step forward. Folding his arms across his chest, the trainer leaned back on one leg as he looked Doug slowly up and down. He wore an incredulous expression, as though he simply didn't know where to begin. Starting from the ground up, he indicted each item of Doug's clothing in turn: his shoes were too pointy, his jeans too wide, his T-shirt loose and badly cut, his blazer cheap and ill-fitting. His look, the trainer summarised, was 'All kinds of wrong'. Doug began to protest that this was not his usual style and that he had actually chosen the outfit he was currently wearing in an effort to emulate trainers based on his observations the day before. At this, the trainer began to laugh, and the others soon joined in. When he recovered his composure, the trainer continued his assessment, now turning his attention to Doug's receding hairline. Intent on making an example of him, the trainer swivelled to face the audience and, still pointing at Doug's head, proclaimed: 'If you're losing it, take control and shave your head. It's very masculine and very alpha.' This time Doug didn't protest but instead smiled tepidly. Having finished with Doug, the trainer dismissed him and moved on to the next student.

Though the tone of the trainer's delivery was certainly critical, this encounter was not marked by the kind of symbolic violence that typifies makeover culture more widely, as self-designated experts inflict their tastes and values on people of lower social status than themselves (Weber 2009). As a white man with an elite education who now holds a high-powered corporate job, Doug held significantly more material power than the trainer who was administering fashion advice. Yet, while Doug was in possession of economic and social capital, he supposedly lacked the kind of cultural capital that translates into heterosexual appeal and therefore constitutes a critical marker of masculinity. When we met a week later for our interview, I was curious to see whether or not Doug had implemented the trainer's advice. As I approached the coffee shop that evening, it was clear that he had anticipated my suspense and was standing outside wearing a hoodie. Seeing my questioning expression, he grinned and raised his hand to pull back his hood, revealing a closely shorn scalp. Doug had shaved his head completely, and, under the hoodie left unzipped at the front, I could see he was also wearing the kind of close-fitting T-shirt he had been told to buy in order to draw attention to his toned physique. In one hand he carried a shopping bag filled with other fashionable accoutrements, having decided to do some last-minute shopping ahead of our meeting.

Once we sat down, Doug explained that, although he had always thought of himself as stylish, he recognised now that his former fashion sense had not been conducive to seducing women: 'It wasn't the look that [the trainer] had, which was a threatening look. And I like that look.' By 'threatening' here, Doug is referring to a masculine aesthetic that signals sexual potency and desirability. Inverting the postfeminist masquerade described by Angela McRobbie (2009), where women get done up to mask the 'threat' they pose to men in a context of gender equality, this is a form of gendered aestheticisation intended to elicit heterosexual desire by amplifying men's physical differences from women and thus foregrounding the sexualised danger they may pose. Although inverted, this kind of masculine aesthetic nevertheless functions as a 'strategy for re-establishing gender relations within the heterosexual matrix' (ibid.: 88). That this look is explicitly articulated in terms of 'threat' further highlights the ways in which straight white men are able to resignify conventionally feminised practices in ways that shore up rather than destabilise the association between masculinity and power (Bridges 2013; Bridges and Pascoe 2014).

Not all men who participate in the seduction community seek to cultivate the 'threatening' look adopted by Doug in line with the advice administered by trainers. For Brent, a young black man, doing so would have been actively detrimental and quite possibly dangerous. In our interview, he explained that, despite having grown up hating formal wear – which his family pushed upon him for occasions such as weddings – he had more recently taken to wearing suits while practising seduction. Describing this transition, Brent said:

> I was under the hip-hop influence – I thought it was all about the baggy jeans, bling bling, big jackets. Before I was all about oversized clothes. But now I'm willing to be more formal. Something that I would never have done in the past, never. Not even, like, if you pointed like a gun to my head, I wouldn't go formal.

Brent's decision to dress more formally was in no small part related to the fact that, when dressed in his previously preferred attire of baggy jeans and outsized T-shirts, women he approached on the street frequently responded as though they felt intimidated or threatened by him. He recounted one episode where a woman he approached ran away clutching her handbag: 'She was obviously, like, "Uh oh . . . bad things gonna happen."'

Brent's experiences vividly exemplify how processes of racialisation organise social space and everyday encounters, as black bodies come to be 'seen' and 'felt' as more dangerous than others (Ahmed 2002: 58; Fanon 1986). That seduction coaching generally does not anticipate this possibility or otherwise recognise the particular difficulties black men may face negotiating public space is indicative of its centring of white male experience. Relating his own sartorial practice to a more general stereotyping of young black men in the UK as '24-7 predators' and 'too sexually charged', Brent went on to explain:

> I can talk to someone – this I'm a hundred per cent sure of – with a track suit on, and, even being the nicest guy on earth, there's a higher chance of her blowing me off than if I go in a suit or if I go in formal wear and do exactly the same thing. Like, just how you dress, just changes it

drastically. So, yeah, there's, like, a lot of stereotypes. People don't realise it, but there are.

Adopting formal wear as a classed and racialised signifier of respectability – associated with money and power and thus functioning as a marker of masculine 'having-made-it-ness' (Edwards 2011: 60) – Brent attempts to moderate some of the negative perceptions he faces and thereby mitigate the impact of racism in his day-to-day life. That Brent is a university student and thus has little need to wear a suit highlights the extent to which the dominant imperatives of business and enterprise have come to organise masculinity around the goals of 'neoliberal market achievement, racial anonymity, and professional success' (Weber 2009: 180).

Through its emphasis on personal transformation via conspicuous consumption, the seduction industry reproduces a broader cultural logic whereby 'particular forms of modernised and upgraded selfhood are presented as solutions to dilemmas in contemporary life' (Gill 2008a: 442). This improved mode of selfhood is implicitly white and middle class. While wealthy white men such as Doug seek to fashion themselves as sexually 'threatening' by adopting aspects of urban street style, young black men such as Brent attempt to ameliorate the danger they are assumed to pose by adopting the executive look of business and entrepreneurship. That such discrepancies go largely unremarked upon within the seduction industry evidences the ways in which seduction training very often presupposes a white middle-class body and further demonstrates that 'racism is far beyond the fixative properties' of makeover culture (Weber 2009: 177).

Making men

For those who become involved in the seduction community, trainers embody the possibility of achieving greater control and choice in their relationships with women. Having read the books and blogs in which these men document their transformation – referencing a past in which they were lonely and unpopular while showcasing a present in which they enjoy near constant access to beautiful women as part of a more generally enviable lifestyle – students are very often in thrall to those whom they see as having realised an idealised form of masculine selfhood. As James related in our interview: 'You see the guys that are good at it, like the finished products, and you want to be that.' What marks trainers out as distinct from other men is their capacity to transform themselves into masculine exemplars by achieving success with women. In this they embody a contemporary masculine ideal predicated upon the ability 'to make things happen' (Schrock and Schwalbe 2009: 280), specifically as applied to the intimate realm, though with implications far beyond this. Through a variety of coaching practices seduction trainers attempt to cultivate in other men the dispositions of body and mind they themselves have realised. Impressing the amount of labour involved in this undertaking, trainer Danny explained: 'It's a massive learning curve for most guys. Because it's so big. You're trying to teach self-development, female psychology, the actual technical side of things – there's a lot to learn. I mean, it's not easy, you know, it might take months or years.' Seduction training can thus be thought of as a remedial process, whereby men whose gender performance is deemed deficient – by themselves or others or both – are taught to inhabit more closely the category of masculinity.

Judith Butler's *Gender Trouble* puts forward an understanding of gender as a series of performances or enactments that take on the appearance of being natural through their repetition over time. For Butler, it is by acting like 'women' and like 'men' that we become 'women' and 'men'. In this sense, gender is not simply a performance, but is performative: it brings into being what it names. She writes:

> Gender ought not to be construed as a stable identity or locus of agency from which various acts follow; rather, gender is an identity tenuously constituted in time, instituted in an exterior space through a *stylized repetition of acts*. The effect of gender is produced through the stylization of the body and, hence, must be understood as the mundane way in which bodily gestures, movements, and styles of various kinds constitute the illusion of an abiding gendered self. (Butler [1990] 2011: 191)

Building on the work of Butler and others, Jack Halberstam argues that 'there is a distinct difference between masculinity and performance and femininity and performance' (1998: 238). Through an examination of female masculinity, Halberstam further contends that, where femininity is 'proximate' and 'easily impersonated or performed', masculinity is 'precise' and therefore 'resilient to imitation' (ibid.: 28). Because masculinity is, to a greater extent than femininity, defined by 'realness', its enactment must be muted and restrained in order to be culturally legible: 'all the emphasis is on a reluctant and withholding kind of performance' (ibid.: 239).

Seduction training lays bare the performative character of gender in general and masculinity in particular as heterosexual men are taught not only how to dress but also how to speak, walk, think and feel. While effecting a change of appearance often represents a necessary first step, seduction training is more fundamentally geared towards reshaping masculine sexual subjectivity. Through a variety of teaching mechanisms, trainers attempt to inscribe in other men the 'styles of the flesh' (Butler [1990] 2011) they themselves embody and which are taken to represent the successful enactment of masculinity. In order to do so, they must find ways to make their own corporeal style and embodied dispositions both visible to and practicable by others. Where at one time many relied on instructional guidelines – in the form of autobiographical seduction handbooks or seminar-style DVD packages – increasingly trainers are producing and distributing in-field videos. As discussed in chapter 1, in-field content involves trainers filming themselves, or having themselves filmed by someone else, while they are interacting with women. This material is then often annotated through voice-overs or explanatory subtitles so that trainers can highlight specific gestures, stances and mannerisms, explaining to students exactly what they are doing and why at any given moment of the interaction.

In a popular adaptation of the in-field format, many trainers host screenings of their in-field footage and provide live in-person commentary. I attended one such event towards the end of my fieldwork, held on a weekday evening on a university campus in central London. Having arrived late, I stood for a moment outside the door to the seminar room before entering. Through the glass panel I could see an audience of about forty men, sitting in the dark and watching a video playing via the overhead projector. Standing at the front of the room was a trainer I had met at a number of previous events, his filmic double appearing on screen. Squeezing into the already packed room, I took the seat that was produced for me and, like the two men I sat next to, began to take notes. In the video, filmed in central London, the trainer is talking to a woman on the street. In the seminar room, he stands to one side of the screen, narrating each aspect of the interaction.

Lining up the next video, the trainer promised the audience that the next set was 'super high quality' – the woman an off-duty model he had met during London fashion week. Instead of beginning the video from the initial approach, he fast-forwarded to the end of the interaction, explaining that by this point he had been 'escalating on her for an hour'. Having paid a professional cameraman to spend the day filming his interactions with women, he was now getting impatient, and said: 'This was the second approach of the day, I was, like, "I want to get more out of this," like, "Wrap it up."' Finding the point in the video he wanted, the trainer pressed the play button. He appeared on screen, evidently about to kiss the woman he was standing with outside a tube station. As he leaned in, the on-screen kiss was cheered by the audience. Almost yelling over the din, the trainer commanded: 'Just push it super hard, get the make-out and walk away – always leave her wanting more.'

Satisfied that he now had his audience's full attention, the trainer began the video from the start of the interaction. On screen, he appears slowly running up behind the same woman, this time in another part of the city. To the audience, he explained: 'Part of the mentality of being a guy is doing the choosing. You do the choosing, not her.' In the video, the trainer jogs a little way ahead of the woman and raises his hands, gesturing for her to stop. As she came to a halt in front of him, he gestured emphatically to the audience and exclaimed: 'Easy, so easy!' For the next few minutes they stand talking in the street, the trainer providing a running commentary throughout. Every so often, he paused the video to draw the audience's attention to various aspects of his body language and physical demeanour, occasionally referring back to prepared notes. Having decided to go for a coffee, the pair begin to walk down the street together, the cameraman following close behind.

At this point, the trainer goes over the importance of planning the logistics of an interaction: 'You have to know where you're going to go, where you're going to lead her – because ultimately you want to lead her to the bedroom.' Elaborating on this point, he explains: 'The key to all this, the key to everything, is to meet girls and for them to trust you.' Looking up at the screen as the couple sit down together on a park bench a few minutes later, the trainer said to his audience: 'She's, like, completely following me around now. I could take her anywhere.' After a few minutes, he once again fast-forwarded to the end of the video, to the moment when he leans in to kiss the woman on screen. In the seminar room, he raised his arms expansively and asked: 'Who's going to take something away from this and really do something?' All around me, men were clapping, cheering, raising their hands.

Sitting in darkened classrooms watching videos of other men seduce women, men attending live in-field screenings engage a kind of pedagogical voyeurism. By mediating their interactions with women in this way, trainers are able to elucidate knowledges that would otherwise remain tacit. Whole sequences of interaction become available to be extended or compressed as needed, slowed down, speeded up, or skipped over at will. By adding annotations or providing a running commentary, trainers can pinpoint examples of strong body language and good conversational strategies. They are able to distil precisely the kinds of masculine dispositions they have achieved and to which other men should supposedly aspire. They demonstrate how feeling can be deployed, manipulated, conjured.

Collective screening events additionally function as spaces of more or less anonymous bonding among heterosexual men. Audience members are encouraged to identify with the trainers who appear on screen and whose physical presence at these events implicitly suggests that the exemplary masculinity they have realised is also available to others. The women who are unknowingly made to appear in these videos serve as vehicles through which men enact a kind of homosocial intimacy, even as they largely remain strangers to one another. Such events enable men to place themselves 'conceptually and ideologically within the discourses of masculinity and male sexuality' (Buchbinder 1998: 113), solidifying their identification with other men and against women. This became especially evident in moments of apparent comedy. In one of the videos the trainer at this event showed, the woman he was speaking with momentarily appeared to look directly at the camera, without seeming to realise that she was its target. The audience began to laugh and, bolstered by their enthusiasm, the trainer exclaimed: 'I was shitting it she'd spot the camera!' During another video, while walking with a woman down a busy shopping street, the trainer repeatedly glanced over his shoulder to check that the cameraman was still following them. Sitting down with the woman on a park bench, he turned around momentarily to make sure again that the cameraman was there. Watching this unfold on screen, in the seminar room the trainer said: 'The cameraman braves it in there, and I'm thinking, "Jesus, you're being brave!"' Again the audience erupted with laughter, which was further amplified a few seconds later when the camera wavered behind some shrubbery, the cameraman evidently having lost his footing. Laughing together like this creates a sense of solidarity among men, who are encouraged to bond through their shared deception of women.

With a strong emphasis on experiential learning, virtually all live seduction training events encompass some kind of practical in-field coaching. During these sessions, students approach and interact with women – on the streets, in shops and in cafés, as well as in bars and nightclubs – while being observed by trainers who choreograph their interactions and offer feedback on their performance.[3] In many cases, students are fitted with discreet microphones so that trainers can not only watch but also listen in as they approach and speak with women. After each interaction ends, students rejoin trainers to receive their evaluation. Typically, this will encompass comments about their approach and the manner in which they delivered their 'opener'; their body language, facial expression and tone of voice; the conversational patterns they employ; and the effectiveness of their 'closing' strategy. When trainers are working with more than one student, this is often done in tandem: when one student approaches, the others remain with the trainer, who narrates the interaction and provides commentary on the approaching student's technique; when that student returns, the next student is sent out to approach. Many trainers additionally film students during in-field sessions. Later, these videos are watched collectively, giving students the opportunity to become audiences to their own as well as each other's performances.[4] Through these kinds of media-enabled surveillance mechanisms, every aspect of masculine conduct becomes available for assessment, analysis and improvement.

During in-field coaching, seduction trainers direct their students to think and feel differently about their interactions with women. One of the most common hurdles to be addressed is that of 'approach anxiety', a term which denotes the apprehension and fear some men experience when initiating interactions with women. Within the seduction community, approach anxiety is understood to be rooted in evolution, as Derek explained to me in our interview:

> Back in prehistoric times, what would happen if a male tried to hit on one of the females when he wasn't the alpha male? The alpha male would pick up a rock and he would bash his head in, until he was dead, you know. So, psychologically, in our heads, we're still the same people that we were back then . . . So your whole anxiety about doing something like this is not a real fear, it's a fear that you can't explain. It's not a fear of anything in particular, it's not a fear of her boyfriend coming over, it's not a fear of girls, it's not a fear of anything. It's not even really a fear of rejection. It's a deep-rooted psychological fear of getting killed, potentially, potentially *dying*. Because that's what would have happened. If you messed up, you were *dead*. Know what I mean? Somewhere in our head, our brain is saying: 'Don't do this.' And it never goes, it never goes.

While for Derek and many other men such explanations are compelling, approach anxiety can also be understood as a fear of unmasking the constructed character of masculinity. That is, approaching women may provoke anxiety precisely because this is something men are taught to believe should come naturally to them, and it is a key criterion on which claims to masculinity are evaluated. In this view, approach anxiety is a parallel or prelude to the more widely discussed 'performance anxiety', which manifests 'when masculinity is marked as performative rather than natural' (Halberstam 1998: 236). In each case, the underlying anxiety 'is not, as one might think, an anxiety about doing; it is a neurotic fear of exposing the theatricality of masculinity' (ibid.).

In order to overcome approach anxiety, seduction training often involves students approaching large numbers of women 'for practice', on the basis that this will enable them to become 'desensitised'. During one in-field coaching session I observed, the trainer had his student approach any and every woman that passed by, on and on for hours. Eventually, the student complained that he finds it hard to talk to women in whom he has no sexual interest and would prefer to approach only those to whom he is attracted. Clearly exasperated, the trainer retorted: 'Look, it shouldn't matter. You should be able to talk to any girl. Okay, it might be better if you actually like her, but it shouldn't matter – you should always be able to speak with conviction.' Producing an emotional display at odds with one's own affective state thus becomes a means to realise the kind of detachment deemed necessary to become successful with women. The basis and substance of each interaction is more or less irrelevant, as the aim is not to foster connection but, instead, to cultivate a mindset. It is not enough, however, for this to be a conscious performance. Rather, through seduction training men are expected to realise this emotional style in a deeper way. Later that afternoon, the same trainer scolded one of his more junior colleagues, who returned from an approach smiling broadly and saying: 'She was really nice, I really liked her.' With a withering look, the more senior trainer told him: 'Don't get so excited.' Suitably chastened, the junior trainer quickly masked the embarrassment that flickered momentarily across his face and turned his attention to a student. While boasting about sexual exploits is permissible and, indeed, encouraged, simpler and less obviously strategic forms of pleasure are not.

While seduction training is geared towards the remaking of masculine subjectivity, the form of masculinity elevated here is not equally available to all men. Following a bootcamp course, Anwar described coming to the recognition that he would never approximate the trainers who had taught him over the weekend:

> I'm never going to be like Jasper, you know. This tall, blonde – you know, you know, this *god* of a man who can walk into a room and women melt. I'm never going to be like that. I'm not stupid, I know that, okay. I'm never going to be, you know . . . you know, the smooth, suave, sophisticated Alfie, I'm never going to be, you know, the cool – the cool Max, you know . . . I have a dual personality in the sense that some of me wishes I could be those people. But the reality of it is, I look at my

life and who I am and my job and everything else, and I'm thinking I will never be, I could never be.

Despite having also been coached by a British Asian trainer over the weekend, here Anwar named only white trainers and highlighted physical characteristics such as being tall and blonde to emphasise his distance from them. Yet Anwar's ambivalent desire to 'be like these people' is not a desire for whiteness per se. Rather, it is a desire for the horizons of possibility that whiteness makes available. As Sara Ahmed argues: 'whiteness is an orientation that puts certain things within reach' (2007a: 154). While feeling that he is unlikely to realise the kind of masculinity embodied by seduction trainers, Anwar was nevertheless keen to undertake further training: 'I could go to more bootcamps and just hang about, do a bit of day game, hang about with the PUAs. I'd love to be able to do that, you know what I mean. For me, I'd love to be able to hang around with this crew.'

Masculinising spaces

Ahead of the final session on the second day of a bootcamp event I attended, a trainer went to the front of the room to tell the small assembly of students about the week-long residential programme the company offers in addition to the weekend training course they were already attending. Promising not to take up too much of their time – wary of being accused of up-selling – he began by explaining:

> What is the residential? It's seven days living with us. You live with us in central London. We were in the flat last night and there were about ten girls there – that's just your average night in the residential apartment. What does the course involve? It is a lot of fun, you do get a lot of results, but it is a lot of work as well. If you're not willing to work, you shouldn't apply, because it's a twenty-four seven programme. For seven days you're going to be fully immersed in the world of pickup. Your results will rocket – not from day five, from day one. From day one you'll be working hard, and getting results from day one.

After detailing the application process and payment details – the residential programme offered by this company costs over £4,000, which can be paid in monthly instalments – the manager called upon the current residential client to come and share his experiences thus far with the bootcamp students. Striding from the back of the room where he had been sitting with the trainers, he paused briefly to shake hands with the trainer before looking around the room and saying: 'Where do I start? I mean, it was amazing. Absolutely amazing.'

The residential client began by detailing the numerous sexual encounters he had had over the past week, which included taking a woman home on the first night of the programme and having sex with her, and later having a threesome. Describing his personal highlight, he recounted meeting a woman on the street during a daygame session and spending the afternoon with her. Eventually he took her back to the residential apartment for something to eat, promising they would go out again for ice cream afterwards: 'I started escalating on her, took her to the bedroom. We got it on in the middle of the day. Like, not even four o'clock. That's how my Wednesday went. Absolutely amazing.' Impressing how valuable the programme had been – he has now entirely resolved his anxiety issues – he explained that, while his results had progressed after the bootcamp course, taking the residential programme had produced more fundamental changes in him, such that he now possesses not only the skills but the belief system necessary to be successful with women. Enjoining those attending the bootcamp to find a way to pay for the residential programme, no matter what their financial situation, he concluded by saying: 'I was destroying girls. They were just melting in my hands. It was fantastic.'

Residential programmes and bootcamp courses offer men access not only to a particular service – that of seduction training – but to a particular experience. Those who pay to attend these events, at a typical cost of several hundred if not thousands of pounds, are afforded temporary access to the lifestyle trainers enjoy as a homosocial collective. The seduction industry must thus be understood as part of the 'experience economy' (Pine and Gilmore 1998), and in this respect it has much in common with other sites of commercial sexual exchange. In an auto-ethnographic study of strip clubs in the United States, Katherine Frank (2003) describes how clubs afford men the opportunity not only to look at women's bodies but to enjoy – however fleetingly – an atmosphere of glamour and luxury. In this way, strip clubs offer men a space to enact 'masculinising practices' (Connell 2000), where they can cultivate a sense of themselves as authentically masculine. Similarly, in her work on sex tourism in Costa Rica, Megan Rivers-Moore argues that one of the major reasons North American men travel abroad to buy sex is because doing so allows them to access both sexual and *social* experiences they otherwise cannot afford. Sex tourism thus encompasses 'transnational masculinising practices', whereby crossing borders enables men to 'claim a level of social status that would be unavailable to them at home' (Rivers-Moore 2012: 866).

In the context of the seduction industry, paying to attend commercial events offers men the opportunity to participate in an exclusive form of homosociality in which women are abundant and circulate freely as objects of exchange among men. Enrolling on seduction training programmes – especially where these involve a live-in or holiday-abroad component – thus permits men to live out their very own 'fantasy-reality' (Frank 1998) in a manner similar to that offered by other kinds of sexualised entertainment and touristic practices. What differentiates the seduction community from these other arenas of commercial sexual exchange – apart from the lack of direct remuneration for sexual access to women's bodies[5] – is that the masculinising practices in which men engage in this setting are expressly intended to translate into other spheres. In contrast to the delimited forms of enhanced status that commercial strip clubs and sex tourism can offer, attending a weekend bootcamp or week-long residential programme is not simply an 'outlet' or 'escape'. Rather, seduction training events promise to enable men to cultivate a set of skills and dispositions that can be *carried into* other areas of life. The key difference, then, is that the seduction industry has an expressly pedagogic function.

Commercial training events provide a forum for men to cultivate and then demonstrate heterosexual prowess in the presence of other men, thereby laying claim to a more dominant or authoritative form of masculinity. This was readily evidenced by the sense of confidence that attending events inspired in many men. In our interview, James explained:

> It's that kick up your arse that you need. Outside the bootcamp obviously the thought of approaching somebody that you've never met – especially if she's hot – it's quite daunting. But they give you that sort of goal, and before you know it you're walking over to her, you know. And even just having them there, just being with other males, it's like you've got the confidence then. You feed off each other's confidence, in a way.

For James, it is the presence of other men that creates the performance imperative necessary for him to face the challenge of approaching women. Far from constraining or undermining men's sense of themselves as masculine – a dynamic that often manifests in their relationships with men elsewhere – seduction training provides a space in which men can affirm themselves as masculine. This is an opportunity worth paying for precisely because 'heterosexual confirmation must be diffracted somehow back through the patriarchal structure, then recognized and authorized by other men' (Buchbinder 1998: 110).

This sense of affirmation can continue beyond the temporal confines of the training event itself. Anwar described the high he experienced in the immediate aftermath of a bootcamp weekend:

> I was on cloud nine when I left. I was confident, I was laughing, and everybody noticed. I mean *everybody noticed*. I went to a work do afterwards and everyone was going, 'What's happened to you? You've just become a completely different person!' Laughing, confident, not taking any – not cowering to the good looking AMOGs[6] in the room. *None of it.*

Enabling men to confirm their masculinity among men, the seduction industry is premised upon and reinforces the patriarchal dispensation of power wherein 'men come to depend for their definition as masculine upon their being recognised as such by other men' (Buchbinder 1998: 65). Yet in allowing men to experience themselves as masculine in ways they seemingly cannot do elsewhere, the seduction industry can create a kind of dependency. As Anwar went on to describe, the come-down after the initial high was dramatic: 'I have to admit, a week later I went into depression.' Because of this, he was weighing up further training options, with a residential programme top of his list: 'It isn't cheap, but I just feel, on the whole, for six and a half thousand . . . you get a whole week, and you get a place to live and hang out. So I'd love to do it, and I'd love to get better at it.'

The seductions of community

For many of those who attend live training events the opportunity to spend time with trainers constitutes a major part of the appeal. Recalling how he felt as a student at his first training programme, Jack – now a trainer himself – explained: 'I remember that from my course, I recognised guys and I was, like, "Oh my God, it's you!" And then I was hanging out with them, and it was amazing. I was, like, "Oh my God, I'm hanging out with really cool guys!"' Given that the sociality of seduction training programmes is a significant part of the experience, it is important for trainers to create a sense of camaraderie. As in other forms of market-based intimacy, this does not occur without significant efforts on the part of those staging the experience. One of the most crucial aspects of a trainer's job is thus to subtly erase the commercial interests that mediate their relationships with students, such that this coming together appears to be based on genuine friendship. As Jack later explained:

> The whole idea is to make the student feel very included and part of the group. More like, 'Oh, we're all going out together, and we're all friends and we're going to help you out with this.' We try to bring them up as

much as possible, make them feel included in the group – as if they were coming on a night out with us and we'd instruct them along the way.

To produce this kind of affective dynamic – a concerted if not necessarily contrived form of sociality – trainers must actively manage their relationships with students in order to create an enjoyable and memorable experience. Part of what the seduction industry markets to men, then, is the promise of fraternity. It is perhaps for this reason that the language of community persists, even as this formation has become heavily commercialised; brotherhood remains a powerful selling point.

For some of the men I interviewed, awareness of the financial interests at play in the trainer–student relationship created a certain ambivalence. Doug, for example, said:

> It was a client relationship, which always feels uncomfortable when you try and socialise within it. Or maybe it doesn't to most people, but I always think at the back of my mind, 'Whether or not this person likes me, he is effectively paid to like me and be nice to me.' Which I have in business a lot, too. It creates a power dynamic and a power imbalance.

While acknowledging that the relationship is underpinned by commercial imperatives, Doug nevertheless went on to claim that the camaraderie he experienced while attending the event was genuine: 'But I got on quite well with most of the trainers, and I think some of them liked me.' Others tried to downplay or dismiss the commercial nature of these relationships entirely, as when Antonio – who had undertaken training with a different company – described his experience of the bootcamp: 'They seem like really cool guys. They're just doing it because . . . like, it's genuine, I think that these are genuine people. Not trying to sell something.' Thus while relationships between trainers and students obviously have a commercial component, this should not be too much on display.

Where students were confronted with evidence that the intimacy they shared with trainers had been feigned or performed, this could be deeply upsetting for them. When I met Derek, who had completed a bootcamp course and then a residential programme in quick succession, he had recently begun an unpaid internship with the same company. Working alongside the trainers who just a few weeks previously had been his teachers prompted an emotional crisis, as Derek came to realise that the friendship that had been extended to him during his time as a student may not have been entirely genuine. In bitter tones, he recounted that, when he had been their student, trainers had really seemed to like him and had promised that they would continue hanging out together once the programme finished. However, no such unpaid companionship had materialised: 'It was, like, "Oh yeah, we'll hang out some time, after you've finished the course." But it's bullshit. It's all bullshit.' Derek went on to describe the anger he felt on becoming privy to the discussions trainers have about students after work and during staff breaks:

> They're bitching about students, like, 'Oh yeah, that guy, he's got no fucking chance, we're not going to be able to help him.' All this sort of stuff. And I'm just thinking to myself, 'You fucking son of a bitch,' you know. It's just like . . . these people are in a fucking position of trust, people look up to these people. Like, God, I remember when I came along I was like, 'Wow, these people are gods, these people are not normal, you know, they've got a skill set that I really desire.' And when I heard that, it really spoilt it for me, because I'm thinking to myself, 'Well, I wonder what they were saying about me when I came on the bootcamp', you know? 'Who's that fucking retard', you know?

Confronted with such deceitful behaviour, Derek found the memory of the homosociality he had enjoyed during the bootcamp and residential programmes was irrevocably tarnished. The trainers he had hoped to become friends with not only revealed themselves to be duplicitous but exposed the essentially profit-orientated character of trainer–student relationships. In this way, the fantasy of community the seduction industry offers up was shattered.

Yet whether or not the promise of fraternity is realised – even briefly – depends very much on the particular trainers and students involved. Where some students I interviewed felt genuinely welcomed and included by trainers at events, others described being virtually ignored. These dynamics of inclusion and exclusion, of attention and inattention, are informed by unspoken assessments trainers make about the masculine capital their students possess. George, a short and soft-spoken Chinese man, described being overlooked by trainers at a weekend bootcamp: 'To be really honest, I don't think the trainers paid much attention to me. They didn't really talk to me that much.' Moe, a tall and well-built Middle Eastern man, had a wholly different experience of the same event: 'Very, very cool guys, really. And I felt very welcome. I mean, it was my first time in England, and it was great.' Significantly, while George had been taken with the rest of the bootcamp cohort to a mid-range club in tourist-dense Piccadilly, Moe had been singled out by trainers as one of two students to be brought to a high-end club in west London. When I asked Moe what he thought of the other students on the course, he sighed and said: 'I understand you're there to get help, but you have a responsibility to take action as well. Some people maybe don't understand that. The instructor can lead you, but they can't take you all the way. You have to push that little extra as well.' While seduction training events enjoin men to celebrate 'masculine sameness in the face of a variety of potentially disrupting differences' (Wiegman 2001: 367), the forms of homosocial intimacy elaborated here are not extended equally to all men.

That the sociality made available via training events appeals to many heterosexual men is demonstrated not only by the commercial success of bootcamp courses and residential training programmes but also by the sheer number of men who otherwise try to find ways to participate in these spaces. Alongside the trainers who are paid to teach and the students who pay to attend, many of the events I observed involved men who were neither teaching nor learning in any official capacity but who nevertheless found some reason to come along. They included former students, who dropped by with or without invitation to catch up with trainers and meet new students, as well as former company employees who occasionally joined in the in-field training sessions. Indeed, the appeal of participating in the seduction industry is such that free labour is exceptionally easy to come by, with many companies offering unpaid internships, such as the one Derek took up. During my fieldwork I met a number of men who were taking the same training programme again for a second or third time, and many others who had taken numerous training courses with different companies. Men who are unable to access the commercial spaces of the seduction industry – likely because they are unaffordable to them – often frequent its well-trodden urban geography, hanging out around Oxford Street hoping to get a glimpse of trainers in action. On one occasion, a young man who could have been no more than fifteen or sixteen years old approached the thirty-something trainer I was observing and said: 'Hey, man, I'm a big fan of yours, I've seen all of your videos.' The trainer shook the young man's hand and chatted with him briefly, asking how long he had been in the game, before wishing him good luck. When I asked him about this later, he simply shrugged and said: 'It happens all the time.' I later discussed these observations with Jenny, a woman who works in the industry; she nodded in recognition and said: 'I always say they're in it for the social life.'

Yet despite its trappings of fraternity and promises of brotherhood, the seduction industry is a constantly shifting constellation of alliances and antagonisms. Relationships forged among men in this setting are often highly fragile, frequently giving way to back-stabbing and betrayal. Though many of the trainers I interviewed described having close friendships with other trainers – living together, travelling together, seducing women together – these relationships regularly and sometimes spectacularly collapsed. On a number of occasions, relationships between trainers who were friends when I first met them later broke down, such that when I met one or the other again I was told that they were now bitterly at odds. At other times I learned of such feuds via public vendettas conducted over social media. The generally fractious character of the industry is well known to those who work within it, and indeed these hostilities are often catalogued by the industry's self-appointed chroniclers under titles such as 'Greatest PUA fights of all time' (Kenny 2012). Very often, business interests are at the root of the conflict, such that friendship is sacrificed in the interests of profit. While the promise of community is seductive, this is an industry that breeds weak social ties.

'Professional friendship'

Not all training services on offer in the seduction industry conform to the episodic model of bootcamp and residential courses, as some trainers prefer to work with students on a one-to-one basis over extended periods of time. One such trainer, Rahul, invited me to observe his training sessions with Gavin, a student he has been working with for a number of years. We met on a Saturday morning at a train station, where the pair began the day with a business-like breakfast during which they reviewed Gavin's short-, medium- and long-term goals. After breakfast, we went down to the main plaza, where Gavin began to approach women while Rahul and I watched. After each approach, Rahul congratulated Gavin on his performance with a high-five, saying: 'You're amazing!' After an hour at the station we took the tube into central London and went to a games arcade, where Gavin and Rahul played a few rounds on the punching machine game.

As we went to leave the arcade, Rahul stopped and walked back to the ticket desk, where a woman was working alone behind the counter. He spoke to her for a minute or two, then returned with an added swagger in his step; Gavin seemed impressed and asked what had happened, but Rahul was coy and said little, telling him simply: 'I'll *definitely* be coming back next week.' Just before 12 p.m., three hours after we had met, Rahul announced that it was time for lunch. For the next hour, I made only occasional contributions as Gavin and Rahul discussed industry gossip and reviewed a film they had recently watched together as part of their weekly online 'hangout' sessions conducted over the Google communication platform. After lunch, Gavin made a few more approaches, before we met up with some friends and students of Rahul's later in the afternoon. By 6 p.m., when Rahul decided that it was time for dinner, I was deeply perplexed by how little time Gavin had actually spent approaching and talking to women; by my count, he had made fewer than ten approaches over an eight-hour training session, none of which had lasted more than fifteen minutes and many far less than this.

When I interviewed Gavin a few weeks later, I came to better understand his relationship with Rahul. While based on and enabled by a commercial exchange, for Gavin this was a relatively inconsequential aspect of their relationship. Gavin viewed Rahul as a trainer – on whose services he estimated himself to have spent in the region of £5,000 – but also as a friend. Responding to a question I asked about their relationship, he explained: 'We had a discussion about this. He sees me more as a client, which is fine. I see him as a friend, but we keep it professional.' I asked him to elaborate:

> We keep it professional, you know . . . he wants to see me as just a client. Personally I can see him as a friend. I mean, he's a friend as well as a coach to me, but he was discussing this with me, and I think he was saying that he wants to . . . obviously he wants to keep the professionalism there. So, ahm . . . you know . . . like, take for example, he won't tell me stuff about his other clients as well, because of client confidentiality. I mean, even if we were friends, he wouldn't tell me anything about his clients. You know, like if someone was going, 'Oh, go on mate, you can tell me about it', sort of thing. I mean, I respect that as well, I respect that. I mean, I'd say we've got a professional friendship, so to speak. We've got a professional friendship.

The 'professional friendship' enumerated here by Gavin – the boundaries of which appear to have been determined entirely by Rahul – signals a profound reordering of the social and cultural parameters within which intimate relationships are configured. As Elizabeth Bernstein has argued in her work on commercial sex: 'the spheres of public and private, intimacy and commerce, have interpenetrated one another and thereby been mutually transformed, making the post-industrial consumer marketplace a prime arena for securing varieties of interpersonal connection that circumvent this duality' (2001: 398; 2010). Gavin's characterisation of his relationship with Rahul as a kind of market-based intimacy between heterosexual men – a seemingly platonic parallel to the better known phenomenon of 'professional girlfriends' (Hoefinger 2011) – exemplifies precisely this interpenetration, suggesting that such dynamics now extend well beyond the realm of commercial sex.

For Bernstein, it is crucial to understand that it is not simply that particular forms of intimacy are being commodified – rather, the meaning of intimacy is being transformed in much more fundamental ways. In her work on the 'outsourced self', which explores how intimate relationships are being reconfigured by their availability on the open market, Arlie Russell Hochschild (2012) has begun to consider the potential implications of these kinds of transformations. One possible ramification she identifies is that, for some people, ordinary and unpaid forms of intimacy seem to fall short by comparison with their commercial counterparts. To this end, it is worth noting the comparison Gavin made between the dynamics that characterise his relationship with Rahul and those he shares with other friends:

> Like, if I'm still with some of my old friends, if I get rejected by this super-hot girl, I'd have some of these friends who are looking at me thinking, 'See Gavin, I told you you'd get rejected.' That's why I'm less likely to approach in front of them. With Rahul it would be like, 'Don't worry about it, no, don't worry about it, just work on your confidence, this is what you need to do, and you can get the next one.' You know, somebody who's encouraging.

For Gavin, the relationship he has with Rahul offers greater benefits and rewards than the more conventional – non-commercial – friendships he shares with other men. Where his other friends might discourage or dissuade him, Rahul is an unerring source of support and encouragement. As such, paying for homosocial intimacy – while not necessarily the descriptor he would himself use – is an unproblematic and indeed beneficial arrangement for Gavin and for many other men who engage seduction training services.

Examining the relational dynamics and affective textures elaborated among men involved in the seduction community, it becomes evident that the commercial interests at stake here effectively capitalise on the 'privatising effects' (Richardson 2010) that men's homosocial relationships often impose. This cultural formation offers men a means to negotiate a tension inherent in the very structure of male homosociality: in order to ward off criticism from other men and to participate fully in certain rituals of homosociality, men are expected to be able to demonstrate heterosexual competency to other men; yet, at the same time, the conventional ordinances of homosociality prevent men who lack this critical marker of masculine status from seeking advice from those who possess it. By virtue of their temporally and spatially bound character, commercial training events create spaces for men to pursue heterosexual competency with and among men in a manner that will supposedly enable them to bolster their status among men elsewhere. Yet, while the seduction community is largely populated by men, in fundamental ways this industry has women at its centre. In chapter 3 I take up this issue by examining how the forms of expertise elaborated in the seduction industry make heterosexual intimacies knowable and liveable in some ways, while foreclosing and delimiting others.

3

Manufacturing Consent

It's Sunday morning and still quiet as I walk with a trainer and his student around Soho. The student is nervous, even more so than he was yesterday, and becomes increasingly dispirited as one woman and then another brushes past him. He asks the trainer what he's doing wrong – everything was fine yesterday, so what's the problem now? Is he approaching from the right angle? Is he smiling enough? What about his hands, should he raise them higher? They go over some technical details, before the trainer tells him not to worry so much, saying that it's not worth analysing the first few sets. The student still seems tense, but nods and says: 'I just need to get one out of my system.' After a few more failed attempts – where women either decline to stop entirely or cut the conversation off once he has delivered his opening line – he manages to speak briefly to a woman who had been walking quickly down a narrow thoroughfare. She too walks away after a moment, her manner hurried. Coming back towards us, fists stuffed into his pockets and gaze averted, the student mutters: 'Bitch.'

The rest of the session doesn't go much better, and towards the end the trainer decides to do a demonstration. He scans the now congested street and then darts into the crowd. He runs after a woman and stops her, but as he's delivering his opening line she's looking around, incredulous, and asks: 'What's going on?' The woman tells the trainer that he's the third man to approach her that morning, all of them saying the same thing. He feigns surprise and attempts to laugh it off. She shakes her head and goes to walk away, but as she does so the trainer steps to the side and blocks her path. Looking at her intently, his face cloaked in sincerity, he gently places a hand on her shoulder and offers a reassuring smile. Her mouth twists slightly, but she stays, and a few minutes later he's giving her his phone and telling her to enter in her contact details. When she finally walks away, the trainer returns to the small group of students who have gathered to watch and tells them: 'You have to disregard what the girl says and be self-assured. Really self-assured.'

It's the final in-field session of the day and already dark out. We've just emerged from a café when suddenly one of the trainers begins jogging down Carnaby Street, running after a woman in a bright green coat. Another trainer tells all of the students to watch – this is their chance to see one of the best in the business do a live approach – but his eyes begin to wander as he's speaking. Abruptly, he runs off, saying: 'I'll do these two.' Seconds later he is talking to two tall blonde women, both dressed in black. The students continue to stand outside the café, looking from one trainer to the other. To my right is a third trainer. I can feel him twitching in anticipation as a woman in a woolly pink hat walks by, and then he too is weaving through the crowd, eventually stopping her a short distance past where the first trainer is standing with the green-coated woman. The cameraman filming the in-field session cannot believe his luck – three trainers at once, all on the same street, all picking up. Panning from one to the other in quick succession, he laughs and shouts: 'All trainers go!'

In a discussion of pornography and cultural politics, Stephen Maddison asks: 'What forms of sex are fostered by neoliberal ideologies? And in what kinds of social relations do these forms of sex take place?' (2013: 102). Maddison argues that the pursuit of sexual pleasure has become a form of labour, with pornography users engaging elaborate practices of searching, sorting, filing and storing. In this way, 'pornographic pleasures, in all their accessibility, standardization and dependability, satisfy the need for work-centric patterns of social relations' (2013: 110). Maddison's analysis resonates with those of scholars elsewhere, who contend that the intersubjective dimensions of eroticism are being hollowed out by an economic system that exhorts individuals to responsible self-management while at the same time normalising insecurity and precarity (Gregg 2013; Power 2009; Tyler 2004). These approaches recognise the fundamental interconnectedness of sex and work, love and labour, eros and economics.

What is less evident in existing analyses are the specifically *gendered* dimensions of neoliberal sex. This chapter takes up this issue by examining the system of expertise elaborated in the seduction industry, which puts forth a particular understanding of heterosexual sex. I consider how seduction partakes in and extends a more general systematisation of sex that has been in progress for decades. I hone in specifically on the concept of 'last-minute resistance', or 'LMR', which refers to the supposedly token objections women make prior to having sex and prescribes a range of methods by which this can be overcome. Examining how men negotiate seduction knowledge-practices in the context of their interactions with women, I detail some of the sexual stories shared with me in interviews. I go on to interrogate how professional seducers and career pickup artists establish authority by claiming to have deciphered the 'truth' of sex for women, an authority that is bolstered by drawing on and receiving endorsements from evolutionary psychology. I then discuss how research by feminist psychologists challenges this presumption of 'truth' by foregrounding women's experiences and revealing just how pervasive dynamics of coercion and violence are in heterosexual sex, dynamics that are further complicated within the context of postfeminism. I conclude, finally, by arguing that seduction is a specifically *masculinist* mode of sexual conduct, which not only thoroughly rationalises sex but excuses men from having to engage with women as relational subjects.

While engaging questions of knowledge and expertise, I should make clear that the analyses developed in this chapter are not concerned to debate whether or not the tactics and techniques made available within the seduction industry actually enable men to 'seduce' women. That is to say, I do not attempt to adjudicate whether or not these knowledge-practices are effective, as research elsewhere does (Hall and Canterberry 2011). Rather, by engaging a Foucauldian framework that seeks to examine the constitution of truths rather than to reveal falsehoods (see Foucault [1980] 1984, [1985] 1990), I trace the connections between this system of expertise and the broader patterns of coercion and violence that pattern women's intimate lives. In doing so, I refuse to accept the premise that, simply because some women go along with and indeed may endorse the use of seduction techniques, these practices are therefore unproblematic. I thus join other feminist scholars in rejecting the pervasive assumption that choice represents the bottom line of feminism, as though, 'so long as a woman's actions or circumstances are considered a result of her own choices, no further analysis or problematisation of them is welcome or warranted' (Stuart and Donaghue 2011: 99).

Systematising sex

In her work on the social ordering of emotional experience, Arlie Russell Hochschild offers up the concept of 'feeling rules' to describe the norms and expectations that 'govern how people try or try not to feel in ways "appropriate to the situation"' (1979: 552). Elaborating on this idea in *The Managed Heart*, she gives the example of a bride on her wedding day:

> Drawing on her understanding of the general rules for how brides should see and feel and seem, the bride makes herself up. She acts like a bride. When everything goes well, she experiences a unity between the event (the wedding), the appropriate way to think about it (to take it seriously), and the proper way to feel about it (happy, elated, enhanced). (1983: 60–1)

Hochschild's analysis is useful in understanding the system of expertise elaborated in the seduction community. For sublimated in all seduction knowledge-practices is a recognition of the implicit feeling rules of heterosexuality, particularly as they pertain to women. This knowledge formation is underpinned by myriad socially regulated and culturally enforced assumptions about how a woman *should* feel when given a compliment, how a woman *ought* to respond when told she is attractive and desirable. In this way, seduction attempts to tap into and manipulate the emotional conventions that mark out gender divisions and 'without which men and women would not reproduce their roles and identities' (Illouz 2013: 3).

One of the most popular seduction models to have emerged from the London scene is the Daygame Blueprint. Borrowing its aesthetic and conceptual motif from the world of engineering – where blueprints reproduce technical specifications for the design of buildings and other infrastructure – this model elaborates four distinct phases of interaction and prescribes specific techniques to be employed at each stage. The product website explains that the Blueprint is 'not a set of scripted lines or routines' but serves instead as a 'sequential, phase-driven approach to interacting with strangers'. Through a combination of in-field videos and step-by-step instruction, the programme enables users to 'deconstruct what it really takes to meet and seduce women during the day' (Moore and Barre 2016).

Like other seduction models, the Daygame Blueprint codifies heterosexual intimacy into a linear series of stages, outlining four key phases of interaction: Capture, Attraction, Rapport and Seduction. In the first of these, men are told how to stop women in the street using an 'attention snap' – which breaks the standard rhythm of public interactions – and are given detailed advice about what to say and how to position themselves physically. 'Assumption stacking', which involves making observations about the person rather than asking questions, enables the conversation to continue in a seemingly spontaneous and authentic way, though the general conversational pattern is almost wholly predetermined. The Attraction phase outlines a series of techniques to be deployed in rapid succession in order to build momentum, with 'assumption stories' – whereby narrative is layered onto the assumption statements already made – used to create a sense of liveliness that also facilitates 'self-amusement'. Techniques of 'challenging', disagreeing or questioning things a woman says, and 'push/pull', indicating and then disavowing sexual interest, are deployed to create tension and uncertainty. In the Rapport phase techniques of 'deep rapport' and 'emotional connection' are introduced to foster a sense of trust and intimacy, as men are enjoined to guide women

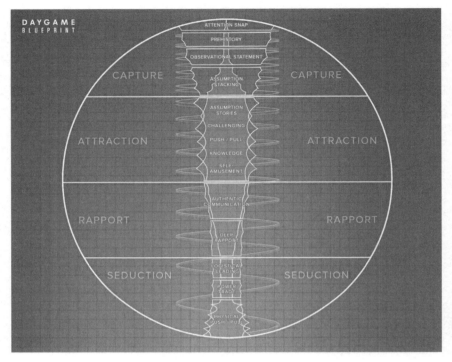

Figure 3.1 The Daygame Blueprint

towards emotionally rich conversation topics designed to ensure 'she'll feel like she's known you forever' (Moore and Barre 2016). The Seduction phase necessitates 'logistical leading', on the basis that, in order to seduce women, there are 'a few objections you have to overcome in order to prevent her from feeling bad about it' (ibid.). This phase further encompasses a range of psychological strategies and physical techniques. As in the Attraction phase, 'push/pull' is used to create tension but now takes a physical rather than a conversational form. Bodily contact is progressively increased and then decreased in an effort to circumvent the possibility of women resisting men's advances, again by creating ambiguity about where the interaction is going.

The Blueprint model both reflects and reproduces a more general systematisation of sex that has been in progress for some time. Building on the work of Antonio Gramsci, specifically his writings on the emergence of a new sexual ethic under Fordism, the sociologist Gail Hawkes contends that, from the mid-twentieth century onwards, 'legitimate sexual acts and sexual pleasures were those which corresponded to the Fordist production process – repetitive and reproducible detailed tasks with a single endpoint in mind.' Sex came to be understood as a product, the outcome of a 'preordained labour process' (Hawkes 1996: 105). These same logics have become amplified within contemporary constructions of heterosexual sex. Discussing how managerial imperatives manifest in sex advice dispensed by men's magazines, for example, Anna Rogers describes how the reader is invited 'to ensure his sex life is "well planned", "controlled", "efficient" and "effective"' (2005: 186). Sexual pleasure and intimacy are framed as achievements to be pursued in line with production methods more commonly associated with the realms of science and economics, as the so-called science of sex – based in the study of brain chemistry, hormones and erogenous zones – enables its rationalised administration. Arguing that the commercialised management of everyday life now extends to the intimate sphere, Melissa Tyler contends that 'sexuality has also become yet another aspect of the lifeworld in which the work ethic seemingly reigns supreme' (2004: 100).

With the emergence of post-Fordism as a new regime of capital accumulation under neoliberalism, these patterns are shifting. Where Fordism was characterised by rigid rationalism, post-Fordism necessitates greater flexibility, as the actual production of goods becomes secondary to their marketing. Considering the impact of these developments on the realm of sexuality, Stevi Jackson and Sue Scott (1997) contend that post-Fordism's heightened emphasis on adaptability and versatility has not served to expand our collective sexual imaginary but has instead constrained it yet further. In their view, post-Fordist sexuality is not so much a departure from its Fordist predecessor as an intensification of existing tendencies towards the systematisation of sex and the extension of managerial logics to the realm of emotional life. Just as post-Fordism represents a new means to realise capitalist goals of maximising profit within changing market conditions, 'so post-Fordist sex is still geared to the maximisation of male pleasure within the context of the commodification of sex' (Jackson and Scott 1997: 566).

As a mode of sexual conduct, seduction centres on the instrumentalisation of feeling through orchestrated displays of spontaneity and cultivated performances of authenticity. On the Blueprint website, Yad Barre – crediting himself as 'the God Father of Day Game' – discusses the origins of this method:

> My own frustrations and struggles with women as a young man led me
> to spend thousands of hours studying interpersonal communication

and testing everything out in the real world to see if it actually produced results. I quickly realized that bars and clubs were no place for me. Getting dressed up like a 'cool kid' to compete with tough-looking guys for superficial women was not my idea of fun; not to mention, given my looks, success in these situations was basically impossible. I turned my attention towards meeting women in everyday situations and in doing so, became the driving force behind the creation of a new way of meeting women – 'Day Game'. (Barre 2016)

The key innovation of the Blueprint, according to Barre, is that it enables men to meet women in the daytime, thereby circumventing the comparative dynamics at play in bars and clubs. This is presented as distinctly advantageous, not simply because it precludes direct competition with other men in an already overcrowded sexual marketplace but, more importantly, because it harnesses the emotional power of media-administered ideals of heterosexual romance. As Barre explains elsewhere on the site:

> The reason women watch romantic comedies and read romantic fiction novels is because it plays into their fantasy of how they'll meet the guy of their dreams. In any classic romance story, the woman meets the man by some spontaneous moment and it's almost always during the day. Yet no one ever approaches a beautiful woman when she's going about her day, apart from the occasional wolf whistle from a construction worker. Once you learn how to strike up a conversation with a beautiful woman during the day, you'll play into her fantasy of randomly meeting the guy of her dreams just like in the movies. She'll believe that YOU are the guy of her dreams. (Daygame 2016)

Drawing on the codes and conventions of genres overwhelmingly aimed at and consumed by women, the Blueprint effectively enables men to exploit conventional romantic scripts. As Barre later goes on to explain: 'The dream of getting "swept off her feet" is very real. And with a little study and practice, you're able to give her an experience that she's only seen in movies.'

Romance – intimacy's dramatic mode – is choreographed through a series of pre-planned phrases and gestures that stand in for or better enable the flow of feeling. And, although the Blueprint is presented as an underlying structure rather than a literal script, the five-module training programme not only provides a general pattern of interaction but offers numerous examples of specific statements or conversation pieces that can be used in the course of a given interaction. Mediating intimate encounters in this way, the Blueprint embeds marketing logics into intimate encounters through its insistence on the carefully coordinated management of feeling. Through this emphasis on emotional orchestration – readily exploiting the codes and conventions of heterosexual romance played out in popular media culture – the seduction industry exemplifies the workings not only of post-Fordism but of what Eva Illouz terms 'emotional capitalism', 'in which emotional and economic discourses and practices mutually shape each other' (2013: 5). It is not that seduction empties sexual encounters and relationships out of their emotional content altogether. Rather, these encounters are laden with feeling, as performances of desire, intimacy and trust are deployed tactically as a means to gain access to women's bodies.

Sex in the social factory

Where the capacity for mass production was a key enabling mechanism of Fordism, post-Fordist production regimes allow for what business and management literature terms 'mass customisation' (Gilmore and Pine 1997). In this context, production processes are organised in such a way as to be able to manufacture the same basic product with only slight variations between individual items, thereby ensuring efficiency while also creating more marketable customised products. Similar logics underpin the Daygame Blueprint and other seduction models, as users are enjoined to enact sexual encounters according to a set formula that can be endlessly repeated with minute modifications in order to produce seemingly unique encounters with any number of women. Indeed, the Blueprint was specifically designed to lend a sense of authenticity and spontaneity to each encounter, while at the same time standardising sexual interactions by ordering them through a linear progression of interactional patterns.

In his book *Daygame* (2012), discussed in chapter 1, Tom Torero details more than a hundred sexual encounters through a compendium of field reports. A series of short extracts – each referencing a different interaction – serves to convey the programmatic approach enumerated here:

> I followed the usual first date plan: beers on the balcony of the *Punch and Judy* Pub in Covent Garden and then maybe cocktails in a smaller bar (p. 103).

> I told her to pick a DVD from the girl-friendly pile next to my laptop that I had accumulated in the last few months (she chose *Marley and Me* which I had seen twice that week already) (127).

> A few days later on her day off we met around lunchtime for a second date – my standard – the *Clipper* boat trip from Embankment to Greenwich and back (124–5).

> I did my usual routine of taking her up to the balcony where she could lean over the rails and watch the street show below, giving me an excuse to stand behind her for some easy kino [kinaesthetics or touch] (119).

> She stopped again, saying she didn't normally do this, and I used the tried and tested '*I know, it's okay, I understand.*' After that it was back on (75).

> I went for the Torero signature move of getting my dick out (217).

With repeated references to the 'usual', 'standard', 'tried and tested' and 'signature' techniques he employs, the stories catalogued by Torero present sex as a kind of production process. All interactions are progressed according to the same basic formula, which is continually adapted and refined so as to ensure maximum effectivity and efficiency. Torero's descriptions convey little sense of desire, instead projecting a 'methodological approach' centred on 'the performance of precise processes with machine-like regularity' (Rogers 2005: 188). The interactions he has with women are based on a rehearsed form of spontaneity that requires a great deal of advance planning and hidden labour. While there is an element of variability across these encounters – thus producing the custom output – the basic production system remains the same. Here the affective and embodied dynamics of attraction, intimacy and desire are brought in line with post-Fordist regimes of flexible accumulation: sex is 'rapidly manufactured' and subject to 'short-lived consumption patterns' (Hawkes 1996: 105).

Discussing the entry of managerial logics to the intimate sphere, Tyler contends that this imperative 'does not simply repress sex, but suppresses (or rather arrests) the inter-subjectivity of eroticism' (2004: 101). She further raises the prospect that such an orientation entails a 'corresponding threat to imagination and ingenuity' (ibid.: 82). Her analysis suggests that the optimism of much sociological work on intimacy and sexuality, notably that of Anthony Giddens (1992), tends 'to ignore the potentially de-humanizing effects of an instrumentalized hedonistic ethic which is driven more by performance imperatives than a genuine ethic of erotic pluralism and mutuality' (Tyler 2004: 99). While seduction may be inventive in the limited sense of producing interaction, it actively curtails the imaginative dimensions of eroticism. Partitioning sexual encounters into a series of phases – where the affective and embodied dynamics of attraction and intimacy are simply necessary if somewhat tedious precursors to sex – seduction reduces sexual encounters to their most basic elements. There is a radical emptying out of the intersubjective, which sharply delimits what it is possible to do and be with others, making it difficult if not impossible 'to engage in the ethic of mutuality within which erotic sex is ideally embedded' (ibid.: 101).

It is thus unsurprising that practising seduction over an extended period of time frequently gives rise to a sense of boredom or ennui, sentiments clearly in evidence in the autobiographical writings of many professional seducers. The latter half of the seduction guidebook *Daygame* is filled with references to a mounting sense of monotony – for example: 'It had been a crazy week – on Saturday I'd fucked the older Slovak in the care home, on Sunday I fucked the English nanny in the afternoon and that night I'd fuck the Romanian, and was about to fuck my regular Slovak girl. Four girls in three days – I was getting bored of sex' (Torero 2012: 378). The apparent overdevelopment of Torero's seduction skills – he was, by this point, apparently rather too proficient in seducing women – creates a sense of dispensability which leads him to concoct ever more elaborate plans. In quick succession, he realises what can only be described as the most generic catalogue of heterosexual male fantasies, including sleeping with a stripper, having a series of threesomes and dating a model. Even as Torero appears to revel in this lifestyle of debauchery, a growing listlessness persists until, finally, he declares:

> The novelty of having lots of sex with hot girls had really worn off. I was sleeping with girls just for the sake of it, not because I necessarily liked them as people or even because they were good looking. As soon as I'd slept with one and she'd left the house, I was texting another trying to get them out on a date and sleep with them. There was no more excitement of the chase, no more of a buzz from a technically perfect pick-up. (Ibid.: 447)

Having perfected the procedural manoeuvres of seduction, Torero describes becoming increasingly alienated from the actual experience of pursuing and sleeping with women. Coming near the end of the book, this admission may have been included as a kind of literary device, a way for Torero to round out the story of his transformation and position himself as ultimately aspiring to greater things.[1] Whatever its intended rhetorical function, such statements readily exemplify the 'de-humanizing effects' of which Tyler (2004) warns. There is an almost wholesale foreclosure of mutuality and reciprocity, as sex is reduced to a series of technical feats and intimacy to nothing more than a matter of impression management.

'Last-minute resistance'

One of the most commonly referenced knowledge-practices within the seduction industry – and one that has attracted significant criticism from feminist commentators – is that of 'last-minute resistance', or 'LMR'. The concept encapsulates the idea that women offer 'token' resistance prior to having sex as a way to protect their reputation and prescribes a range of tactics and techniques by which these objections can be managed. In many ways, LMR represents the lynchpin of all seduction theory and practice, not only because it is continually referenced and discussed but because it epitomises the idea that the affective and relational dynamics that typically precipitate heterosexual sex can be wilfully produced by one party over another.

During the latter stages of my fieldwork I attended a seminar in Covent Garden on 'same-day lays' or 'SDLs', but which ended up focusing almost entirely on LMR. I arrived at the venue just before 6 p.m. to find about twenty men were there already, casually milling around and chatting to one another as they waited for the talk to start. Mark, a trainer I had interviewed some months before, who was the evening's scheduled speaker, arrived a few minutes later. We chatted briefly before the organiser called for everyone's attention and the event got under way.

After being introduced, Mark outlined the main themes of his talk, explaining that this would cover the origins and antecedents of LMR as well as the precise means by which this can be offset and overcome. He began by stating that, 'Obviously, if a girl says "no" and she really means it, you respect that.' He paused then and looked around the group, his gaze finally resting on me, leaving me in no doubt that this cautionary note was squarely intended for my benefit. Looking around the audience once again, he then immediately went on to say: 'Fortunately, 99 per cent of the time she doesn't really mean it.' The problem, Mark explained, is that women are socially conditioned to police their sexual behaviour for fear of being called 'sluts'. Impressing this point, Mark told the audience: 'Women love sex – even more than we do.' With a knowing look, he added that, while this may be hard for men to believe, multiple neurological studies have proven that women experience sexual pleasure far more intensely than do men.

Over the next hour, Mark explained both the theory and practice of LMR. Much of this content was familiar to me, as I had already heard him discuss it elsewhere. Throughout his talk Mark continually restated the potency of female sexual arousal, claiming that the key to overcoming

LMR is to turn a woman on so much that she loses the capacity to think logically. Reiterating this point a number of times, Mark said: 'Arousal is the most important thing. You need to shut off the logical part of her brain.' He went on to say that, if a woman expresses doubts about having sex – for example, by saying something to the effect of 'I don't usually do this' or 'I think we should stop' – it is important not to ask questions or to talk to her about her feelings. Instead, he maintained that the best strategy is simply to agree with these statements and rehearse them back – such as by saying, 'I know, we really should stop' – and then continue to escalate the interaction anyway. He explained that, by agreeing with the woman verbally, she will have less reason to object as you continue to escalate the interaction physically. Even better, Mark told the audience, is to make these kinds of statements before the woman has a chance to do so herself, for example by saying things such as 'This is moving really fast, but it just feels so right', or 'This is crazy, we're being so naughty – I love it!'

Again reiterating the importance of 'disengaging her logical mind', Mark explained that careful logistical planning is key to both avoiding and overcoming LMR. He noted the importance of always working out the logistics of sex in advance – for example, by going to bars and clubs near to where you live: this is to ensure that the route home is short enough that the woman won't have too much time to think about what she's doing. Grinning slyly, Mark then pulled a set of keys from his pocket and chose one, holding it up for the audience to see. He explained that this key, which can be easily bought online, gives him access to any disabled toilet in the city and can be used to have sex with women in bars and clubs without having to take them home at all. Acknowledging that this is a more advanced strategy, he then went back to the logistics of getting women home, stating that, if a woman goes home with a man, sex is practically guaranteed: 'She knows it as much as you do.' Any objections beyond this point are 'shit tests', deployed to challenge a man's resolve and thereby establish his sexual worthiness. Mark explained that, in order to pass these 'shit tests' successfully, it is crucial not to question or reason with the woman. Instead, he advised his audience to de-escalate physically for a few minutes before then re-escalating. A simple way of doing this, he said, is to go from touching her breasts to stroking her face or hair. Slowing the interaction down in this way allows you to appear to pull back while maintaining physical contact, thus making it easier to re-escalate the interaction once the woman has relaxed.

If she's still reluctant after this point, Mark pronounced that there's only one way forward: 'You have to get her to orgasm.' Again impressing that men and women have different arousal patterns, he advised men to bring women to orgasm using their hands or mouth, claiming that, after women have orgasmed, they 'almost always want to be fucked.' If this doesn't work, and LMR continues, the final measure is to implement a 'freeze-out' by disengaging from the interaction entirely, withdrawing physical contact and emotional connection. As an example, Mark suggested getting up from the bed, turning on all the lights, taking out your laptop and checking your email. He cautions that this needs to be framed in the right way. The woman should not feel that it is punishment for not agreeing to sex. Rather, it should seem as though you are genuinely respecting her wishes. Mark explained: 'If a girl says, "Stop", and you do, then she has no rational reason to be annoyed with you.' Done correctly, he reiterated finally, freeze-outs are an extremely powerful means of overcoming LMR, as the woman will almost inevitably invite you to come back to bed and allow you to re-escalate. Shoring up his authority on the subject, Mark claimed that these techniques have enabled him to sleep with over two hundred women to date. He then took a few questions from the audience before delivering the inevitable sales pitch, detailing the various training services he offers and handing out business cards. He thanked everyone for attending and wished them good luck for the night ahead. As he began to collect his things, a number of men gathered around him to ask follow-up questions and book appointments for one-to-one consultations.

While this was one of the more comprehensive lessons on last-minute resistance I observed, almost all of the events I attended included discussion of the problem and the means by which it can be dealt with. Conceptually, LMR derives much of its rhetorical force from the repeated assertion that women love sex. In this way, it appears to dispense with the patriarchal presumption that women are inherently *lacking* in sexual desire, as it is claimed that women experience *even greater* sexual desire and pleasure than men. Acknowledging that women's sexual expression can be inhibited by cultural norms that corral women into policing themselves in an effort to protect their reputation, it seems to align with feminist critiques of the sexual double standard whereby 'men's sexual behaviour is relatively free of social constraint while women's sexual activities are judged and punished more harshly' (Flood 2013: 95). In a more explicit example of this, elsewhere Mark voiced opposition to the term 'slut' being used in a derogatory way against women, contending that: 'There's nothing wrong with women enjoying the same things men do.'

All this is notable in light of the emphasis feminists often place on the importance of women's pleasure in heterosexual sex, understood as a kind of index or marker of gender equality and therefore a crucial component of 'intimate justice' (McClelland 2014). Yet while the conceptual underpinnings of LMR may seem to parallel feminist critiques of the social ordinances that limit and constrain women's sexual expression, and to endorse feminist demands that women's sexual pleasure to be taken as seriously as men's, the ends to which LMR is put are not consistent with feminist goals of ensuring women's agency in the context of sexual encounters and intimate relationships. Under the precepts of LMR, men are exhorted to fulfil the desires women are *presumed to have* but are purportedly unable to expressly articulate. What is more, by insisting that women's verbal communication is not simply ambiguous but deceptive and misleading, LMR licenses men to *disregard* what women say and to do so in the earnest belief that they are in fact *fulfilling* women's unspoken and unspeakable desires. Insofar as consent is considered at all, it is presented as something that can be secured through tactical manipulation and emotional engineering, often after the fact.

The concept of LMR thus remains firmly within the terms of the double sexual standard from which it initially appears to seek distance: because it is always already assumed that women are unable to express their desire for sex, there is little room within this formulation for women to legitimately refuse sex. In this, the seduction industry exemplifies a more general cultural tendency 'to twist and corrupt empowerment discourses so that they become cliched, commodified, detrimental, and ultimately disempowering' (Fahs 2011: 275–6). Despite allusions otherwise, within this context heterosexual sex remains centred on and equated with the desires of men, while nominally appearing to take women's desires into account. Although there is an acknowledgement of the social forces that can limit women's ability to articulate their sexual desires, there is no corresponding consideration given to any of the dynamics which may limit their ability to communicate a desire *not* to have sex. Within this framework of understanding, it is difficult to envision any situation in which a woman's 'no' would legitimately be heard as such, as women are portrayed simultaneously as *unable* to act on their desires when they refuse sex but as necessarily *fulfilling* their desires when they consent to sex.

Buying in

Ali also attended Mark's seminar. In our interview, I asked what he thought of the advice Mark had offered. Ali explained that, while the material was probably 'more advanced' than he required at the moment, it had been interesting nevertheless: 'You know, hearing stuff like [women say], "I'm not going to sleep with you", when that really means, "I *am* going to sleep with you, but I don't want you to judge me", or something like that – so, I guess it's interesting hearing his take on it, yeah.' When I asked Ali whether to not he agreed with Mark's advice, he responded:

> Yeah, probably. Well, I mean, he's so much more advanced than me, that it'd feel almost arrogant to kind of say . . . until I've actually had as much experience as him – if I have as much experience as him – then I can judge it more. But at the moment I'm kind of just taking it as advice from a guy who's way more advanced in this area of life and obviously makes a living out of it.

He went on to explain further:

> It's almost like having faith, in a way, in what someone says, and then putting it into practice to see yourself. Because with a lot of things, and especially in this, if you don't believe that something will work, you probably won't make it work. Like, if you don't believe you can do something, you probably won't. I think that's the first step to achieving anything, that self-belief. So sometimes I guess you just have to have a bit of faith in what you're being told and kind of trust. Maybe it'll work, maybe it won't – but I'll test it out and give it a fair try and see what happens.

Ali's reasoning here suggests a willingness to test out the tactics and techniques Mark outlined, while at the same time he cites an impetus to 'make it work'. Conspicuous by its absence is any recognition of sexual encounters as sites of mutual negotiation, as attention is instead focused on the efficacy of seduction tactics. Ali's reflections are testament to the considerable authority accorded to those who establish themselves as experts in the seduction industry, such that men may be willing to follow their directives simply as a matter of faith.

Another participant, Ralph, raised the subject of Mark's talk with me when we met some weeks later. While questioning some of the claims Mark had made – particularly women's willingness to have sex in public toilets – Ralph felt there was a lot of value in recognising that women enjoy sex, explaining: 'I understand exactly what he meant by that. You know, it's a big realisation to understand that women actually love sex.' However, he then immediately went on to problematise this idea:

> I think you've got to be careful about it, because it could lead to rape. Guys thinking, 'You love it bitch.' You know – you understand what I'm saying there? You know, it could actually – in the mind of someone

twisted, it could lead to rape. Because, where the guy's thinking, 'You're just saying you're not enjoying this ...', yeah? You know, so, as long as the guy's sort of got his head screwed on.

With these latter comments, Ralph demonstrates a much more ambivalent attitude towards the kinds of knowledge-practices put forward by Mark and elaborated within the seduction community at large. He simultaneously heralds the idea that women enjoy sex as a 'big realisation' for him personally, while claiming that this idea could incite sexual violence 'in the mind of someone twisted'. Ralph thus absolves Mark of any responsibility for the content of his teachings, claiming that these would be problematic only in the hands of a deranged person – never mind that Mark had been speaking to a group of complete strangers about whom he knew nothing whatsoever. In keeping with cultural understandings of sexual violence more generally, Ralph imagines rape as a crime perpetrated only by aberrant individuals rather than as something that ordinary men do to ordinary women in ordinary places and at ordinary times.

Other participants raised ethical qualms about certain seduction techniques but often described being prepared to implement them anyway. Doug, for example, spoke of his discomfort in using tactics he described as 'not dehumanising' but 'definitely not respectful'. Nevertheless, he attempted to rationalise their use:

> The more I learn about PUA theory, the more it lowers my respect for people. Specifically, women. Because it's terrible that that's what guys have to do. I would really like to live in a world where the nice guy got the girl. That's not what happens. I think most PUA theory basically works and . . . it saddens me slightly that that is what works. But, given that it is what works, that's what I have to do.

While Doug finds some seduction tactics morally suspect, he places the locus of blame for their supposed effectiveness on women, thereby implicitly clearing himself – and, by implication, other men who use them – of any potential wrongdoing. Crucially, it is not a lack of *understanding* that is at issue here but, rather, a *willingness* to disregard women's perspectives and experiences in order for men to pursue their own sexual wants and desires.

Elsewhere, Ravi voiced discomfort with certain attitudes he saw among men involved in the seduction community:

> I've seen many people there, extremely misogynist. Their view on women, their view on people, their view on life is very shallow. Maybe – I don't know if those are right or wrong, if that really helps you in pickup

> or not, but those are things I don't identify with . . . I've seen pickup
> artists that see girls as commodities, as sex objects, nothing more than
> that. They don't care about their feelings, their emotions. Those I think
> are misogynistic behaviours. Maybe these are some essential character-
> istics to be a good pickup artist, I don't know. I'll find out later, but as of
> now I can't identify myself with those qualities.

In response, I asked Ravi what it would mean for him if such attitudes
proved to be essential traits of successful seducers. He replied: 'Then I'm
far below. Far below that level. So I have a long way to go then, if those
are really essential. I don't know if they are essential or not. If those are
essential, then I still have a long, long way to go.' While problematising
what he saw as a tendency towards misogyny within the seduction community, Ravi describes being prepared to adopt this same disposition if it
proves to be essential to achieving sexual success.[2] Like Doug, he is willing
to reconcile himself to attitudes and practices he regards as ethically
dubious, demonstrating that, in the seduction community as elsewhere,
'the subjectivity offered to men is one where getting sex is more important
than being a morally "good" human being' (Farvid and Braun 2013b: 123).

Given the authority accorded to seduction trainers and the methods
they prescribe by many of the men I spoke to, it is possible to view their
capitulation as a form of 'reflexive impotence' (Fisher 2009), a sense that,
however lamentable the system may be, it is ultimately inescapable. This
sense of inevitability was especially evident when Doug spoke about
'negging', a technique that involves making statements about a woman
that contain a negative element or which are otherwise open to a negative
interpretation so as to undermine her confidence:

> I mean, like, you know, negging. I would like it if that did not work. I
> would like to be in a world where that wasn't used. But, it seems that
> it *does* raise your chance of having a girl be interested in you, and so
> guys will neg girls. So, I don't actually feel like guys that use that are bad
> people, they're just rationally responding to the incentives that are laid
> out to them. I feel slightly less . . . I feel less respect for those women
> who are more likely to be interested in the guy who negs them, because
> that's not what I would like to have as what attracts women. I completely
> understand why men will do that. I understand why people respond to
> the incentives they're given, it's always perfectly logical. The part that
> sometimes bothers me is why are they given those incentives? Why has
> someone decided to set it up in such a way that this is what you have to
> do to get ahead?

While indicting women for responding favourably to such manipulative tactics, Doug's blame lacks a clear target, as he bemoans an unknown 'someone' for constructing this arrangement. He resigns himself to employing such techniques in order to 'get ahead', a phrase that perfectly encapsulates the neoliberal logic whereby one's own self-interest must be advanced above all else. The belief that there is no alternative legitimates the use of seduction tactics as a matter of necessity, such that this becomes 'a self-fulfilling prophecy' (Fisher 2009: 21).

While some participants queried the ethics of seduction – if only in the context of our interviews – others had no such compunctions. Harry, for example, gave a vivid account of how he had begun implementing techniques he read about in a book called *The Sex God Method* (Rose 2008). This book – popular within but also well beyond seduction circles – outlines a programme for heterosexual sex based on the premise that women's most fundamental sexual desire is to be physically and psychologically dominated by powerful men. According to Harry:

> Women respond to the physical and the drama and the temperament of someone that really knows what they want and they're quite forceful with it. So, a girl will like to be pinned down, or talked dirty to, maybe hit . . . So if me and a girl are together, I will just push her down – if I want her to suck my cock, I'll push her down by her shoulders, so she can go ahead and do that. And because I know that girls respond to it, I can push them up against walls, and grab their arms behind their back, and bite them, push them down onto the bed, push them into different positions that I want to do at that time, because I know that they respond to that. And, you know, it's not going to be as exciting for a girl if I just say, 'Oh, let's do this position, or let's do this.' I'll just make it happen, and she has to be fine with that.

Here Harry gestures to the importance of women's pleasure as he claims that verbal communication is less sexually exciting for women. Yet his phrasing suggests that the women involved do not necessarily have much choice in the matter: 'I'll just make it happen, and she has to be fine with that.' His purported knowledge of women's sexual desires – knowledge he has gleaned from a book written by a man for other men – serves as an authorising mechanism to pursue a relation of dominance and submission that is not discussed or agreed upon with individual partners but always assumed in advance and enacted with impunity. Indeed, Harry appears to believe he has good reason to disregard women's stated desires entirely, as he later told me: 'What girls will say they want and what they respond to are just two completely different things.' Whatever the predilections of individual women, who may well enjoy sexual power play, the assumption that all women secretly desire to be sexually overpowered by men 'sets up murky conditions for consensual sexual relations and ripe conditions for sexual coercion' (Antevska and Gavey 2015: 620).[3]

The kind of obtuse reasoning to which buying into seduction can give rise became evident in a number of interviews where men spoke about pursuing sex with women who strongly resisted their advances. Stefan, for example, described an encounter with a colleague with whom he was sharing accommodation for the evening as part of their work arrangements. Having had dinner together, the woman invited him to watch a movie in her room, which he took as an invitation to have sex:

> I started kissing her and she said 'No'. Then she said, 'Oh, I'm not too sure if we should do that so quickly.' And I said, 'Come on, what do you – I mean …', and then I didn't go on about it, I didn't ask why or whatever, I just said, 'Enjoy it.' Because this was again her sort of programming or ego kicking it, trying to lie to herself. Sometimes I have the feeling the woman has to lie to herself. She wants it, but then again, the conditioned mind says, 'Oh no, no, I have been taught to be a good girl and whatever . . . I can't just let it happen.'

Relating this story, Stefan positions himself as capable of reading between the lines to decipher women's true wants and desires. When faced with expressions of discomfort and uncertainty, he momentarily begins to engage these before quickly reverting to the directives prescribed within the seduction industry for dealing with such resistance. He does not try to talk to this woman about her feelings but instead proceeds regardless, telling her simply to enjoy the experience. Rationalising this in the context of our interview, Stefan claims that she was not seriously objecting to sex but was in fact deceiving herself. Extrapolating from this encounter, he contends that this is a common tendency among women and underscores the legitimacy of his actions on the basis that, as he had determined from the outset: 'I know what she wants.'

In our interview, Rahul described an encounter that exhibited many similarities with that shared by Stefan. Having met a woman earlier that day on the train, they had later gone for a drink together at a bar not far from his home. Recounting what happened when they decided to go for a drive together afterwards, Rahul explained:

> When we got in the car, that's when it got a bit more physical. I started undressing her, but we didn't have sex then. It's almost as if she kept stopping me – this has happened before as well. So, you know, I had her

> breasts out, but she wouldn't let me go any further than that. And then we drove, I said to her, 'Let's go to my place, we'll watch a movie.' So then we went to my place, but then we parked near my house. It was like cat and dog, literally. I was in the car, chasing her in the car, right, and she was playing hard to get. I was just playing the game because I knew that she wouldn't let me seduce her. It was like she wanted to have sex, but she wanted to make it a bit difficult. She was one of those personality types that wanted to be broken through.

Like Stefan, Rahul claims to be able to intimate women's desires, thereby permitting himself to disregard verbal objections and physical resistance. He further contends that, despite this woman's protestations, she wanted to be overpowered by him. Also like Stefan, Rahul generalises from this experience, as he later went on to contend: 'A lot of women are looking for that – they just want that real strong man.' He proceeded to describe, apparently without concern, that this encounter was interrupted when police arrived to investigate reports of a woman screaming. Rahul managed to reassure them that nothing untoward was happening, and they left shortly afterwards. Notably, he told me this story in response to a question I had asked about his best sexual experiences.

Significantly, in each of these stories – which are not isolated examples among my participants – both Stefan and Rahul position themselves as *licensed* to contravene women's stated desires because they know what women 'really' want. Women are positioned as by turns naive or duplicitous, a construction which authorises men to direct and control all aspects of heterosexual sex – *even and especially when women resist their advances*. While men who participate in the seduction industry do not unquestioningly accept the knowledge claims made in this setting, the majority of those I interviewed buy into this system of expertise. Conducting themselves in accordance with seduction precepts, their capacity to relate to women as relational subjects – whole persons whose thoughts and feelings are just as important as their own – is radically diminished. Instead, an ethic of self-interested individualism prevails.

Masculinist sex

While the seduction industry codifies techniques of emotional orchestration to a greater degree than may be seen elsewhere, it is important to acknowledge that it did not invent such patterns of interaction. As Anthony Giddens notes, performances of romance have long been the 'stock in trade for most Lotharios' (1992: 60). Research within masculinity studies further demonstrates the various ways in which heterosexual men style themselves as desirable to women using certain emotional repertoires. Thus Máirtín Mac an Ghaill describes a cohort of 'fashionable heterosexuals' who make themselves attractive to women 'by writing ascribed female definitions of desirable masculinity onto their bodies' (2000: 204). Elsewhere, Michael Flood documents the activities of men who profess to be 'smooth' and 'sensitive', willing to 'do the work' necessary to access sex by providing women with 'talking, dancing, flirting, compliments' (2008: 349). While such men may think of themselves and be seen by others as relatively egalitarian on account of their emotional expressivity, to accept this view too readily is to overlook how romance 'enables the relative stability of male power over women in heterosexual relationships' (Allen 2007: 139).

In his work on masculinity and morality, Michael Schwalbe argues that male supremacy – 'the materially and ideologically enforced condition where males are more highly valued than females, enjoy greater rights to self-determination, and command vastly more institutional power' (1992: 29–30) – entails a narrowing of the moral self among men that can be described as masculinist. Highlighting the importance of role-taking in everyday interaction, Schwalbe contends that, 'When we truly feel with the other, we are forced to reckon with the weight of the other's feelings as equal to our own. It is this, it seems, that men so often fail to do vis-à-vis women' (1992: 37). From Schwalbe's perspective, it is not that men do not take on women's perspectives and experiences at all, as role-taking of some form is required for any kind of communication to take place. Rather, men who take up a masculinist subject positioning tend to role take only in ways that are projective and inferential, not in ways that are receptive. That is to say, the masculinist self does not enter into feeling *with* or allow itself to be affected *by* others. As a result: 'while the masculinist self contains impulses to role take in the ways necessary to overcome women's resistance as objects, it lacks impulses to role take in the way necessary to receive their feelings as subjects. The masculinist self is equipped, in other words, to deal with women as sources of technical rather than moral problems' (ibid.: 42).

Despite its emphasis on emotional orchestration, seduction is a masculinist enterprise. Women's feelings are to be engaged with and understood only insofar as this is held to be conducive to the pursuit of sex. This dynamic is readily exemplified in the seduction stories told by professional seducers in their books and blogs. Nick Krauser is a British pickup artist who maintains a popular blog and has produced numerous autobiographical seduction hand guides as well as video products. In a post entitled 'Belgrade diaries 2015 – part two', he describes having sex with a nineteen-year-old woman he had met in the city a few days previously:

> I decide to take a chance and walk her directly to my apartment. I murmur something about charging my phone and how she can smoke in the garden. She comes in. She's just accepting my lead.
>
> My main thought is to keep her in the garden until her momentum to go to a bar has died. I put two chairs out and we just sit drinking water as she smokes. We make small talk for about twenty minutes. I don't push hard. I just want to stabilise the 'this date is in my apartment' frame. There's almost no kino and I don't try to kiss.
>
> After her cigarette I suggest we go inside, where the only place to sit is on the bed. Then I go to kiss. She fights me off a little until I just grab her neck, throw her back onto the bed, and kiss her. Then she likes it. The next twenty minutes are a technical masterclass in beating LMR. Her body is screaming out for sex but she's determined not to do it.
>
> Gradually I get her top off and tits out. Damn they are good. Then I'm fingering her. She's moaning feeble protests and not really making any effort to disengage. Then I get my dick out and put her hand on it. 'We're not going to have sex' she says as she starts giving a handjob. It's time to get sneaky. I pull my trousers off and finger her while I'm kneeling between her legs. When I judge her to be at maximum arousal I just put my dick in and rawdog her. I don't want the pause while I put on a condom.
>
> Her eyes briefly go wide, she whispers 'don't' and then I'm fucking her. Within ten seconds she's all-in, arms and legs wrapped around my back, pulling me in. It's dirty, raw, hard sex. Fucking awesome.
>
> Afterwards I interview her. She tells me she really didn't plan to have sex but once it started she loved it. She also tells me she really enjoyed the process of being skillfully seduced – knowing what I was up to and just appreciating the skill of it. She rated the sex 9/10 so I told her to tell the sister (heh!) but she reckons it'll be a secret from everyone. (Krauser 2015)

In an unabashedly predatory tone that is characteristic of his writings more generally, Krauser flaunts his skills as an expert seducer, able to meet and have sex with women with a minimal investment of time and other resources. The woman he describes in this story is clearly positioned in technical rather than moral terms: indeed, this is precisely the language he uses to describe overcoming her resistance. The 'interview' he conducts with her after sex – a relatively common feature of the lay reports he and other well-known seduction trainers post online and publish elsewhere

– serves an important rhetorical function, demonstrating that his actions were justifiable on the basis that she is purported to have ultimately enjoyed the experience. Projecting pleasure and inferring contentment, Krauser licenses himself – and, by extension, the readers of his blog – to pursue their own sexual agenda at all points, no matter what women may say, think or feel.

While the sexual stories related by trainers such as Krauser routinely emphasise the supreme efficacy of seduction techniques, elsewhere this narrative unravels. In the very first comment posted in response to the above field report, a commenter writing under the handle 'Slush Panties', says:

> Hey Nick!!!
>
> Had a similar situation last night. I'm 32. In Ukraine. Daygamed a really tall hot ass 21 year old. On the street she was very shy. Wasn't sure how strong of a lead it was.
>
> Texting was very boring but she agreed to come out last night. Took her to a cafe and again she was very shy and the conversation was boring. She wouldn't even tell me if she likes ukrainian men or if she's dated many men but.....when i physically escalated she happily allowed it. I was rubbing her long legs, kissing her, pulling her shirt out and looking down at her tits.
>
> Told her I wanted to leave and go for a walk. She agreed. Didn't tell her where but just walked straight back to my place. No objections once we got there.
>
> As soon as we got in I started kissing her and laid her on the bed. Had her down to her panties and had my cock out. Was fingering her and trying to fuck her but she wouldnt let me stick it in. At one point she was on top of me rubbing her clit on my knob but still refused to fuck. With one last ditch effort I was on top of her with my cock on her hole but couldnt get it in. Wtf?
>
> She left my place soon after and hasnt responded to a text today. She obviously wanted it.

This post clearly illustrates how seduction knowledge-practices encourage men to view sex as the outcome of their own skilful manoeuvring. There is a categorical assumption that, when properly implemented, these techniques guarantee sex. Indeed, this commenter appears to be entirely at a loss as to why this woman refused to have sex with him, given that, by his own assessment, 'She obviously wanted it.' Unable to understand why she may have left so abruptly, he regards her refusal to communicate with him after this encounter as unfathomable. In this way, seduction relies on and reinforces a worldview where 'women are indeed valued – for their capacities to satisfy impulses; they are also seen as deserving understanding – because they can present all sorts of annoying technical problems. What they are not seen as is subjects whose thoughts and feelings are of equal value to men's' (Schwalbe 1992: 42).

Codifying sexual interactions via carefully choreographed displays of romance, seduction limits the extent to which men actually take on and engage with women's feelings. The intense emotional labour they perform – conjuring intimacy, creating trust – masks the extent to which seduction is undergirded by a masculinist conception of women not as persons but, rather, as problems to be negotiated or objects to be overcome. After all, it is only by refusing to enter into feeling *with* others that the unencumbered pursuit of one's own self-interest can be sustained. The masculinist self is thus predicated not only on dis-identifying with women but on remaining insulated from women's perspectives and experiences. The simultaneous emotional intensity and emptiness of seduction should permanently disabuse us of the myth of male emotional inarticulacy (Rutherford 1992) and further caution against any uncritical endorsement of the idea that male emotional expressivity is necessarily a good thing (Allan 2015; de Boise 2017; de Boise and Hearn 2017). For all its pretences of novelty, all of its claims to expertise, seduction ultimately serves to impede sexual mutuality and deepen sexual inequality. It is at once highly emotional and deeply chilling – a truly 'cold intimacy' (Illouz 2013).

Claiming truth

In a blog post entitled 'Players outrank scientists in the art of seduction' (2014a), Krauser argues that seduction techniques are effective because they are based in empirical evidence superior to that gathered by more conventional researchers. He begins by citing an article written in 2014 by another industry figure, Rollo Tomassi, which outlines the biases and limitations of research in the social sciences:

> Now, imagine for a moment that, today, all men had to build on was the antiseptic studies and controlled experiments of a social science academia firmly steeped in a feminine-primary, feminine-correct social context … Only the PUAs of then and now have had the unfettered freedom to perform in-field social experiments, and relate their collected evidence and observations with other men; the types of which social science has been forbidden from due either to ethical considerations or by feminine-primary social conventions.

Following this line of reasoning, Krauser contends that the body of evidence the seduction industry has produced over the past fifteen years is of greater validity and reliability than existing academic knowledge. His claim for the higher authority of seducers is based on the belief that the only way to produce valid data is to conduct research at first hand in a naturalistic setting. Krauser outlines his own empirical method: 'Go hit on some actual women in real live environments, try to fuck them, then figure out what went well and what didn't.' As testament to the effectiveness of his own seduction methods, he cites his track record of results, claiming: 'I'm having sex with girls who are, on average, 16 years younger than me and two points hotter. That should be impossible under the deterministic explanation.' He concludes with an admonishment to his readers: 'Stop acting as if scientists are the authority on seducing women. When academia disagrees with successful players, it's the academics who are wrong. Just look at their wives' (Krauser 2014a).

It is not without a certain irony, then, that a number of academics have set out to verify scientifically and, indeed, lend support to the system of expertise elaborated within the seduction industry. In an article published in the peer-reviewed journal *Evolutionary Psychology*, Nathan Oesch and Igor Miklousic argue that, 'Despite its provocative label and origins outside of academia, [the seduction industry] is founded on solid empirical research as well as first-hand courtship and relationship experience' (2012: 901). The authors develop their argument via an analysis of a popular seduction handbook by an American pickup artist known as Mystery, entitled *The Mystery Method: How to Get Beautiful Women into Bed* (2007). Like other seduction models – many of which take their cue from this early instigator – the text portions heterosexual interactions into three distinct and linear phases: Attraction; Comfort and Trust; and Seduction.

Reviewing the tactics prescribed in the first phase, Oesch and Miklousic posit that these 'exploit evolved cues for what women generally find attractive in men' (2012: 901). The authors go on to examine the use of touch – referred to in seduction parlance as 'kinaesthetics' or 'kino' – in the Comfort and Trust phase. This too they deem to be substantiated by scientific research, as touch serves 'an adaptive function in bonding, both in human and non-human primates, involving complex psychopharmacological chemicals including oxytocin, endorphins, dopamine, and various other neuropeptides' (ibid.: 904). Discussing the tactics advanced in the final phase, Seduction, Oesch and Miklousic endorse the *Mystery Method* 'seven hour rule' – which premises that women generally need to spend seven hours with a man before they will have sex with him – on the basis that 'women typically require more time and intimacy to develop the same amount of passion as men' (ibid.). Arguing that 'there is in fact a substantive degree of psychological research to support many claims made by the Community', Oesch and Miklousic posit that 'this knowledge could be an important aid to couples reducing conflict, frustration and finding fulfilling relationships' (ibid.: 905).

Towards the end of the paper, the authors note that there may be 'unrecognised ethical implications' (Oesch and Miklousic 2012: 905) arising from the use of seduction techniques, citing research by feminist communications scholar Amanda Denes (2011). In a highly divergent reading of *The Mystery Method*, Denes contends that this and other seduction guides 'privilege biological responses as "truth" and position women's bodies against themselves' (2011: 411). To this end, Oesch and Miklousic acknowledge that seduction material 'has the potential for abuse' and 'urge caution . . . especially in the context of short-term relationships where sexual activity is the sole objective.' However, they immediately go on to say:

> On the other hand, in the context of helping people to initiate long-term, stable relationships, we argue that informed male behaviours are not so unlike women attempting to manipulate perceived attractiveness through the use of perfume, cosmetics, clothing, liposuction and cosmetic surgery, and thus disrupt normal mate choice by men ... Therefore, if such practices allow men to approach, attract, and connect with women in similar fashion, we wholeheartedly endorse the ethical practice of such materials for establishing meaningful long-term relationships. (2012: 905)

Oesch and Miklousic thus admit that seduction techniques may impact negatively on women, yet they assert the legitimacy of these tactics on the basis that they are equivalent to women's engagements in fashion and beauty practices. In doing so they adhere to the kind of moral indifference that characterises evolutionary psychology more widely, where ethical concerns are routinely dismissed as having fallen prey to the 'naturalist fallacy': 'mistakenly inferring an ought from an is' (Buss and Schmitt 2011: 780). Yet, given that Oesch and Miklousic explicitly endorse the use of seduction techniques – rather than simply claiming they are empirically well founded – this charge cannot hold, as 'is' is collapsed with 'ought'. In referencing but not actually discussing Denes's work, Oesch and Miklousic perpetuate the 'dismissive recognition' of feminist scholarship within academia more generally, 'whereby the epistemic status of feminist work is both asserted *and* denied' (Pereira 2012: 296).

One might wonder why academics such as Oesch and Miklousic feel the need to weigh in on these issues and provide an academic alibi for the seduction industry. Whatever their own personal motivations, it is clear that there is a distinct affinity between the two fields, as arguments from the seduction industry come to provide evidence for claims made in evolutionary psychology, and vice versa. In this respect, the seduction industry exemplifies the workings of 'chronic reflexivity', whereby 'knowledge about social life systematically feeds back into social life itself' (Heaphy 2007: 76). At the same time, evolutionary psychologists routinely make use of popular instructional sex and relationship texts to inform their research and provide support for their own studies (Cameron 2015). What practitioners in both of these arenas have in common is a shared belief in the existence of a universal 'truth' of sexuality, which each claims to have discovered via their own particular scientific method. The ultimate effect of this is that purported differences between women and men – and the inequalities these occasion – are naturalised as a matter of 'genetic inheritance' (Cameron 2009: 175).

In *Inventing Our Selves: Psychology, Power, and Personhood* (1998), Nikolas Rose examines the powerful role played by the 'psy disciplines' in organising contemporary subjectivity. While not concerned with evolutionary psychology specifically – he focuses instead on fields such as psychology, psychotherapy and psychiatry – Rose's observations nevertheless apply here. Following Foucault (1972), he argues:

> Truth is not only the outcome of construction, but of contestation. There are battles over truth, in which evidence, results, arguments, laboratories, status and much else are deployed as resources in the attempts to win allies and force something into the true . . . Truth, that is to say, is always enthroned by acts of violence. It entails a social process of exclusion in which arguments, evidence, theories, and beliefs are thrust to the margins, not allowed to enter "the true".' (Rose 1998: 55)

Though the seduction industry – aided and abetted by evolutionary psychology – claims to have discovered the 'truth' of female sexuality, it does so only by ignoring the perspectives and experiences of women themselves. In this regard it perpetuates broader cultural patterns whereby 'the claim to know the "truth" of sex for women can be converted into hard capitalist cash from those seeking to know' (Sonnet 1999: 177). Meanwhile, research undertaken by feminist scholars – research which centres women's perspectives and experiences – offers a radically different portrait of heterosexual sex.

In her work on the cultural scaffolding of rape, the feminist psychologist Nicola Gavey describes the way in which, during the 1970s, feminists began to examine how normative understandings of heterosexuality and heterosex are 'patterned or scripted in ways that permit far too much ambiguity over distinctions between what is rape and what is *just sex*' (2005: 2). The catalyst to this discussion was the discovery – through a combination of consciousness-raising activities and scholarly enquiry – that, although experiences of sexual coercion and violence are widespread among women, they remain largely absent from public discourse. As Gavey describes:

> To say that women often engage in unwanted sex with men is paradoxically both to state the obvious and to speak the unspeakable. While this assertion will not come as a surprise to many women, it embodies a subjugated knowledge which usually remains private and hidden. Unwanted and coerced sex are thus an aspect of some women's experiences of oppression which have remained to a large extent unrecognised, yet implicitly condoned, and often encouraged. (1992: 325)

Engaging a Foucauldian frame, Gavey examines how 'technologies of heterosexual coercion' facilitate patterns of heterosexual relating whereby men's interests are routinely given precedence over and above women's. A key issue here is the positioning of women as passive sexual subjects who are expected to fulfil men's desires regardless of their own wishes. In this way, the gendered conventions of heterosexual sex set limits on women's agency, such that sexual coercion can inhere not only in specific acts and practices – such as verbal bargaining, emotional manipulation, threats of violence or use of force – but also in social norms and cultural expectations, 'the invisible networks of power that operate in heterosexual sex' (Gavey 2005: 10).

Gavey's research is supported by an extensive catalogue of scholarship which documents unwanted sex as a pervasive feature of women's intimate lives (Baker 2010; Barker 2013a; Bay-Cheng and Eliseo-Arras 2008; Brown-Bowers et al. 2015; Chung 2005; Gavey 2005; Hlavka 2014; Patton and Mannison 1998; Sieg 2007). In a study of women's sexual subjectivities in the United States, the psychologist Breanne Fahs found that being pressured into sex was so commonplace that 'it is not a matter of *if* women have experienced coercion, but rather a matter of *how, in what context,* and *what the coercion meant to them*' (2011: 26). This question of meaning and context is indeed critical, not least in a postfeminist terrain where women are continually exhorted to style themselves as 'liberated' and 'empowered' sexual subjects. As Rosalind Gill explains: 'For young women today in postfeminist cultures, the display of a certain kind of sexual knowledge, sexual practice and sexual agency has become normative – indeed, a "technology of sexiness" has replaced "innocence" or "virtue" as the commodity that young women are required to offer in the heterosexual marketplace' (2007a: 72; 2008b; see also Evans et al. 2010). While in some respects this may seem like a positive development – women are, supposedly, afforded the right to claim ownership of their sexuality – it has also led to more troubling developments.

Throwing this issue into sharp relief, Melissa Burkett and Karine Hamilton (2012) examine the disjuncture that exists between women's stated beliefs about consent and their ability to act on these beliefs in the context of a given interaction. The women they interviewed not only endorsed but actively promulgated the idea women should 'just say no' when faced with unwanted sexual advances. And yet, in the context of their actual lived experience, they were very often unable to do this. Interview participants thus related encounters where they were cajoled into sex, manipulated into situations where they felt they could not refuse sex, or were ground down by sustained pressure over time. For Burkett and Hamilton, these already well-documented patterns of coercion have become all the more insidious because women are now accorded 'compulsory sexual agency', whereby 'it is a given that all sexual choices are freely made' (2012: 817). The women in their study continually blamed themselves for submitting to unwanted sex 'because they perceived sexual choices within the prism of a postfeminist sensibility which renders forces outside individual responsibility obsolete' (ibid.: 829). As such, they were resistant to labelling their experiences as coercion or violence, even when they found these experiences deeply upsetting. The authors conclude: 'Ultimately, the compulsory sexual agency of postfeminist sensibilities negates the on-going negotiation of consent because women can no longer express distress if genders are now equal' (ibid.: 828).

These issues have recently become the focus of public attention in the UK and elsewhere amid renewed feminist activism on issues of sexual violence, particularly among younger generations of feminists who have taken up the language 'rape culture' (Keller et al. 2016). The seduction industry is often directly implicated in such discussions, with cultural commentators raising the possibility that the knowledge-practices elaborated in this sphere may be harmful to women. And yet within the seduction industry – which specialises in the provision of sex advice for heterosexual men – such issues go almost entirely unacknowledged. In this regard, the seduction industry can be seen to propagate what the philosopher Charles Mills calls an 'epistemology of ignorance', a form of unknowing or non-knowing that supports inequality (1997, 2007). Introducing a collaborative project that builds on Mills's formulation, Shannon Sullivan and Nancy Tuana summarise the concept as follows: 'Sometimes what we do not know is not a mere gap in knowledge, the accidental result of an epistemological oversight . . . a lack of knowledge or an unlearning of something previously known often is actively produced for purposes of domination and exploitation' (2007: 1). While Mills is concerned specifically with dynamics of white ignorance in the maintenance of racial inequality, he holds open the possibility that similar dynamics apply in relation to gender.[4]

The seduction industry sustains a specifically gendered and masculinist epistemology of ignorance, one that systematically privileges men's perspectives and experiences far above women's. While purporting to have deduced the 'truth' of female sexuality and enumerating a seemingly novel form of expertise, this system of knowledge is composed of more or less wilful and deliberate exclusions. In particular, and despite the groaning weight of evidence available and the cacophony of discussion currently taking place about dynamics of sexual consent, seduction instructors steadfastly refuse to acknowledge the capacity for harm contained within their teachings. Where power differentials are acknowledged – as in platitudes about 'social conditioning' in the case of LMR – it is only so that they can be more readily exploited. The seduction industry thus colludes in maintaining uneven power dynamics between women and men in the context of heterosexual sex, encouraging men to take up a masculinist subject positioning that insulates them from women's pain. This kind of strategic ignorance is necessary to maintain men's power and privilege in the intimate realm, not least because, 'If [women's] pain were to be fully felt, its roots in the patterns of domination that sustain masculinist selves in other ways might become obvious. The pain that men cause women would then become men's pain and men would be motivated to destroy the masculinist selves sustaining it' (Schwalbe 1992: 42).

The fine print of seduction training terms of service statements demonstrates just how much effort goes into maintaining this epistemology of ignorance. For, while seduction trainers are loath to discuss ethical conduct when they teach men how to seduce women, they are sure to try to cover their backs legally. In lengthy terms and conditions clauses, seduction training companies attempt to absolve themselves of responsibility for any harm that may arise as a result of men utilising their advice. Indeed, many go so far as to claim that the advice they provide – through a compendium of educational courses, instructional guidebooks and video tutorials – is not advice at all. Exemplifying this, PUA Training (2017b) includes within its terms of service the following statement:

> You understand that all materials and content are intended for information and entertainment purposes only and do not constitute professional advice. Therefore they should not be relied on to assist in making or refraining from making a decision, or to assist in deciding on a course of action. PUA Training does not guarantee and does not promise that following any of its methods will ensure any particular results. PUA Training shall not be liable for any loss or damage arising out of, or relating to any such reliance.

This assertion contrasts markedly with claims appearing elsewhere on the company website, where products are advertised with invitations to 'begin reaping the benefits of almost unlimited power and choice with women' (PUA Training 2017a). Similarly, the Daygame Blueprint terms of service include a clause titled 'No Personal Advice', which stipulates that:

> The information contained in or made available through this Site (including but not limited to information contained on message boards, in text files, in products, from services, or in chats) cannot replace or substitute for the services of trained professionals in any field, including, but not limited to, psychological, financial, medical, or legal matters . . . Further, you should regularly consult a lawyer in all matters relating to interacting with other people to assure yourself you are behaving in compliance with law, including but not limited to laws related to harassment, assault or other similar laws.

Acknowledging the potential for harm – indeed highlighting the possibility that harassment and assault could take place under the auspices of seduction – draws attention to cracks in the edifice of ignorance so carefully obscured from view elsewhere. That companies who sell seduction products and administer seduction training services feel the need to employ this kind of legalese and distance themselves from the very basis of their businesses – teaching men how to have sex with women – surely begs the question of just how oblivious trainers are to issues of coercion and violence.[5] And while the purpose of these statements is clearly to exempt companies of any legal responsibility, whether or not they actually succeed in doing so is a question that would have to be answered in a court of law. In any case, and whether they are willing to acknowledge it or not, trainers remain morally culpable for any harm that may be done to women as a result of their patronage.

The patterns of intimate relationality enumerated in the seduction industry, and the willingness with which many men buy into them, further evidence the production of distinctly antisocial forms of sociality and subjectivity within neoliberalism. Exacerbating this situation are postfeminist imperatives of 'liberation' and 'empowerment' which imbue women with uncompromising agency in sex as in everything else, rendering deeply embedded modes of inequality all the more insidious. As a cultural formation, the seduction industry not only promotes a masculinist subject positioning among men but bends heavily towards masculinism as 'the point at which dominant forms of masculinity and heterosexuality meet ideological dynamics, and in the process become reified and legitimised as privileged, unquestioned accounts of gender difference and reality' (Whitehead 2002: 97). In chapter 4 I extend this analysis further by examining how seduction acts as a conduit for social grievances by promising men greater control in their intimate lives.

4

Seduction and Sexual Politics

In August 2017 the Daily Mail *ran an article with the headline '"British women are entitled and overweight": Seduction expert who's dated 200 Russian ladies says men should look to Eastern Europe to find a beautiful, intelligent wife' (Brennan 2017). The seduction expert in question is Richard La Ruina, founder of the UK-based company PUA Training and author of* The Natural Art of Seduction: Secrets of Success with Women *(2007) and* The Natural: How to Effortlessly Attract the Women You Want *(2013). The Mail piece details his transformation from a man who struggled to meet women to one who 'could easily go out in central London on a Friday night, kiss a girl and probably take them home after.' As he entered his thirties, however, La Ruina became 'unhappy with the calibre of single British girls'. After spending a couple of years in Eastern Europe – his business in the UK and its subsidiaries in the US, Italy and Brazil providing for him financially – he decided to move to Moscow 'with the single purpose of finding his future wife'. Over the next few years, La Ruina claims to have dated 'over 100–200 beautiful women'. He met his 'perfect match' in 2015, proposed to her some months later, and the couple were married the following year. Included with the article – around which the text is based – is a cache of some twenty-five photographs, encompassing pictures from their wedding day alongside an array of seemingly candid images of La Ruina with some of the other women he has been involved with over the years.*

As the title of the article suggests, La Ruina believes that his decision to move abroad is symptomatic of wider problems in the UK:

> *In general, I think British women are entitled, overweight and less feminine. They want a guy who is successful, good-looking and chivalrous even though they don't have much to offer in return. And they want the man to be a gentleman even though they refuse to fulfil the traditional role of the woman in the household and take care of their looks. English women just think they deserve to be with a man like that.*

Expanding on these points further, La Ruina goes on to argue:

> *I've met so many successful, nice British guys who are struggling to find a girlfriend in the UK dating scene – because English women are looking for too much.*

> *They're too confused and they don't make pleasant wives. Meanwhile Eastern European women are gorgeous, ladylike, accomplished and have traditional family values . . . They are much more straightforward, refined and in control of themselves – you won't see them swearing, getting drunk in a nightclub or going home with someone on the first date like most British girls. And obviously, looks and beauty play a huge factor too. Tall and thin girls are the norm in Eastern European countries.*

Strategically placed in the Daily Mail's 'Femail' section, the article sparked vociferous debate among readers in below-the-line-comments. Entering into the broader media churn, it was shared over 6,500 times on social media.

This chapter examines the sexual politics of seduction. It begins from a recognition that seduction is at once a self-making project and a world-making project, as men who take up the knowledge-practices on offer within the seduction community use this system of expertise to renegotiate their relationships vis-à-vis women and thereby recalibrate the wider terrain of gender relations. In developing this analysis it is important to foreground the fact that, while PUA blogs and forums form part of the vast internet territory known as the manosphere (Ging 2017) – the vitriolic politics of which have come to play an outsized role in a political landscape marked by new instantiations of anti-feminism and popular misogyny (Banet-Weiser 2015) – my research has focused not on these ideologues but on those who participate in this sphere primarily for their own personal benefit. This, however, is not to say that their involvement is in any sense apolitical, as La Ruina's commentary – moderate in comparison to some of his peers – clearly demonstrates. Rather, sex becomes politics by another means. That is, seduction functions as a way for men both to gain greater control in the intimate realm and to address perceived imbalances in the gender order.

Articulating aggrievement

In interviews, I routinely shared with participants my central research question – 'What makes seduction so compelling for those drawn to participate in this sphere?' – and asked if they had thoughts on this. Some had not previously given the matter much thought, as was demonstrated by the heavily prefaced and somewhat halting responses they gave. James, for example, began by saying: 'Ahm . . . yeah, probably . . . actually, I never really thought of it, but just thinking about it now ...' Similarly, David said: 'If you think about it – like, again, a lot of questions you're asking aren't things I've thought about, and I'm sort of thinking about it on the spot, so I hope I'm coming up with something comprehensible, something that makes sense.' Once we had alighted on the topic, however, most participants spoke about this issue at length. Those who work in the industry tended to have the most fully formed opinions, and many trainers offered highly detailed arguments regarding the various social and cultural developments that had precipitated and propelled the industry. Overall, discussion of this issue – why seduction appeals to men – constituted the single most extensively discussed topic across all interviews. When compiled for analysis, this corpus totalled close to 40,000 words. Such volubility suggests that there is a good deal at stake in explaining the appeal of seduction among heterosexual men.

For almost all of the men I spoke to, it was evident that the take up of seduction expertise pointed to deeper social issues, a sentiment also expressed by La Ruina in the *Daily Mail* article. Mark indexed this when he discussed the reasons men become involved in seduction: 'If there weren't a problem, then we [trainers] wouldn't exist.' Similarly, when describing the kinds of men he coaches, Danny commented: 'They're completely normal guys, very stable, normal jobs – just the average Joe basically. Very normal people. Most of them are cool, they don't have any psychological trauma or stuff like that – at least it's not obvious. So it just goes to show, that there's something not right in wider society.' Many participants claimed that seduction is something all men need, with both Rahul and Elijah each separately stating that 'Every man needs this.' In the same vein, David posited: 'It's this humongous thing that people need, that society needs, that men need.' William took this one step further by asserting men's prerogative to access the forms of expertise the seduction industry makes available: 'It's every man's right to learn it and to do it.'

In explaining the underlying source of the problem, some highlighted issues around technology, contending that the copious amount of time many people now spend online has impaired interpersonal skills in society at large. Others spoke of the pressures of living in an 'on demand' and 'throwaway' society in which relationships of all kinds are increasingly dispensable. A few men, mostly those who had come to live in the UK from abroad, spoke about seduction as a means to traverse cultural difference and learn the otherwise unspecified codes of dating and relationships. But, whatever other reasons participants might mention in passing, what they came back to time and time again was the belief that large-scale shifts in the gender order have created a kind of impasse between women and men that is most keenly felt in the intimate domain. Constantly in the background, unnamed but very much present, feminism functioned as a structuring absence in these discussions. It was continually alluded to and invoked by proxy, as participants employed a whole host of related but less definite terms, including 'equality', 'equal rights', 'emancipation', 'liberation' and 'political correctness', to get at this issue. Overall, the term 'feminism' itself was used on only a handful of occasions by just three of more than thirty participants. In this way, participants reproduced a broader postfeminist logic whereby feminism is backgrounded even as it is invoked (Gill 2007c; McRobbie 2009; Tasker and Negra 2007).

This tendency to talk around rather than about feminism was readily demonstrated in my interview with Antonio. Responding to a question about why seduction appeals to men, he explained: 'I think this is due to, first of all, this whole emancipation stuff.' As Antonio began to expand on this point, I interjected to ask what he meant by 'emancipation'. He continued talking without responding to this, such that I eventually had to interrupt to ask if he was referring to *women's* emancipation. He responded: 'Yes, exactly, yeah. I don't think necessarily that it's bad or something – I've just observed the result, I mean, the impact on the other side. I don't want to judge if it's bad or not good or . . . or good or something.' Notably, Antonio reacts to my introduction of the term 'women' here – a word that has taken on a political charge of which the word 'men' is utterly devoid – by immediately impressing that he is not *against* women's emancipation. Instead, he claims neutrality while nevertheless contending that women's emancipation has had negative implications for men. Through this rhetorical pattern, Antonio attempts to negotiate a positioning that allows him to appear supportive of gender equality, while at the same time raising questions about the consequences of this.

Overall, responses to the question of why seduction is compelling to men were organised around three main lines of argument or 'interpretative repertoires', composed of 'recognisable themes, common places and tropes' (Wetherell 1998: 400). Recognising that interpretative repertoires form 'part and parcel of any community's common sense, providing a basis for shared understanding' (Edley and Wetherell 2001: 198), it is worth highlighting that, while the arguments participants invoked have much to do with shared systems of meaning elaborated within this sphere, these are not dissociated from or discontinuous with broader cultural frameworks of understanding. Rather, they rely on and reanimate extant discourses about gender and sexuality in the contemporary UK context, specifically through recourse to evolutionary narratives of sexual difference, concerns about the feminisation and emasculation of men, and the belief that the pursuit of gender inequality has now gone too far. Together, these repertoires work to construct a view of seduction as an altogether necessary and justified response to the damages wrought by feminism, damages that are perceived most acutely and protested most vigorously in the intimate sphere.

'It's just evolution of the species': evolutionary imperatives

> In an account where men's need for sex is incontestable,
> this makes women very powerful indeed.
>
> (Mooney-Somers and Ussher 2010: 362)

Towards the end of our interview, I asked Ralph if he had any thoughts as to why the particular form of expertise on offer in the seduction community appeals to so many heterosexual men. In response, he stated simply: 'Because guys have got dicks.' After a pause, he continued: 'That's not the end of my answer, but that's reason number one. Men have a higher sex drive. The idea for most men about not being in the mood is . . . you know, that's something we can't really get our head round.' Answering the same question, George likewise pointed to physiological determinants: 'I think it's about the physical part of the man. Because we've evolved to have lots of relationships with lots of women, so that you probably spread lots of seed, so that you have more offspring.' Adam similarly argued: 'It's just natural selection, it's biology, you know. If you don't get it sorted out, your genes aren't going to be passed on. It's just evolution of the species, dressed up in many different guises, but that's what it is. It's evolution of the species.' Elsewhere, William positioned himself as a translator of male experience: 'It's very hard to understand, like, the mindset of an alcoholic if you're not an alcoholic. And men have this ridiculous desire – it's our number one biological desire – to procreate. And that is a physical pain; that is a physical need. And, unless you're a bloke, you're not going to know what that feels like.' Later he elaborated on this point: 'The desire for sex and short-term pleasure is billions of years old. That incessant desire for beauty and beautiful women and sex – that's part of us, you know.'

Statements of this kind figured repeatedly across interviews, with participants making sense of and justifying seduction by claiming that men have an incontrovertible need for sex. These arguments clearly instantiate what Wendy Hollway terms the 'male sexual drive' discourse, composed of the following assumptions: 'First, the sexual drive is a natural propensity that men have. Second, it makes them want to have sex with women (note the heterosexist assumptions). Third, it is normal and healthy not just because it is natural but because it is the product of a biological necessity – an evolutionary imperative – which ensures the survival of the human species' (1984: 63). The male sexual drive discourse has been shown to profoundly influence heterosexual men's sense of themselves as gendered and sexual subjects (Gavey et al. 1999; Mooney-Somers and Ussher 2010; Terry 2012) and is commonly invoked by men to account for practices such as watching pornography and paying for sex (Antevska and Gavey 2015; Grenz 2005; O'Connell Davidson 1995). As such, it is not entirely surprising that men engaged with seduction also cited evolutionary imperatives. Yet the *frequency* and *ease* with which these were invoked by many of those I interviewed was striking, as was the *confidence* and *conviction* with which they were presented. It quickly became evident that this was not simply an explanatory frame that could be reached for when convenient; rather, it functioned as a deeply held and embodied belief. Those who employed this repertoire were utterly convinced of their own evolutionarily ordained need for sex and felt compelled to explain why they and other men must conduct their intimate lives in accordance with such biological dictates.

The tendency among participants to rationalise seduction through recourse to an evolutionary discourse of male sexuality could, perhaps, be partially explained by the fact that, as a form of expertise, seduction borrows from and is informed by sociobiology and evolutionary psychology. Indeed, popular texts such as *The Red Queen: Sex and the Evolution of Human Nature* (Ridley 1993), *The Evolution of Desire: Strategies of Human Mating* (Buss [1994] 2003) and *Sperm Wars: The Science of Sex* (Baker 1996) are frequently included on seduction reading lists and cited by well-known industry figures as major influences. As such, many of those who engage with seduction are liable to have a heightened awareness of and familiarity with evolutionary narratives of gender and sexuality. However, evolutionary imperatives were invoked not only by men with long-standing involvement with seduction but also by those who had been involved in this community-industry for relatively short periods of time. George, for example, had only recently attended his very first event. And while it is logical that those already sympathetic to evolutionary perspectives are more likely to be drawn to seduction because of the pre-existing fit between their own worldview and the one promoted in this setting, to follow this line of reasoning too closely would be to lose sight of the way in which social life has increasingly come to be understood and experienced through an evolutionary framework.

The linguist Deborah Cameron refers to this 'new biologism' as one facet of a wider Darwinian turn wherein 'the most powerful explanations of how humans think, feel, and act are those which appeal to the principles of evolutionary theory' (2009: 175; 2015). Cameron charts the outsized influence of evolutionary psychology in shaping both academic and popular understandings of gender and sexuality, as exemplified by texts such as *Men are from Mars, Women are from Venus* (Gray 1992). Rosalind Gill further examines how narratives derived from evolutionary psychology flourish in sex and relationship advice media, cultivating a representational pattern that 'employs exaggerated and stereotypical descriptions of male and female behaviour' and reifies a reductive view of men as 'testosterone driven and motivated by a desire to "spread his seed" among as many women as possible' (2003: 50). Writing in the US context, Martha McCaughey argues that male sexuality has become lodged within an evolutionary narrative that has become corporealised: 'quite literally incorporated into living identities, deeply shaping these men's experiences of being men' (2008: 84).

For a number of men I interviewed, the evolutionary discourse of male sexuality functioned as a 'lived ideology' (Billig et al. 1988).[1] So overwhelmingly obvious were the evolutionary antecedents of seduction for some participants that even my raising this for discussion appeared deliberately obtuse. Early in my interview with Jay, I asked why he personally had become interested in seduction. Apparently confused, he responded: 'Who wouldn't be interested? I mean, like, evolutionary [*sic*] speaking, people want to procreate. That's what you want to do. And if this could help you with it, then shouldn't you *naturally*, like *biologically*, be interested?' Noting his gender-neutral phrasing, I asked if this was the case for both women and men, to which he responded: 'I mean, at least for men. Because of how the dynamic works between the sexes, it's more of an active role for guys to go out and pursue. Because it's an active role, it makes sense that you should actively try to improve your skills. So, I mean, it seems very natural. That question is weird.' Laughing at this latter comment, I pointed out that there are many men who have no involvement with the seduction community. Considering this for a moment, and again using gender-neutral language, Jay responded: 'Yeah, but there are a lot of people who don't know about it. Or it might be just a bit hard for them and they lack the willpower.' From Jay's perspective, seduction is innately appealing to heterosexual men because it provides them with a means to advance their reproductive strategy over other men. It is, in a sense, a kind of evolutionary adaptation. The possibility that men may be indifferent towards or even critical of seduction is rendered untenable, explicable only by some personal failing or deficiency.

The kind of dogged belief in evolutionary imperatives at work here feeds into and finds parallel with the 'capitalist realism' that enables and sustains neoliberalism (Fisher 2009). Indeed, evolutionary narratives have much in common with neoliberal rationalities, as both promote a logic of individualism centred on profit maximisation – whether this is defined in terms of finance or progeny. In her work on 'genetic individualism', the anthropologist Susan McKinnon examines this interrelation and argues that evolutionary narratives play a crucial role in upholding neoliberal capitalism by naturalising 'a conception of human life that reduces social relations and human behaviour to the product of self-interested competition between individuals' (2005: 43). Evolutionary narratives – in their constant rehearsal across the contemporary mediascape – help to maintain a situation where neoliberal capitalism comes to be seen as natural and inevitable, however unfair this system may be. Popular TV programmes such as *The Apprentice* dramatise the ethos of social Darwinism – centred on natural selection and survival of the fittest – by inviting contestants to compete in the 'corporate jungle'. Inequality is turned into 'an exciting competition for survival', as workers are told that in order to succeed in the workplace they need to adopt 'a strategy grounded in individualistic, meritocratic notions of hard work, initiative, talent, and perseverance' (Lair 2011: 82; see also Couldry and Littler 2008). Elsewhere, David Graeber (2014) argues that evolutionary theory is itself being reinterpreted through the lens of neoliberal capitalism; where old-school social Darwinists viewed nature as a marketplace, neo-Darwinists assume 'not just a struggle for survival, but a universe of rational calculation driven by an apparently irrational imperative to unlimited growth'. In this version of evolutionary theory, life has no purpose unto itself, but instead becomes 'a mere instrument for the propagation of DNA sequences'.

Crucially, then, it is through their *convergence* with neoliberal rationalities that evolutionary imperatives come to be experienced by heterosexual men as deeply felt and embodied truths. Yet, while frequently asserted as a self-evident fact, the claim that seduction is an expression of a deep-seated evolutionary imperative contains a rather glaring contradiction. That is, though many of those I interviewed argued that seduction appeals to men precisely because they are driven by an evolutionary imperative to reproduce, none were actually trying to *fulfil* this imperative by fathering children. In fact, all appeared to be actively taking steps to *prevent* this possibility, chiefly through the use of contraceptives. When I asked Adam to explain this apparent contradiction, he reasoned:

> Well the thing is though – all right, maybe it's not the actual passing thing on, but you still have that desire, the need to actually – you know, you still have that need to go and have sex, whether it's going to result in children or not. That desire, that human desire is still there. The thing is, human desire – it doesn't matter if there's a thin sheet of latex or you're on a chemical – humans are going to be human.

Despite the conspicuous discrepancy between men's understanding of themselves as driven by biological mandates to reproduce and their deliberate avoidance of procreative sex, evolutionary imperatives still provide an apparently incontrovertible rationale for seduction's appeal. Men are understood to be at the mercy of biological drives, subjugated by their own physiology, programmed by evolutionary determinants that direct all aspects of their behaviour. The pursuit of sex is naturalised as an expression of an essential male nature which it is pointless to deny. Not only this, but through the logic of procreation – even where this is deliberately thwarted – seduction takes on moral weight, framed not as a self-interested endeavour but as a veritable service to the human species.

One of the most worrying aspects of all this is that the evolutionary discourse of male sexuality frequently stultifies moral and ethical considerations. Jay, for example, expressed discomfort with certain elements of seduction practice but rationalised these as natural and thus beyond critique. Recalling a recent training event he had attended, he described being 'disturbed' when watching another attendee – a man in his fifties – approaching women in their late teens and early twenties. Though uncomfortable with this at the time, in the context of our interview he reasoned: 'But then, again, biologically, men would be attracted to young women. Because young women are fertile. That's just a biological fact.' Jay went on to relate his unease when listening to a seduction trainer claim that all women crave a sexual 'master'. Again, he determined to put aside these moral qualms, reasoning: 'That made me uncomfortable, but actually it kind of makes sense biologically.' Understanding sex as a male physical necessity conditioned by evolutionary imperatives effectively enables heterosexual men to abdicate responsibility for their actions, on the basis that these are determined by forces at once deep inside themselves and yet utterly outside their control. Moreover, this same logic occasionally lent itself to the claim that it is *men* who are exploited by the seduction industry, the marketing of which appeals to deep-seated desires beyond conscious awareness. Thus Ravi argued: 'They are exploiting some inherent weakness of male psychology. Men are always – since prehistory – men are always attracted to beautiful girls, and they want to have sex with as many as possible. The pickup industry is exploiting that weakness in their psychology.'

In order to account for the historical specificity of seduction as a contemporary formation, the evolutionary repertoire had to be supplemented by a further rhetorical manoeuvre. Thus, as well as claiming that men have a preordained biological need for sex that stands to benefit the human species, participants argued that this need has become frustrated. William argued: 'It's certainly hard for guys in Britain or America to meet women in a normal fashion, I would say.' Mark similarly claimed: 'At the moment, an ordinary guy has pretty much no way to get a woman. Social dynamics are such that . . . it's just impossible.' Danny stated: 'It's not actually easy to get laid, it's not easy. Even typically easy women, you still need a bit of game. You do need to know what you're doing. You can't just whip your dick out, it takes a bit more.' These statements denote a shift in register whereby it is claimed that men's ability to access sex has somehow become impeded. Though unnamed, the implied culprit here is feminism. Jay pointed to this when he highlighted the growing disjuncture between societal expectations and biological imperatives, claiming: 'It's become mostly equal. Women have become much more independent. And although societally it's better, in terms of sexual satisfaction and relationship-wise, it's deteriorating. Social and economic factors have changed, but biologically, the biology has not changed a lot with it.' Similarly, William concluded a lengthy discussion about the problems gender equality has brought about in Western societies by saying: 'In terms of opportunities, obviously then that ought to be addressed. But in terms of who we are and our biology, then [sighing heavily] that's kind of set in stone.'

While participants regarded gender equality as acceptable at one level, they very often also held that biological differences between women and men cannot be submitted to the ideological demands of gender equality. This line of reasoning accords with the postfeminist logic whereby campaigns for equality are considered to overlook the immutability of sexual difference: 'Feminism was deemed to have lost its way when it tried to impose its ideological prescriptions on a nature that did not fit' (Gill 2007b: 265). Evolutionary imperatives are mobilised not to *deny* women's right to social and political equality per se but, rather, to frame the pursuit of equality in the intimate and sexual sphere as *fundamentally untenable*. Cast as a biological fact honed through thousands of years of evolution, sexual difference comes to be regarded as fixed and unchanging and thus 'an inappropriate target of political analysis or intervention' (Donaghue 2015: 363). Where social relations between women and men are framed as 'subject to the laws of *nature*, rather than man' (Edley and Wetherell 2001: 452), any attempt to reshape these relations is liable to be cast as supremely ignorant and potentially delusional, tantamount to a denial of evolution itself.

'Your whole masculinity gets lost': masculinity undone

> The notion of a 'crisis' of men/masculinities can be seen, then,
> as a desire to change culture in order to maintain a 'natural' gender order.
> (Whitehead 2002: 61)

When explaining the emergence of the seduction industry and the appeal of the expertise it promotes, participants made frequent reference to what they saw as the 'feminisation' and 'emasculation' of men. Discussing this during our interview, which took place in a bar near Covent Garden, Danny gestured to a group at a nearby table, saying: 'Over the years, over the decades, the roles have started to blur. So you've got a lot of feminised men. For example, the guys behind us.' Turning around, I saw four young men sitting together around a table, fashionably turned out in skinny jeans and designer T-shirts. Shaking his head in disgust, Danny continued: 'Look at that guy! He's got his legs crossed – that's very feminine.' For other men I spoke to, patterns of feminisation and emasculation manifest in how 'nice' men have become, a quality that always seemed to be deemed excessive in men no matter its quantity. Antonio lamented: 'We're educated to be nice, always friendly and always like "Yes, sir", and so on. And then your whole masculinity gets lost.' For Ali, the media plays a crucial role in this: 'Just from TV and advertising, it ends up with a lot of guys being so nice that they just become really effeminate, killing any attraction between a man and a woman.' Elsewhere James described the difficulties he had faced overcoming his own geniality: 'I think I've been too nice in the past, in a way. And I know that I need to be, you know, not like that, but it's hard to do because it doesn't come naturally to me.'

Within this repertoire, feminism was often implicated through references to 'equality' and 'political correctness'. Kalim argued: 'Modern society has almost emasculated the male individual, because we're in an egalitarian society where everybody is seen as the same. We are told, we are reminded time and time again, that we are equals. And so it's easy to overlook our core masculine essence.' In a similar vein, Ali posited that 'Political correctness might have a part in it. Men and women being equal has made men not want to behave in an overtly masculine way. And while that may be beneficial in some ways, it also makes them less able to be attractive to women.' Jenny felt that contradictory expectations currently placed on men have produced an impossible predicament: 'Men aren't allowed to be so alpha, because they're considered sexist, so they can't be chauvinistic. They can't be too metrosexual, because then they're considered undesirable, too nice or too beta male.' In the background here is a censorious feminism which inhibits sexual expression. In a more concrete instantiation of this – indirectly referencing the infamous 'Antioch rules' which prescribed affirmative consent procedures for university students – Mark postulated: 'Some people certainly advocate for asking permission at every step of the seduction, like "Oh, can I hold your hand, oh, now can I touch your shoulder, and now can I touch your back?', and so on. I can't honestly think of a more unattractive way to seduce someone.' By this view, masculinity has not so much been undone as actively prohibited.

Single mothers loomed large in discussions of feminisation, reflecting a more general pattern whereby parents and especially mothers are blamed for a whole range of societal ills as part of the new landscape of 'parent-citizenship responsibility' (Jensen and Tyler 2012). Expanding on comments he had already made about this, Danny argued:

> A lot of single mothers. A lot of single mothers raising boys. I mean, there are exceptions, but generally I think that the guys that are particularly bad are the ones from either single-mother households or households where the dad was extremely beta, extremely beta, like an extremely weak male. So they kind of, like, saw that as the definition of masculinity, and hence it's meant that they've struggled with women, because they've had very bad, weak role models.

As though to give credence to Danny's theory, James related his own experience of being raised by women to broader patterns of emasculation:

> I think for me, personally, and I guess maybe it's again a result of a cultural shift, where a lot of guys . . . I'm just speculating, like, but my dad left when I was quite young, so it's been absent, that father figure. I was obviously raised by a lot of women. There was a lot of women around and I didn't have that . . . and then I picked things up off my mum, and it's, like, picking up female traits rather than male traits, and maybe that's . . . obviously there's a lot of divorce and that nowadays, and it's the mother that always has the kids. Maybe that has an effect on a lot of guys. Because I know a lot of nice guys.

For Danny and James, as for many other men I spoke to, masculinity is understood as a matter of intergenerational transference, such that a lack of strong male role models brings about its loss or attenuation on the basis that: 'only fathers and other men, not mothers, can properly develop masculinity in their sons, since masculinity by this definition is a matter of making men more manly' (Gardiner 2002: 101).

Within this framework of thinking, seduction comes to be seen as a means of returning to men a form of masculinity that has been lost or forfeited. Rahul argued: 'Men in Western society have drifted away from who they really are and that core primal instinct of being a raw animal and going for what they want. So, definitely, every man would benefit from this, without a shadow of a doubt, because it will make them stronger.' Adopting a more personalised register, Kalim stated: 'This is a part of my masculinity that I was missing. So for me this is about getting in touch with my masculinity. I think that's what the industry offers.' Ali posited that 'It's almost like reconditioning yourself', while Harry said: 'It can be a way to unprogramme a lot of things that society has put into your head.' At the same time, many participants were keen to emphasise the benefits of seduction for women, with Rahul contending that, through seduction, 'men develop so many skills that benefit the woman', and Jay adding that the industry 'helps men become the men that women want'.

In claiming that men in the UK and in Western societies more generally have become feminised and emasculated, participants often made reference to contrasting iterations of manhood belonging either to the relatively recent past or to societies believed to inhabit a different temporal order. These other masculinities were typically denoted as 'real', 'hard' and 'strong'. Exemplifying this, and clearly referencing feminism without naming it directly, Adam explained:

> The thing is, it's really hard to be an out and out man. You know, even if you look at who are supposed to be the most manly men – like footballers – if you look at footballers they're all metrosexual. It's not like George Best, drinking, smoking, fighting – you know what I mean? So I think men are being . . . I think you've got to be careful what you wish for. I think women wanted a much more equal world. And I think now we have it. I don't think men are above women, but I think that there are certain roles where men . . . that whole thing, women keep going, 'Where have all the real men gone?', you know? I don't think women have brought themselves up, I think they brought men down. You know what I mean? I think men have really lost their roles.

There is a clear sense here that some kind of embargo has been imposed on what is imagined as a previously hegemonic and unproblematic form of masculinity of which the footballer George Best – who came to fame in the 1960s and 1970s – is held up as an exemplar. Underpinning this construction is the belief that 'there was once a golden time of unproblematic, stable gender, when men were men, women were women, and everyone was happy with their social roles' (Gardiner 2002: 14). While the accuracy of this image could be complicated by Best's record of violence against women – at one point he landed his wife in hospital on Christmas Day – such logics find a ready alibi in the contemporary cultural belief that women today 'long to surrender to an unreconstructed man' (Downing 2013: 93). Adam's use of the well-worn idiom 'be careful what you wish for' serves as an indictment of feminism and the problems this is seen to have produced for women as well as men.

Yet while 'real' masculinity was often situated in the past – masculinity is, after all, a nostalgic formation, 'always missing, lost, or about to be lost' (Gardiner 2002: 10) – there was some uncertainty among participants about whether or not recapturing this would mean returning to traditional gender roles. Danny discussed this in relation to the seduction concept of 'polarity', which he defined as 'the plus and minus, the black and white, the contrast'. Arguing that polarity is a crucial component of attraction – 'you literally *have* to have polarity, otherwise there's no attraction' – he explained: 'Where game is good is basically telling men to be men, you know. So it's trying to regain some of that polarity. It would make them happier, and also I think it would make the women happier, if we went back to those roles.' Having pointed to the gender order of the 1950s as a period of social harmony characterised by clearly defined gender roles – with women as housewives and men as breadwinners – Danny added a note of caution: 'I genuinely think that, as long as you don't overdo it, those roles have worked really well for millennia.' I asked Danny what he meant by 'overdo it', to which he responded: 'You don't have to be a mindless gorilla. I'm not talking about wife beating or anything like that.' He went on to elaborate: 'For me, it's about men being more dominant. But dominance should start with the man himself. So the man should be able to control and dominate his own emotions and his self first. Take responsibility for himself, for his thinking, for his life, for his body. That sort of thing.'

Elsewhere, William also discussed the need for polarity in relationships and spoke about how much he had learned while travelling in Russia and the Balkans: 'It's fascinating to study. I love watching Russian men and

Serbian men. It's literally stepping back in time, so you can learn some stuff from these guys.' When I asked him to elaborate, William said:

> These are men that look after themselves, they do physical work, they go to the gym, they fight. Especially in Serbia, the men are really massive, it's amazing. Massive guys. So that's the good polarity. The bad polarity is that it's clearly sexist, coupled with homophobic and racist. You could say everything that feminists argue for [laughing] is yet to be established in these countries, you know.

With this latter commentary, William acknowledges the problems associated with traditional forms of masculinity for women and other Others. Nevertheless, and despite his awareness of these issues, he holds Serbian and Russian men up as the standard bearers British men should model themselves on in order to recover their masculinity and rebalance the gender order. The capacity for violence is important in underwriting 'real' masculinity here, as William emphasises physical size and readiness to fight as admirable characteristics of Serbian and Russian men. Indeed, the violence of both groups looms large in the cultural imaginary through displays of 'muscular nationalism' (Banerjee 2012) – Serb forces notoriously having propagated mass rape in the Bosnian war of the 1990s and the Russian president Vladimir Putin having famously maintained an iron-like grip on power for almost twenty years. While masculinity's ideal form is held to have been lost or prohibited in the West, it is claimed that this can still be found in societies supposedly untouched by the corrupting influences of feminism.

In claiming that men in the UK have become feminised and emasculated, a considerable number of participants made reference to the 1999 film *Fight Club*. Adapted from Chuck Palahniuk's eponymous novel and directed by David Fincher, *Fight Club* depicts the travails of an unnamed protagonist (Edward Norton). Through an apparently chance encounter with the enigmatic Tyler Durden (Brad Pitt), the protagonist goes from being an insomniac office worker to becoming the leader of a clandestine network of fight clubs and, later, the commander of a paramilitary organisation. Towards the end of the film, the protagonist learns that his insomnia has caused him to project Durden as a dissociated personality and that they are in fact the same person. Revelling in the depiction of bashed, bleeding and bruised white male bodies, the film inspired an outpouring of cultural commentary and academic writing on the plight of modern men. Reflecting on this and considering the film's enduring appeal among young male audiences in particular, Sally Robinson (2011) argues that 'the response to the film becomes almost as interesting as the film itself.'[2]

For a number of men I interviewed, *Fight Club* provided a kind of short-hand to describe the patterns of feminisation they saw all around them, and as such is worth considering in some detail. Comparing participation in the seduction community to involvement in the underground clubs depicted in the film – where the capacity both to inflict and to endure intense physical pain restores manhood – Danny explained: 'A lot of the natural alpha traits I might have had were beaten out of me through school, through parents, through everything really. And game gives you that awareness to try and recapture some of that, you know, *Fight Club* style.' Elsewhere, William claimed: 'A lot of men get into pickup for men. Not in a gay sense [laughing], but in a brotherhood sense, you know. It's *Fight Club* all over again. It's all about male camaraderie, because we lack that as men, we lack that bonding.'

When I asked Moe if he had any thoughts as to why seduction appeals to many men, he asked: 'Have you seen *Fight Club*?' I nodded and he continued:

> I can see a lot of similarities to that movie and to what is in – I mean, this generation of weak men who were raised by their mothers. I mean, it's good to be raised by your mother, but it takes a *man* to raise a man. I think you need that masculine power. I don't know how you explain it, but I think that's a very fundamental thing. And I think many men have lacked that.

Moe's mention of 'this generation of weak men who were raised by their mothers' references a well-known quote from the film. In a scene that is both demure in its domesticity and highly homoerotic – part of a broader sequence intended to underscore the growing intimacy between the two central characters – the unnamed protagonist sits on the bathroom floor talking to Durden as he bathes. Indicting their father(s) for having advised him/them to accede to a conventional middle-class lifestyle by going to college, getting a job and getting married, Durden pronounces: 'We are a generation of men raised by women. I'm beginning to wonder if another woman is really the answer we need.' Paraphrasing this sentiment, Moe dispenses with the second half of the quote, an omission that is notable precisely because it is necessary to maintain a view of the seduction community as analogous to the network the film portrays. Similarly, William's claim that the seduction community is '*Fight Club* all over again' elides the fact that the homosociality made available to men in the seduction community centres men's relationships with women in a way that has no parallel in the film.

While *Fight Club* is unquestionably concerned with themes of male crisis and, indeed, was marketed as 'a glorious satire of our "crisis of masculinity"' (Whitehead 2002: 49), its main target of critique is not the feminising influence of women, whether as mothers or intimate partners. Rather, the men who are drawn to participate in the film's underground fight clubs rage against the colonisation of their bodies and minds by consumer culture. They regard themselves not so much as a generation of men who have been feminised or emasculated by women as a generation of men who have become so thoroughly enslaved by the pursuit of wealth and material goods that they have lost any sense of themselves as embodied male subjects. The centrality of this theme to the film is evidenced by the progression of the original fight club – in which mostly white middle-class men come together in the basement of a local dive bar to fight one-on-one – into the militant political organisation Project Mayhem. Under Durden's lead, the men band together to wreak havoc in the financial districts of major American cities, before eventually conspiring to eliminate by way of dynamite the central enabling mechanism of contemporary capitalism: debt.

This, then, is a film about the ravages of a capitalist economic order that systematically undermines men's ability to relate to themselves and to one another. Undoubtedly, it privileges the male experience by routing its critique through the spectacular display of bleeding and breaking male bodies, which are transformed through brute force and sheer will into fighting machines. The anti-capitalist credentials of the film are, admittedly, deeply contradictory, produced as it was by a major Hollywood studio and harnessing the then considerable star power of Pitt. And yet it contains the possibility of fostering a critique of capitalism by showcasing the 'profound existential dis-ease' (Gill 2014) this economic system produces. This possibility, however, is continually circumvented in community readings of the film which displace a narrative of male disempowerment vis-à-vis *capitalism* and instead centre a story about male disempowerment vis-à-vis *women*. Indeed, some participants disavowed the anti-capitalist politics of the film altogether, as when Danny concluded: 'It would have been a perfect film had they not become homeland terrorists in the end.' Without trying to suggest that those who referenced *Fight Club* have simply misread the text, it seems important to recognise how this particular manner of decoding the film actively forecloses any recognition of the ways in which contemporary capitalism propagates the kind of disillusionment depicted so spectacularly in the film. Instead, attention is focused on the supposed attenuation of men's power in relation to women rather than on the workings of an economic system which disempowers women *and* men.

The discourse of masculinity in 'crisis' that has been such a persistent feature of public discussion – in areas such as education, employment and health – since at least the 1990s encourages men to understand whatever difficulties they experience in gendered terms. Elevated to the status of cultural common sense, the logic of crisis enters into everyday sense-making practices, both individually and collectively. Yet, while men's experience of powerlessness is real, in the sense that 'men actually feel it and certainly act on it', it is not true, in that 'it does not accurately describe their condition' (Kimmel 2005: 40). Meanwhile, the underlying causes of so many of the difficulties men may face in their lives – difficulties that are rooted in a range of hierarchies and inequalities far beyond those of gender – go unexamined. Where men's suffering is framed only and ever in terms of their relationship to women, disparities among men structured by class, 'race', nation, religion and (dis)ability cannot be acknowledged. After all, 'it is only in their ubiquitously cited and definitively enforced demarcation from "women" that the deep and pervasive divisions between men can be ignored' (Segal [1990] 2007: xi).

'You can't have it both ways': intimate inequality

> It is the selective and unfinished character of the feminist revolution that has made intimate and sexual relations so fraught with difficulties.
>
> (Illouz 2014: 61)

In our interview David complained that, despite claiming equality with men, women themselves remain reluctant to undertake the awkward business of expressing sexual interest and initiating romantic encounters:

> Women still expect men to approach them. They talk about equal rights and all this kind of stuff, but women will not approach men. They don't need to – they've got thousands of men approaching them. Why would they need to approach a man? So, unfortunately, this whole equal rights is only applicable in some respects.

Invoking a similar line of reasoning and sounding equally resentful, Antonio stated: 'We are educated in a way that we think that women and men are equal. Because we are constantly being told that we are equal, we are equal. But at this level it's not equal – because we have to do everything and they expect us to.' With these statements both David and Antonio draw attention to what they and many other participants regarded as women's intimate advantage – the various social arrangements and psychological dispositions that accord women greater power than men in sexual relationships. In doing so, they problematise not so much the social norm whereby men are expected to take responsibility for initiating heterosexual encounters as the fact that this norm persists alongside a demand for gender equality. Like many of the men I spoke to, they are frustrated with what is experienced as a constant exhortation to accept equality, evincing a sense of 'gender fatigue' (Kelan 2009). Even without being mentioned directly, feminism is again cast as an imposition.

Through this repertoire, participants drew on a more widely circulating cultural narrative which positions women as the primary beneficiaries of social change (McRobbie 2009). Pointing towards the various rights and opportunities now afforded to women, particularly in education and employment, men claimed that such shifts should have been accompanied by adjustments in the intimate sphere. Exemplifying this, Mark indicted women for trying to reap the benefits of both systems: 'Now women are, thankfully, in an almost equal position with men on the work scene. Not yet fully – in some countries there's still a gender pay gap, which I'm against. On the other hand, the social norm of a guy buying a girl drinks and whatever is still there. So what gives? You can't have it both ways.' Proudly displaying his egalitarian credentials by attesting that he is against pay inequality, Mark argues that women's new-found wage-earning potential ought to have made redundant the social niceties that accompanied their historically unequal status with men. He presents gender equality as a *fait accompli* in the UK by suggesting that the fight for pay equality is a battle that has long since been won – despite official figures indicating that this is far from being the case (ONS 2016). Invoking a by now familiar logic which displaces feminism elsewhere (Koffman and Gill 2013; Scharff 2013), Mark contends that feminism is no longer necessary in egalitarian societies such as the UK, while maintaining that it still has a role to play in less 'enlightened' countries. Though his criticism is directed towards social norms rather than women per se, there is nevertheless a palpable sense of resentment here, as Mark implies that women have deliberately contrived this situation – or at the very least knowingly exploit it.

Later he went on to argue that, while for heterosexual men it is nearly impossible to access casual sex, for women this is readily available: 'That's another power dynamic, because women feel like they have the power to get one-night stands when they want. Which is true, they do have that power right now.' Impressing this point, he invited me personally to test his thesis: 'Just do it sometime if you don't believe me. Go to a club, walk up to however many – say ten guys – and offer them, straight away, not even an introduction, offer them sex. See how many accept. I dare say around eight.' While Mark's intention in making this statement was clearly to highlight the ease with which women can apparently access casual sex, his suggestion that I go to a club to 'offer' men sex remains within a framing whereby sex is understood as something women 'give' to men rather than engage in for their own pleasure. When I responded to Mark's proposition by asking whether the outcome of his proposed experiment would depend on the individuals involved, he replied with obvious irritation: 'Well, yes. But, by and large, any woman does not have to make any considerable effort to get laid, if that's what they want. Whereas a man, nowadays, has to make an insane amount of effort.'

The belief that women enjoy unimpeded access to casual sex – a decidedly unfair arrangement given men's supposedly greater need – was commonplace among men I spoke to and interviewed. That this belief so often functioned as a means to explain and justify men's engagement with seduction demonstrates that 'gender retrenchment is secured, paradoxically, through the wide dissemination of discourses of female freedom' (McRobbie 2009: 55). Obscured from view are the myriad inequalities which can inhibit women from pursuing casual sexual encounters, including risk to reputation, lack of sexual reciprocity and fear of violence. Instead, it is the postfeminist sexual subject who 'knowingly and deliberately plays with her sexual power' (Gill 2008b: 41) that looms large in these accounts.

Yet while many participants complained about men's disadvantage vis-à-vis women in negotiating sexual encounters – a common complaint among heterosexual men in general (Mooney-Somers and Ussher 2010; Pleasants 2011; Seal and Ehrhardt 2003) – few actually wanted to *change* the cultural scripts which dictate that it is men's role to initiate contact. Thus when I asked men if they would like to see women take a more active role in this, only David embraced the possibility unequivocally: 'It's great! I think, you know, women want 50 per cent of everything, they want equal rights, why can't they do this as well? And just approach men – I think more of them should do that.' When I put the same question to Antonio, he sighed with exasperation and said: 'That's not the thing. The thing is more that we are educated in a way that we think that women and men are equal, but there are certain exceptions.' Later he added: 'It's not good to make everyone equal, in the sense that men are not women. You have to understand the difference of the genders.' In a more overt manifestation of this logic, Jack emphasised the need to maintain clearly defined gender roles: 'Guys feel like they have to make the first move and lead the way –

which is right, which I think is right, you know, traditionally. I'm a believer in certain values and I think guys should always make the first move, as it were, and lead the way.' Magnanimously, he added: 'Of course, it's up to the woman to say, "Yes, I like him", or "No, I don't".'

When I asked Derek how he felt about women approaching men, he was initially ambivalent: 'Sometimes I'm okay with it, and sometimes I'm not okay with it. Sometimes I'm like, "What the fuck?", you know. Like, "I'm the man here, you know, why are you trying to take my role?" But sometimes I'm alright.' He went on to recall a recent encounter with a woman he had approached on the street. Though a few minutes into their interaction Derek had concluded that this woman was 'almost perfect', his feelings changed when she suggested they go for a drink together later that night: 'I found it a bit off-putting, actually. I'm not used to that sort of thing, for somebody actually being up for it *that much*. I'm used to it being a bit more of a challenge than that. It was a complete role reversal.' Unsettled by what he saw as unconscionable forthrightness, he exited the interaction a few minutes later with a noncommittal agreement to get together another time. Derek's description of this woman as 'up for it' invokes the classed and gendered vocabulary of the postfeminist 'phallic girl', 'a young woman for whom the freedoms associated with masculine sexual pleasures are not just made available but encouraged and also celebrated' (McRobbie 2009: 83). His ambivalence demonstrates that the feminised forms of phallic power that give rise to 'conflicts and anxieties on the part of young women in regard to what they might now expect of sex and intimacy within the heterosexual matrix' (ibid.: 86) are also a cause for disquietude among heterosexual men.

This all suggests that, while heterosexual men may endorse equality in principle, this does not necessarily mean that they accept or enact it in practice (cf. Lamont 2014). Ultimately, while many participants complained about the perceived impetus for men to initiate sexual encounters and relationships, few wanted to see women take a more active role, as this would undermine the binary logic of sexual difference that structures heterosexual interaction. Rather, the source of their frustration was the perceived *incongruity* between demands on men to accept gender equality while still being expected to undertake the labour of approaching women. As such, the *propriety* of men's role in initiating and directing heterosexual relationships was rarely in question.[3] In one sense, it is little wonder that so many men want to retain the privilege of being socially licensed to initiate conversations with women. Despite the fact that this is often experienced as a burden – the cause of considerable discomfort and anxiety – it also affords men a great deal of agency as it authorizes them to express sexual interest in a manner not typically afforded to women. Yet, at the same time, the social ordinances that govern who can express desire for whom limit the opportunities available to heterosexual men to experience themselves as desirable.

Derek came onto this issue later when he recounted an interaction where a woman shut down the conversation before it had even begun, with a wearied: 'Do we have to do this?' Still angry about her dismissal of him, in our interview Derek spat: 'I was just like, it's just, "It's so difficult being attractive, isn't it? It's so difficult being hot, being good looking, and having people come up and compliment you, it must be a really stressful life." I was disappointed, you know, like what the fuck is that?' When I asked Derek why he thought she had responded this way, he offered a range of hypotheses before reasoning: 'Maybe a couple of other guys had already hit on her that day. Maybe she just wanted to be left alone, you know. I think that's probably what it was.' However, he then went on to contend that this was no excuse:

> But there are ways to deal with it and just be like 'Look, I'm sorry ...'. There's a nice way to take that. If it was me, I'd never get tired of people coming over to me and saying how beautiful I looked, or how amazing I was, you know. Like, how can that get tiring? How can it? And even if you just said 'Thank you so much, you know, I've got to go.' How would that get tiring? Why would that get tiring? There are people out there that would kill for that. People like me would have killed for that a few years ago. That sort of validation from other people.

Derek's comments suggest that he has little sense of what it is like for many women to inhabit public space, facing an onslaught of demands on one's time and attention alongside routine harassment and intimidation. Indeed, he not only contends that to receive attention is a *privilege* but goes so far as to suggest that women should *themselves* politely apologise when met with unwanted advances. Yet, at the same time, Derek's commentary belies an intense desire to be the object of desire, resentment mixing uneasily with envy. Though he expresses frustration with this woman in particular and laterally with women in general, it is arguably the uneven distribution of agency in heterosexual relationships that denies him the opportunity to be desired in the way he evidently wants to be.

The belief that women have an advantage over men often encompassed claims about women's greater psychological attunement, as manifest in references to women's 'intuition'. James, for example, suggested that, as a woman, I likely already have an instinctive understanding of the dynamics he had to learn about through seduction training: 'Maybe to a female who knows all that stuff – your intuition's obviously a lot better – maybe this is, like, "Oh well, this is all stuff I know", but for men it's just like . . . you have to find this. It's a journey, you have to find this stuff out.' Notably, intuition is figured as a quality inherent in women, such that the considerable 'emotion work' (Duncombe and Marsden 1993) women perform in attuning themselves to the needs and desires of others is absented from view.

Claims of this kind were routinely couched in the language of feminist object-relations theory. In but one of many examples of this, Harry argued: 'For women, you're a lot more socially attuned because going to school when the guys were off playing football the girls were, you know, talking with each other. So you're more socially intuitive and more socially aligned then men are.' This statement closely approximates a quote from Carol Gilligan's *In a Different Voice* (1982), which Neil Strauss later used as a chapter preface in seduction handbook *The Game*: 'People used to look out on the playground and say that the boys were playing soccer and the girls were doing nothing. But the girls weren't doing nothing – they were talking. They were talking about the world to one another. And they became very expert about that in a way the boys did not' (cited in Strauss 2005: 289).[4] While the reproduction of Gilligan's argument by participants is undoubtedly testament to the authority accorded to figures such as Strauss, this pattern also exemplifies the *selective* uptake of feminist ideas that is a key feature of postfeminism (Gill 2007c; McRobbie 2009). What is also significant about the appropriation of Gilligan's work in this way is that feminist object-relations theory has long been the feminist theory of choice for academic as well as popular authors on masculinity. Examining this pattern elsewhere, Anthony McMahon argues: 'feminist object-relations theory licenses men not only to speak of the burdens of masculinity but to speak of themselves as, at least psychologically, at a disadvantage when compared with women' (1999: 199). In this way, the material interests men have in maintaining gender inequality are obscured through a *psychologisation* of sexual politics.[5]

Extending claims about women's presumed psychological advantage over men, a number of those I interviewed argued that such disparities are compounded by the emotionally centred content of women's media. Having also claimed that gendered play patterns in childhood set women up with a 'massive advantage, right at the beginning', Derek argued that this is further consolidated via the relational orientation of media aimed at women: 'When you look at women's magazines, and it talks about relationships, it talks about who's sleeping with who, there's all this gossip and stuff. All of that stuff is available to women, wherever you go. For men, there isn't stuff like that. All there is, is just porn. That's literally it.' Paralleling this comment, David argued: 'Dating advice is *always* aimed at women. It's just such a funny world. I mean, why do women need dating advice? You know, like, *men* need it, because we're the ones that are orchestrating and initiating the entire process.' Likewise, Gavin claimed: 'If you look at what's there for women and what's there for men . . . you know, women have *Cosmopolitan* saying "Sex rules that will please your man", "How to drop down a dress size to make your man sexually excited over you", you know, "How to attract a man." Women have these sort of things to help them.' Gavin went on to add that women also benefit from empathetic friendships with other women in a way men do not: 'And also, women as a group are a lot more supportive of each other. Like saying "Oh, don't worry, your boyfriend's a dick", you know, "You can find a better man", you know, "I know how you feel." With men, we don't get that. In normal society, men don't get that.' Even as he envisions women's friendships to be characterised by mutual empathy and understanding, it seems that these women are not as empowered as the bylines of women's magazines might suggest, as their conversations about men appear to involve a great deal of commiseration.

Clearly, there is a certain irony to women's magazines being held up as examples of women's supposed psychological advantage over men, not least because women's magazines often devote themselves to exhaustively detailing the various kinds of work women must undertake – emotional, aesthetic, sexual, domestic – in order to please and appease men (Gill 2009). But there is also an unacknowledged contradiction at work here. While participants repeatedly claimed that women 'don't have to do anything', as David put it, they also cited the sex and relationship advice dispensed by women's magazines as a central means through which women secure an intimate advantage over men. Paradoxically, then, while claiming that women are not required to expend any effort to attain and maintain sexual relationships, media directed at women to facilitate precisely this aim were taken as evidence of women's advantage in the intimate realm. Such discursive flexibility allows the form of expertise elaborated in the seduction industry to be figured as analogous to cultural resources made available to women. Thus Adam argued: 'Men haven't had the beauty industry and the fashion industry like women have. If you think about what that's all about, it's making women look as best they can so they can get the best possible partner. Men just now have an industry that's equal to that.'

Framed as a kind of equivalent to fashion and beauty practices, seduction comes to be seen as a means to redress an imbalance currently tipped in women's favour. Again, it is somewhat ironic that these industries are held up as evidence of women's privilege, given the very real psychological and physical harms the beauty-industrial complex perpetrates (Wolf 1990; Elias et al. 2016; Jeffreys 2005).

At times, the claim that women enjoy an intimate advantage over men spilled over into the claim that it is men who are disadvantaged in society at large. This was demonstrated in my interview with Mark when, less than ten minutes into our discussion, he launched into the following diatribe:

> Most men feel like women have a lot more power than they do. And, this is quite obvious when you walk into a high-end nightclub, guys will pay twenty pounds just to get in. Women generally don't, if they're hot enough. And the club will go even as far as saying sometimes, 'Oh, no more guys in for tonight, but your girls can go.' I call that discrimination. You know, if that happened . . . if that happened the other way round, you'd *never* hear the end of it. I mean, feminism has done a great deal of good, up to the point at which it advocates equality. But when it steps over that . . . I mean, if you look at Sweden. I was reading a newspaper article about some jobs where now they have a protected quota of female workers in that job. Do you know what that quota is? Sixty per cent. Higher than the number of men. So how's that equality, you know?

Linking together a range of disparate issues, Mark blames feminism – which he, unlike most participants, references directly – for the various disadvantages men face across a variety of settings. In doing so, he draws on more widely circulating discourses in which feminism is understood primarily as an attack on men (Calder-Dawe and Gavey 2016; Edley and Wetherell 2001; García-Favaro and Gill 2015). Yet, as he indicts feminism for the differential treatment of women and men nightclub patrons, Mark rather conveniently overlooks the fact that it is overwhelmingly *men* who control access to these spaces, and that women's privileged entry is part of a broader economy of power in which women function as commodities of exchange *between* men.[6]

Mark's comments again evoke a sense of gender fatigue, as he complains that, were women subject to the forms of discrimination men endure on a regular basis, it would be endlessly discussed. And although he acknowledges the value of feminism in securing certain rights and opportunities for women – thus not repudiating it entirely – he contends that this has now gone too far, with women being conferred advantages over and at the expense of men. Towards the end of our interview, Mark returned to this subject when I asked if he had any thoughts as to the wider social or cultural significance of seduction. Thinking on this for a few moments before responding, he then said:

> The question I always ask myself is why? Why do things happen the way they are? And I don't have an answer about the pickup community. I have a few ideas, a few thoughts, which I have shared. One thing I have noticed is that people in positions of power enjoy denying others the possibility of enjoying the very same things they enjoy themselves.

With this oblique yet loaded statement, Mark implies that women – assumed to be enjoying a host of new-found rights and entitlements – are now denying these same liberties to men. This framing is illustrative of the enormous power attributed to women in the context of postfeminism, such that it is assumed that women are *in a position* to deny to men the freedoms they putatively enjoy. At the same time, his commentary works to *offset or forestall* criticism of the seduction industry, as any kind of critique is always already construed as an attempt to deny men the liberties feminism is understood to have accorded women.

Danny was more forthcoming in his views on feminism than any other participant I spoke to. When in our interview I asked what he thought had brought about the emergence of the seduction industry, he responded: 'That's a tough question. I mean, you would have to look at the economy, feminism, things like that. Women entering the workforce, definitely.' Elaborating on this point, he claimed that women's participation in the formal economy had driven down men's wages:

> What's happened with women entering the workforce, it's just reduced the salary of men. In the forties and fifties, a man could actually make enough money to provide for the whole household. Whereas, now, the same amount of money is split between two people, so now we need to have both parents working in order to survive. Whereas before the man was the sole breadwinner. So really what has happened is that pot of money has just been split in half.

Danny's commentary partially reflects the reality whereby the organisation of the economy around a family wage has been undercut (Fraser 2009), the impact of which has been especially pronounced among working-class men who are unable to access the kind of decently waged work that in the UK has long been a key marker of masculinity (McDowell 2014; Willott and Griffin 1997). Yet by framing this in terms of gender rather than the capricious demands of capitalist labour organisation, Danny implies that women have somehow taken jobs that rightfully belong to men. This is, of course, a pervasive cultural narrative (Kimmel 2013) that some feminists have helped propagate (see Faludi 1999) and which has found renewed purchase in the ever resounding aftermath of the 2008 financial recession (Negra and Tasker 2014).

Following this, Danny went on to claim that higher education for women is a poor use of resources: 'A lot of degrees are wasted by women that end up only doing that job for a little while. Then they become housewives. And they're happy being housewives. So resources are wasted sometimes by women. They're depriving men of actually getting those degrees. There's more competition.' While cloaking his arguments in economic rationality, in questioning women's right to pursue third-level education Danny strikes at a central tenet of postfeminism, wherein women are called upon to take up new opportunities in education as well as employment (McRobbie 2009). From here, he went on to indict the treatment of stay-at-home mothers, again laying the blame for this at the door of feminism:

> In modern day Britain, if you're a housewife, yeah, it's fucking isolat-
> ing, because you're stuck at home on your own watching *Jeremy Kyle*.
> Whereas, in the fifties, most women would have stayed at home looking
> after the kids. They would have looked after each other's kids, they
> would have done loads of fun activities, you know. So it wouldn't have
> been so isolating. So, I think women have been encouraged to take on
> these masculine roles and they're now working in shitty office jobs.
> Whereas, in fact, I think many, many – not all women, but many women
> – would be satisfied with the traditional role of looking after the kids.
> And, you know, would be satisfied by that role.

Danny's belief that many if not most women would be happy as stay-at-home mothers calls to mind Simone de Beauvoir's insightful recognition that 'it is always easy to describe as happy the situation in which one wishes to place [another]' ([1949] 1997: 28). But what is most interesting here is how he uses the architecture of feminist argument to turn feminism against itself. In a final indictment, he went on to pillory the feminist academy:

> Most women, instead of liberating themselves, they've just oppressed
> themselves by working in shitty office jobs. Yes, it's nice if you're
> Germaine Greer, right, and you've got a nice cushy job working at a
> university, writing *The Female Eunuch* and stuff like that. That's awesome.
> Yeah, you've got a great deal there. But most women ultimately end
> up working in these shitty jobs, you know. It's only again the elite that
> benefit, the lesbian elite. And a lot of – a disproportionate amount of

feminists are basically – many of them are lesbians trying to tell straight women what they should want and what they should strive for. You know, and ultimately they're realising actually it's not what they want.

Invoking prominent spectres of feminism – the 'killjoy' (Ahmed 2010a), the 'feminist-as-lesbian' (Hesford 2005) – Danny undermines the very premise of feminism by highlighting its supposed failures. In doing so, he taps into the very real problem whereby feminism has been 'righted', taken over by and for the purposes of individual self-interest and capital promotion (Farris and Rottenberg 2017; Rottenberg 2014). Though Danny was more vocal than many others I spoke to, his arguments nevertheless accord with the general view that seduction is a much needed corrective to current imbalances in the gender order, with men's intimate relationships with women understood as offering both the most immediate point of intervention and the greatest personal yield of a now diminishing 'patriarchal dividend' (Connell 2000).

After the aftermath, into the wreck

The sexual politics of seduction centre around the reassertion of sexual difference. For the majority of men I interviewed, this does not mean a wholesale return to traditional gender arrangements; rather, it manifests in a desire to establish and enforce clearly defined roles for women and men in the context of intimate life. While this is framed as a neutral endeavour, it necessarily involves maintaining and, indeed, strengthening divisions and hierarchies that have long accorded men power over women in private and public life. Seduction also gives rise to a particular programme of sexual politics, as men are encouraged to see and experience themselves as the beleaguered party in a zero-sum game in which every gain for women entails a loss for men. Participation in this sphere frequently exacerbates a sense of frustrated entitlement, as men continually compare themselves to others who appear to enjoy sexual plenty. It sublimates feelings of anger and frustration, directing men to seek power in the context of their intimate lives rather than directing this outwards to contest the wider social, political and economic arrangements that precipitate profound feelings of disempowerment. Where other securities fall away or are placed out of reach, for many men, investing in sexual difference seems a promising way of ensuring some kind of stability in their lives. This, if nothing else, is something they can control.

I want to conclude by outlining what I see as the significance of this for feminist thought and politics, most especially in relation to ongoing theorisations of postfeminism. In *The Aftermath of Feminism* (2009) – one of the first texts to chart the contours of the postfeminist landscape and which has decisively shaped its study since – Angela McRobbie examines the variety of forces through which feminism has been 'taken into account' and 'undone'. One of the most important concepts she develops is that of the 'new sexual contract', part of a wider redefinition of gender relations in the context of global capitalism. McRobbie describes this as 'a form of power which entails negotiation at the social and cultural level with the objective of a settlement within the field of sexuality' (2009: 90). The new sexual contract invites women to take up a range of entitlements and opportunities – to gain qualifications, participate in the workforce, partake in consumer culture, and engage in the kind of recreational sex that has long been the purview of men. The unspoken proviso to all this is that it is granted 'in exchange' for feminism. The new sexual contract thus represents a form of social compromise through which renewed feminist challenges are offset, while at the same time there is a 'subtle renewal of gender injustices' and 'vengeful patriarchal norms are re-instated' (ibid.: 54).

In the many analyses of postfeminism that have since been developed, little attention has been given to the place of men in the new sexual contract. Contributing to a review symposium on *Aftermath*, Vic Seidler notes this issue and questions McRobbie's use of terms such as 'resurgent patriarchalism', on the basis that this suggests 'a reversion to something that we already know' (2011: 706). Reviewing the book elsewhere, Adrian Howe asks why McRobbie privileges the workings of symbolic violence at the expense of examining the many other forms of violence that pattern women's lives, contending that: 'Self-policing is not the only dubious practice constraining the lives of young women entering the new sexual contract' (2012: 112). Howe further argues: 'It might have been anticipated too that a book exploring the post-feminist gender settlement that its author calls 'the new *sexual* contract' would have clocked worrying developments in the sex lives of young women (ibid.: 111).

These discussions highlight the need for feminist scholars to engage with the issue of how men are situated within and negotiate the terrain of postfeminism. For while men clearly have a stake in the new sexual contract – they are necessarily caught up in the bargain – the manner in which they are implicated by and seek to negotiate its terms has not been sufficiently investigated. In more recent writings, McRobbie touches upon some of these issues when she notes that 'to contest male privilege is to risk inhabiting the old space of the radical feminist whose antipathy, it is understood retrospectively, was to "men"' (2015: 17). Further to this, McRobbie posits that there is a reluctance among many feminist scholars to 'resurrect and reinstate "old" categories such as masculine dominance, patriarchy or male power', now deemed 'too crude, possibly essentialist, and theoretically unviable "after" queer theory' (ibid.). She concludes this discussion by arguing: 'This empty space of antagonism to male dominance in work or in everyday life is in need, therefore, of some new feminist theorising' (ibid.).

I agree with McRobbie's comments. Indeed, it strikes me that it is in large part because many feminist scholars have retreated from these issues that recent developments in the terrain of gender politics – marked by misdirected anger and inchoate rage – have taken so many of us by surprise. To this end, and while McRobbie deliberately seeks distance from Carole Pateman's original coinage in *The Sexual Contract* (1988), it is instructive to return to this earlier coinage. What Pateman's analysis foregrounds, in a way I believe much of the scholarship on postfeminism does not, is both the collective dimension of masculine power and the centrality of sexual relationships to the organisation of gendered power dynamics. As Pateman argues: 'The original pact is a sexual as well as a social contract: it is sexual in the sense of patriarchal – that is, the contract establishes men's political right over women – and also sexual in the sense of establishing orderly access by men to women's bodies' (1988: 2). In the case of the seduction community, this analysis readily applies, as seduction is both a self-making and a world-making project to which the pursuit of sexual access is pivotal.

How, then, can feminist scholars go about examining men's brokering with the new sexual contract? Certainly, steps are being taken in this direction, as feminists explore the emergence of newly emboldened and technologically enhanced forms of sexism and misogyny. Yet, in examining contemporary permutations of what seem to be age-old problems, it is crucial that our methods enable us to gain some purchase on the perspectives and experiences of those drawn towards these cultural formations. Such undertakings have become all the more urgent in an era of 'libidinal politics' (Forrester 2017), awash with 'reinvigorated political patriarchs' (Mellström 2017) intent on undoing what not long ago seemed like assured gains. In order for feminists to gain a handle on these issues, it is crucial that we attend to the everyday spaces of contestation through which men's collective power is simultaneously asserted and denied. To do this, it is necessary to undertake research – difficult, uncomfortable, likely exhausting research – with and among those with whom we may most forcefully disagree. For if we allow ourselves to become locked into antagonism, critiquing only from a distance, there will be no possibility for any more expansive dialogue to emerge that might enable us to move towards radical progressive change. Collectively, men I spoke to expressed deep ambivalence about shifts that have taken place in the wider terrain of gender relations. My contention is that it is precisely this space of ambivalence which feminists must address in our analyses of, and interventions in, contemporary sexual politics. To do so, we must 'dive into the wreck', in order that we may find 'the wreck and not the story of the wreck, the thing itself and not the myth' (Rich 1973). Because if we cannot do this, then we have already lost.

Conclusion: Against Seduction

Those who become involved in the seduction community, who take up the knowledge-practices on offer here, are looking for something. Whatever the content of their own intimate ambitions – which in any case often change through their participation in this sphere – the initial foray is typically born of a desire for connection. Claiming expertise and seeking profit, the industry promises heterosexual men that by purchasing its wares and enlisting its services they will find whatever it is they are looking for – choice with women, status among men. Having been seduced by this promise of control, those who buy into this knowledge system apply themselves to the work of seduction, attempting to cultivate the capacities and dispositions said to be conducive to sexual success. What makes seduction so compelling for many men is its meritocratic appeal: it seems to offer a way to undo received masculine hierarchies and rectify the uneven distribution of sexual access among men. In this way, the sexual lottery is transformed into a marketplace where, men are told, their hard work will be rewarded. Promoting an entrepreneurial solution to the very real problems involved in finding and forging intimate relationships – which many today navigate via dating sites and hookup apps that instantiate a similarly market-like apparatus – the seduction industry exemplifies some of the most dubious tendencies of the current conjuncture. Individual self-work is prescribed as the solution for problems that are culturally shared and socially patterned. Labour-intensive and profit-orientated modes of sociality consume other forms of being and relating. Ethical concerns are cast aside in favour of personal promotion and unencumbered self-interest. For these and other reasons I conclude this book with an argument against seduction.

Before elaborating any further, it is necessary to clarify what this argument is not. To be against seduction is not to be against sex. It is not to be against the kinds of interactions and relationships that are often placed beyond the heteronormative bounds of sexual respectability: sex with multiple partners, sex with anonymous partners, sex for money, sex without commitment, sex involving consensual power exchange. To be against seduction is instead to be against sex that is cynical, calculating, disingenuous. It is to be against the packaging of intimacy as a script that can be rehearsed, in which trust is conjured rather than cultivated. It is to object to the giving over of intimacy to entrepreneurialism, not because sex is special – though certainly it can be – but because individual self-work is not and cannot be the answer to the problems we experience in the intimate realm (nor, despite prevailing wisdom to the contrary, can it always be the answer to problems arising in the economic, social and political realms). To be against seduction is to be against the kinds of sexual encounters in which the perspectives and experiences of our partners are valued only insofar as they enable us to more readily manipulate others to comply with our own wishes. It is to be against modes of sexual relating in which our own bodies and desires are turned against us, where the rhetoric of liberation and empowerment is used to corral and subjugate. It is to be against the reduction of sexual pleasure to little more than the mechanical pursuit or procurement of orgasm. It is to be against sex that serves as a means to enhance or affirm oneself over and at the expense of others. It is to categorically refuse any form of sexual coercion, whether through premeditated emotional manoeuvrings or the carefully calculated weight of expectation. It is to absolutely oppose sexual violence in the myriad forms this sadly but predictably takes.

What gets between

As a system of expertise for the management of sexual conduct by and among heterosexual men, seduction perpetuates the already overwhelmingly mediated character of sex and relationships in the contemporary moment. In her 1984 essay 'The uses of the erotic', Audre Lorde decries the tendency to live 'outside ourselves' and 'on external directives only', explaining that, 'when we live away from those erotic guides from within ourselves, then our lives are limited by external and alien forms, and we conform to the needs of a structure that is not based on human need, let alone an individual's' (1984: 58). Lorde continues: 'When we look away from the importance of the erotic in the development and sustenance of our power, when we look away from ourselves as we satisfy our erotic needs in concert with others, we use each other as objects of satisfaction rather than share our joy in the satisfying, rather than make connections with our similarities and differences' (ibid.: 59). As intimacy has become ever more heavily mediated – the subject of an endless litany of injunctions and directives in lifestyle magazines and self-help books, the central focus of attention in much music, TV and film – these external directives become more deeply embedded in our day-to-day lives. They permeate our individual and collective psychology, shaping our innermost desires and orienting us in ways in which we are not fully aware. While the management of sexual relationships has long been regarded as the provenance of women, seduction enjoins men to similarly plan for and direct their intimate lives, supposedly to challenge the upper hand women have for too long enjoyed. A variety of seduction-related media – handbooks, DVD programmes, online content – piles up alongside existing paraphernalia like so much sexual ephemera. Live training events and coaching programmes offer the opportunity to put theory into practice under the supervision of men who apparently enjoy 'mastery' with women.

Having largely circumscribed the role of religion and all but given up on any conception of the social, in the UK today intimate relationships – especially romantic and sexual relationships – have become central to our sense of identity and personal value. At the same time, current social and economic conditions conspire to make these kinds of relationships supremely difficult to cultivate and sustain. In concert with but also to a greater extent than other societies experiencing the shuddering convulsions of neoliberal capitalism, contemporary Britain is marked by a consummate preoccupation with work (Couldry and Littler 2008). For the predominantly middle-class professionals I interviewed, conditions of overwork are such that many felt they had neglected what was invariably understood as a discrete area of life. Some described having had little time for sexual relationships beyond the most perfunctory affairs, absorbed as they were with work or study. Almost all were disappointed either with the kinds of intimate relationships they did have or with the kinds of women with whom they had them. In these circumstances, seduction comes to represent an attractive solution, an effective and efficient means to pursue sexual encounters and manage intimate relationships. Paradoxically, then, the solution to overwork is to transform other areas of life into work,[1] as heterosexual men are exhorted to cultivate a sexual work ethic, to invest in training materials and coaching courses. Cordoned off from other areas of life, sexual relationships become something to 'sort out', a term that came up again and again across interviews, as intimate life is converted into yet another project to be managed.

There is an obvious tension here. Sex and relationships have become increasingly central to our sense of self, yet at the same time the demands of the contemporary workplace are such that for many there is little space to foster and care for these relationships in our day-to-day lives. As this tension becomes ever more pronounced, so commercial solutions proliferate. But as a response to the unsustainable mode of living engendered by capitalism, the seduction industry in turn proffers an equally unsustainable solution. Trainers I spoke to readily admitted as much, noting that, like other chimeric industries – such as the market in fad diets – engagement with seduction frequently begets repeat custom. And despite an avowed concern to help men less sexually fortunate than themselves – with many trainers insisting that, unlike others in the industry, they are not just in it for the money – this was generally regarded as unproblematic: the necessary cost of doing business in a competitive industry. That the industry often fails to fulfil its promises of control was evidenced too by the unhappy attachments some men developed to it, finding themselves compulsively picking up women just to reassure themselves they can do so, alienated from the process but placated, perhaps, by the knowledge that they do not have to be alone. In the writings of those who find fame in this industry, the shifting horizons of sexual expectation are writ large, evidenced in the constant exhortation to seek out conquests that are 'younger, hotter, tighter', as the mantra of one industry figure puts it. Their conquests pile up, sexual partners are enlisted and discarded, the perpetual notch count whittling the bedstand to toothpick proportions. As the desire to accumulate sexual experience fails to abate, so the feats performed become ever more outlandish: teenage girls seduced in front of their parents; women of different ethnicities and nationalities collected like so many totems in a kind of sexual neo-imperialism; strippers and sex workers engaged without payment; girlfriends passed around to other men like prizes.

Writ through by an ethos of competitive enterprise, sexual encounters function as a measure of masculine self-worth, and are thus pursued as a means of testing skills, measuring improvement, affirming desirability. Sex is invaded by the logics of assessment and surveillance that already pervade so many other sites of human relating. The injunction to work on sex and relationships necessarily entails a flattening out of the intersubjective. Despite the constant allusions to and pretensions of artistry, to the extent that seduction involves creativity of any kind, this is the cold intimacy of the advertising or PR executive, who orchestrates emotion in order to close the deal. Like so many other neoliberal delusions, seduction is based in the denial of all that is unpredictable and inexact about human experience in favour of something more readily administrable. It offers up a system of rules and interdictions by which sex and relationships can be managed rather than experienced. It involves turning away from the intricacies of intimacy and, in doing so, turning away from the complexity of our own as well as each other's experiences. The dynamism of sexuality and the poetry that can be found here is circumvented in favour of something altogether more generic. And yet the promise of control proffered by seduction is not only illusory but frequently self-defeating. Where sexual encounters and relationships become a matter of concerted effort, to be pursued and consumed like so many other commodities, disappointment becomes all the more likely as the horizon of expectation continually recedes towards a perpetual vanishing point.

For many men, certainly for the majority of those I spoke to and interviewed, seduction proved not to be the hoped-for elixir for the disappointment and dissatisfaction that patterned their intimate lives. More often, engagement with this system of expertise exacerbated existing feelings of disaffection. Past relationships and current lifestyles seemed ever more inadequate, ex-girlfriends and present partners all the more deficient. In keeping with the meritocratic logics that enable and sustain this industry, the solution to this is yet more hard work. In the seduction industry, as elsewhere in contemporary culture, upgraded selfhood is marketed as the singular solution to all manner of problems. Modelled on the middle-class white men who dominate the upper echelons of the industry, who in turn fashion themselves on men whose material wealth and status they can only dream of emulating, this industry upholds a limited definition of what it means to be a man. The capacity for control – to be exerted over the self and others – is paramount. All that might encroach upon or diminish this is jettisoned. There is a drive towards conformity on the basis that only certain iterations of masculinity are accorded value in the heterosexual marketplace. Those who do not carry the right kind of value are exhorted to model those who do. The self – understood as a product – is to be packaged in such a way as to appeal to 'high-quality' women. In this way, the industry reflects and reproduces wider patterns of racism and classism that organise hierarchies among men. In reconciling themselves to this ideal of masculinity, men accede to the histories that have placed them at a distance from it in the first place. The desires of the successfully remediated masculine subject are, in turn, formulated so that women's appearance – conceived as a marker of masculine status – is valued above all else.

The seduction industry profitably colludes in perpetuating the logic of sexual difference that, despite the emphasis on complementarity, ultimately positions women and men in opposition to one another. This system of expertise reinforces the already pervasive 'two sexes, two cultures' paradigm, whereby women and men are understood as essentially and *properly* different (Potts 1998). By this logic, antagonism in heterosexual relationships is inevitable and therefore acceptable and often eroticised. Women and men are not *supposed* to be able to relate to one another easily; we are practically different species. Rather than seek to throw off this covenant – which has been undermined in so many other ways in recent decades – seduction advocates that men cling on to their assigned masculine role. After all, it is this role which has traditionally accorded men power over women in not only the private but also the public sphere. That it causes men untold harm is for the most part not discussed, stoicism being regarded as a cardinal virtue. For though adopting conventional gender roles in heterosexual relationships may provide a certain amount of reassurance – these roles can be comforting in their familiarity, their well-worn character making them easy to slip into – heteronormativity is by definition restrictive. It sets limits on what it is possible to do and to be in intimate relationships, a site many of us look to for the kinds of freedom too often unavailable elsewhere. For heterosexual men, heteronormativity often means denying the vulnerability inherent in us all.

Patching the system

When we accept the idea that women and men are fundamentally different – despite the considerable evidence to the contrary[3] – we also accept all manner of banal indifference and everyday enmity in heterosexual relationships. While such agonies and antipathies are liable to be experienced as deeply personal, heterosexuality is an institution afflicted by systemic inequalities. Seduction is one among many available patches for a system that at its heart is deeply flawed. What marks out this form of expertise as in some sense distinct is that it is produced predominantly by and for heterosexual men. Providing men with the necessary scripts and stage cues to act out the drama of heterosexual romance – choreographed to give the impression of spontaneity and chance so often played out on the silver screen – seduction obviates extemporaneous affect. As the role of seducer is more deeply inhabited, so the calculated display of emotion all the more convincingly substitutes for feeling. The appeal of taking up this role for many men is that it may enable them to bypass the uncertainty and anxiety that so often go along with meeting new people and moving towards sex or intimacy. What often goes unsaid is that, by inuring themselves to these feelings, men may also limit their capacity to feel other things, to experience joy and wonder in tandem with intimate others, rather than simply wring pleasure for themselves out of others' bodies.

Far from enabling greater emotional expressivity, seduction encourages men to take an instrumental stance towards feeling, redeploying the romantic scripts and narrative devices of Hollywood rom-coms as a route to sex. In this way, physical proximity can be achieved without necessarily having to enter into shared feeling. Enabled in part by this sequestering of emotion, seduction involves a narrowing of the moral self, as men are exhorted to adopt a masculinist subject positioning in which women are regarded in technical rather than ethical terms. Where sex is understood as something to be attained rather than shared, women can all too easily be regarded as objects to be overcome. What begins as banal indifference can quickly give way to studied cruelty.

Feminist cultural commentators have long argued that the tactics and techniques as well as the general mindset and belief system advanced within the seduction industry may promote sexual violence. While often met with accusations of histrionics, these concerns have been borne out. As I was completing this manuscript, American news media reported on a case in San Diego involving two seduction trainers and one of their students, all three of whom were convicted of rape for events that took place in 2013. At the time, trainers Alex Smith and Jonas Dick were employed by a California-based company called Efficient Pickup, and Jason Berlin was their student. As part of their arrangement, Berlin had rented a downtown apartment in which the two trainers lived, and on weekends he joined them for training sessions. On the night in question, Smith and Dick went to a nearby club and later brought two women back to the apartment. While Dick distracted one woman in the living room, Smith and Berlin took it in turns to rape the other woman in the bedroom. She was rendered unconscious and vomited repeatedly during the assault.

A decisive factor in securing the conviction of all three men was the substantial body of evidence the victim herself unearthed. Frustrated that the police were not doing more to investigate – despite the fact that she immediately reported the assault and submitted to a forensic examination – the victim began searching for information about these men online. She soon discovered their links to the seduction industry. Reading through a forum in which they posted about their activities, she found an entry written by Smith describing the night he and Berlin had raped her:

> Jonas and I are both teaching BC [bootcamp] tonight. We run into each other at pull o clock (bar closing). He asks me to Wing for him. I do; within a couple of minutes I'm fingering my girl right outside of the bar in public. Pull back to the spot. 0 LMR [last minute resistance] make her

beg for my dick and I say only if my friend can fuck you too. So we run a train [have sex in succession] on the hoe. I text Jonas to choo choo her but he has to occupy her friend. Her friend came out and I was like 'yeah we just tagteamed your friend' my chick freaked out (cause now she's a slut etc.) I get hit in the face with a high heel. I laugh; we kick them out. (Cited in Zadrozny 2016)

This account, along with the larger cachet of evidence the victim assembled and delivered to the police, was submitted to the court. Handing down the maximum eight-year sentence to Smith – the only one of the three men to plead not guilty and go to trial – Judge Jeffrey Fraser stated:

I've got to tell you, having sat up here for eighteen years, there's a lot of people that have sat in that chair and I can't recall – murderers, rapists, kidnappers – go down that list, I don't know if I've seen one that has been as mean and cruel as you have been. You had your own language, you had your own apartment, you had your own school. That is the only thing that you could say about your school. It was about being a rapist. (Cited in Smith 2016)

During this trial the district attorney argued that there were potentially many more victims yet to be identified, noting that CCTV footage from the apartment complex showed a number of different women accompanying Smith and Dick home before leaving their residence some time later in obvious distress. When their apartment was searched by the police, prescriptions for Viagra, steroids and Xanax were found. DNA samples from all three men were entered into the national database, whereupon Dick was implicated in an unsolved case; he was subsequently charged with and convicted of the forcible rape of a sixteen-year-old girl.

Undoubtedly, there are many in the seduction industry who would decry such crimes as the heinous acts they are. Indeed, when any kind of negative spotlight is thrown on this industry, there are some trainers who take the opportunity to weigh in on the controversy, often garnering publicity for themselves and their companies in the process. Yet, even as they may try to distance themselves from the most obviously egregious examples of violence and exploitation that take place under the rubric of seduction, the industry as a whole remains complicit. Knowledge-practices elaborated within this sphere teach men to regard women not as subjects to commune with but as obstacles to overcome. As such, it becomes permissible – necessary even – to press that bit harder, push that bit further, take that much more. Nothing I saw in the course of my research suggested a serious appreciation of what consent is or how it can be meaningfully practised. Insofar as consent was considered at all, it was as something that can be obtained obliquely or assured after the fact, assumed to be a once-off process rather than a pattern of relating. Nowhere were dynamics of sexual violence discussed or the seriousness of rape deliberated upon, other than in terms of the harm done to men by false accusations. Ethical considerations – beyond the throwaway dictum of 'leave her better than you found her' – simply were not on the table. That this absence of discussion is set within an overall context where men are encouraged to view women in oppositional terms, and to harden themselves against women's feelings, is especially worrying. For some of those who buy into seduction, any and all action can be justified as a matter of self-interest, as their sense of sexual entitlement is bolstered by the belief that men's need for sex is evolutionarily ordained and socially imperative.

The callous disregard so often exhibited by the seduction industry towards women is caught up with its ready exploitation of men. For many if not most men the promise of control the industry proffers will forever remain elusive, no matter how seriously they apply themselves to the hard graft – and expense – of cultivating the prescribed skills and dispositions. The sense of having been deceived – tricked into paying for expensive but ineffectual products and programmes – can give rise to feelings of anger and despair, each of which are found in abundance on forums devoted to discussing the failings of the industry, and which have been linked to devastating acts of violence elsewhere. The perpetrator of the 2014 Isla Vista killings in California, Elliot Rodger – who murdered six people and wounded fourteen others – subscribed to several seduction channels on *YouTube* and frequented forums such as *PUAHate*. In the manifesto he left behind, Rodger blamed women for 'starving' him of sex and outlined plans to get revenge by killing the 'hottest' women.[4]

The seduction industry readily exploits classed and racialised hierarchies among men, with many becoming involved in this sphere out of a desire to be accepted and included in a predominantly white society or to realise, even by proxy, otherwise thwarted aspirations of social mobility. While public displays of prejudice were at one time uncommon among those with a commercial stake in the industry, this is no longer the case. In the past few years, amid a rising tide of racism and xenophobia across Europe and elsewhere, there has been an eruption of racist sentiment within the seduction industry. Attitudes that had heretofore been tempered by business ambition – 'sacrificed in capital's interests' (Gilroy 2013: 35) – have been unleashed. Prominent industry figures now regularly launch invective and violent tirades, particularly against Muslims, on social media. Those with more moderate views – perhaps espousing the kind of cosmopolitan outlook on which many Londoners, correctly or not, pride themselves – look on and say nothing.

Some men who become involved in the seduction industry – the exact proportion is unclear – do so because they are experiencing acute psychological distress. For these men, attending a seduction course may be less intimidating or simply more accessible than seeking professional help from a counsellor or psychologist. A number of trainers I spoke to confirmed this to be the case, with one relating: 'A lot of the people who come on a bootcamp, for them it's almost like a last resort.' While some trainers express concern for the welfare of such men and try to help where they can – often going well beyond their occupational remit, for example, by instructing students to reduce their use of antidepressants – others were only too ready to take advantage of their distress. Though I saw numerous indications of this during my research, the callous disregard with which some men who come to the seduction industry in evident desperation was most forcefully demonstrated by a trainer who laughingly recalled the story of their 'worst student ever'. The trainer described how difficult it had been to work with this young man, whose pronounced anxiety made all the usual training exercises impossible. When pressed about the roots of his shyness, the student intimated that he had been sexually abused as a child by his father. Some time after the course, having initially maintained contact with trainers via *Facebook*, he disappeared from social media. Musing on this, the trainer noted: 'It's the sort of guy who you imagine probably did, might have killed himself. But we don't know; we have no idea what happened with him. And we still laugh and say he was the worst student ever, but God knows what that guy went through.' The cynicism of this statement is difficult to countenance, as is the offhand manner in which the story was recounted. It suggests not so much indifference as an *inability* to deal with the serious emotional and psychological problems that at least some of those who turn to the seduction industry present with. And no wonder. After all, in their legal disclaimers these companies claim to offer not instruction or advice but 'entertainment'. Whatever its pretensions to community, whatever promises of friendship and support are made, this is ultimately a profit-driven industry and a frequently brutal one at that.

Given the enormous problems surrounding mental health – the bleak testament of which can be seen in the alarming rate at which men in the UK and many other societies are killing themselves – it is extremely disconcerting to know that some of those seeking help may find themselves in the clutches of an industry totally unprepared to deal with the issues they face, where those invested with authority and expertise are often more interested in furthering their own bottom line than in helping men in distress. I saw this at first hand during my research. At one bootcamp course, a student – who to my mind should not have been there at all, so evident was his instability – became increasingly agitated during the course of the day. Eventually, standing outside a nightclub while other students inside were being put through their paces, he declared he was quitting the programme and demanded his money back. The trainer in charge of the night-game session spent twenty minutes trying to placate him, but the student was resolute. Finally exasperated, the trainer went to ask the manager if a refund could be arranged. I was then left alone with the student, who grew more and more agitated with each passing moment. He launched into a diatribe about being ignored and mistreated by women, talking loudly and drawing the attention of passers-by. His face became increasingly contorted as his voice became louder and louder. Looking directly at me, while appearing to see past me, he screamed: 'I am so angry. I just want to say, *fuck you, bitch!*' That men experiencing such acute distress – this student's disquietude had been obvious to me from the moment he introduced himself to the group that morning – is a sobering indictment of the extent to which we as a society are failing to deal with mental health problems and their social antecedents. That this failing is being capitalised upon by an entirely unaccredited and unregulated industry – with unknown ends for those whose misery leads them here – is regrettable in the extreme.

Going forward

Where, then, do we go from here? What, if anything, is to be done? I have already expressed uncertainty about the usefulness of mobilising against specific individuals associated with the seduction industry. In the case of transnational campaigns waged against Julien Blanc – which saw the American-based seduction trainer swiftly ejected from Australia and subsequently denied entry to countries including Brazil, Canada, Germany, Japan and Singapore – politicians of all persuasions were quick to line up to support calls for a ban. In the UK, this was frequently articulated in terms of a defence of 'British values', as though the seduction industry did not already exist here. While the fact that Blanc was ultimately denied a visa – a decision taken by the then home secretary, Theresa May – was hailed as a kind of feminist victory, it effectively foreclosed a consideration of the broader issues at stake regarding sexual harassment and violence against women. Denying a visa to Blanc was, in the end, a decidedly simple yet effective measure through which the continued disarticulation of feminism could be assured; postfeminism, after all, operates through a double movement by which feminism is 'undone' by being 'taken into account' (McRobbie 2009). At the same time, the campaign to ban Blanc also played into the hands of flourishing right-wing sentiment in Britain, as some feminists yet again colluded with the operations of the securitised nation-state by invoking border controls as a legitimate mechanism to secure women's rights and freedoms.

Of course, it may be argued that there is a certain symbolic victory to be derived from the success of these campaigns, which ensured Blanc was unable to travel to these countries to teach – at least, for a time. For, while the media had by then long since lost interest, a year later Blanc was once again teaching seminars in many of the same countries that had moved to block his business activities just months before. Not only this, but he was now touring under the honorific of 'World's Most Hated Man', proudly dispensing with the question mark *Time* magazine had included in their original formulation (Gibson 2014). That Blanc could so readily integrate the controversy into his brand identity, and indeed appears to have benefited from this commercially, should provide an important lesson for feminist activists, not least as we seek to negotiate a political climate characterised by newly emboldened and unrepentant misogyny. This is clearly a difficult balance, as on the one hand such sentiments should not be in any way normalized or condoned, yet on the other constantly reacting to every infraction only serves to feed the attention economy of the contemporary mediascape, where outrage of all kinds is cynically channelled in capital's interests.

While the campaigns against Blanc were more or less spontaneous, a more coordinated approach that took the industry's core practices rather than a specific individual as its focus could provide a stronger starting point from which to challenge the workings of this community-industry. To my mind, in-field videos represent the most pertinent target. At an ethical level, the recording and distribution of covertly filmed footage, whether shared freely online or made available to buy, is a gross invasion of women's privacy. Yet under current British law the legality of such practices is unclear. While filming people in public spaces is permissible, filming people in public who have a 'reasonable expectation' of privacy is not (Macpherson 2009). Where established or aspiring pickup artists film sexual encounters with women who are unaware they are being recorded in private settings, or who record such encounters with women's knowledge but later use the materials for purposes of which they are unaware, this is most certainly an infringement. Yet videos filmed in public spaces, such as on the street or in cafés and restaurants, may still constitute a breach. For many trainers, in-field videos are a central part of their branding and business apparatus – and therefore a key revenue stream – with more and more of this content going behind paywalls. A campaign against their production and distribution could look to inroads being made to counteract digitally mediated sexual abuse, including but not limited to 'revenge porn' (Hall and Hearn 2017; Powell and Henry 2017; Salter and Crofts 2015). Activism on this issue could further highlight how the non-consensual production and/or dissemination of in-field videos lays the groundwork for further violations, not least as these media encourage men to view the deception of women as necessary to their own learning and to take pleasure in women's ignorance as part of the rituals of male bonding.

Those with an investment in the seduction industry may feel that, if one of the main problems with this system of expertise is the lack of consideration it gives to consent, then surely the solution is to find ways to integrate this into seduction teachings. This, in my view, is to ignore more systemic issues. It is not simply that seduction trainers neglect to discuss consent, but that the construction of heterosexuality they subscribe to and propagate renders consent virtually meaningless, as women are positioned as unable to act on their sexual desires wherever they refuse sex but as necessarily acting in accordance with their own wishes when they consent to sex. For companies or trainers intent on warding off scrutiny, it is only too easy to tack empty disclaimers about consent onto their products and services, as Real Social Dynamics briefly did in the wake of the Blanc scandal. Meanwhile, the majority of their content and the belief system that underpins it remain fundamentally unchanged. This raises the question of whether or not the seduction industry could be reformed so as to promote more ethical, even feminist, forms of relating, as some have proposed (O'Malley 2014). I would maintain that the answer to this question has to be 'no'. The seduction industry is so utterly steeped in sexism, so thoroughly committed to a programmatic view of sex, that it is difficult to see how it could be meaningfully reformed. Those who want to help heterosexual men cultivate more ethical forms of relationality will, I think, have to find other starting points for these efforts.

It is crucial that any attempt to challenge seduction does not fall into the trap of placing responsibility on women to guard against this, framing seduction as yet another threat to be anticipated and avoided.

Providing advice to women about how to evade or deflect seduction attempts – however well intentioned the occasional features on this in women's magazines may be – is ultimately self-defeating. Not only does this approach collude in the patriarchal dispensation towards ensuring women's safety rather than enabling women's right to take risks (Phadke et al. 2011), but, given the sophistication with which the most practised seducers operate – constantly innovating upon existing techniques – such advice is unlikely to be of much use. Our focus must thus be on men, those already swayed by the promises of control the seduction industry offers up, as well as those who are liable to become so.

At the same time, we must seek to cultivate alternative modes of being and relating. In the UK, there is a desperate need for better sex and relationship education in schools. But our efforts also need to go much wider than this. Such work has been admirably taken up by Meg-John Barker in *Rewriting the Rules* (2013b) and further explored alongside Justin Hancock in *Enjoy Sex (How, When and if You Want to)* (Barker and Hancock 2017a), as well as the range of digital resources they have produced collaboratively (Barker and Hancock 2017b). Further inspiration can be found in the countervailing impulses of queer and anarchist re-envisionings of sex and relationships (Heckert and Cleminson 2011), which seek to promote more ethical modes of intimate engagement through a radical commitment to equality and relational conception of freedom. Art, literature, poetry – and even feminist theory – may provide other starting points. What seems crucial is that the resources we bring together help us appreciate that there is both much more and much less to sex than we are commonly led to believe. There is more to sex because so much of what we currently understand as sex is really sexual simulacra, endless copies of copies of copies of scripts we take no hand in writing. When we follow these scripts, as most of us do most of the time, we deny ourselves the possibility of authoring our own. There is, at the same time, a great deal less to sex than is commonly envisioned, as sexual desirability and performance is so often taken as the singular measure of our individual worth and the key indicator for assessing the health and happiness of our relationships. In distancing ourselves from these kinds of supplied knowledges, we might afford ourselves the space necessary to become alive to other modes of relationality. Though adult heterosexual men may prove the most difficult group of all to reach in this endeavour – relinquishing control or the pursuit thereof so often seen as anathema to masculinity – we must persist in these efforts through our schools and communities, friends and families.

It is also important that, in our efforts to promote change, we do not allow ourselves to become transfixed by this industry, focusing so concertedly on its machinations that we cannot see the wider social, economic and political arrangements that enable and sustain it. The need to reinvent our sexual culture goes far beyond reinventing ourselves and our relationships – though for many of us these will be our starting points and the touchstones to which we continually return. It is also necessary to challenge the larger structures of power through which our everyday practices are shaped. The fate of our private and public institutions are absolutely intertwined. What goes on 'out there' shapes what happens 'in here' – not straightforwardly, but nevertheless indelibly. If we fail to confront the ravages of neoliberalism as an economic and political order that naturalises inequality through its unceasing promotion of competitive individualism in a multitude of contexts – employment, housing, health-care, the environment – then we are effectively paving the way for this ethos to enter ever more deeply into our intimate lives.[5] Likewise, if we do not continually challenge the emptying out of feminism of all political meaning – the rhetoric of empowerment pressed into service to concen-trate power and wealth in the hands of a small number of women whose campaigns for 'equality' depend upon their ready exploitation of other women – then we accede to the prevailing postfeminist consensus that feminism is a spent force. Though the seduction industry represents an especially bald provocation to feminists, it is ultimately the twin rationali-ties of neoliberalism and postfeminism that demand our most trenchant critique and continued attempts at intervention.

I am aware, in writing this, that for many of those invested in seduction – emotionally, socially, financially – my arguments are liable to be read as so much feminist pedantry or liberal sentimentality. But in staking out this position I am ultimately arguing that we *all* demand more from our intimate lives, not as a space of attainment or achievement but one in which we might find the connection with others we are looking for and allow ourselves to be transformed in the process. Knowing these words are liable to be taken in bad faith by some, despite the sincerity with which they are intended, I take heart in the recognition that sometimes it is necessary to strike at existing attachments in order to 'make room for life, to make room for possibility, for chance' (Ahmed 2010b: 20). To be against seduction is not to set ourselves irreconcilably against those who, for whatever reason, become involved in this community-industry. To be against seduction is instead to be against the overwhelming mediation of sex and intimacy that cuts us off from one another and ourselves. It means appreciating that, when our notions of self-worth are too closely tied to sexual performance, there is a limit to the value that we can find here. It means recognising that too much of what passes as 'just sex' is coercive and violent, this 'just' providing cover for all manner of mistreatment. It means refuting a corrosive entrepreneurial logic that diminishes our ability to relate to one another as whole persons. It means refusing to cede any further ground to the dictates of cultural rationalities that dramatically undercut our capacity for empathy and vulnerability. It means challenging, as early and as often as possible, the emptying out of intersubjectivity in relationships of all forms. It means setting ourselves – bodies, hearts and minds – against the kind of instrumentalism that begets indifference to the pain and suffering of others. It means railing against an economic and political system that naturalises the most prosaic forms of indignity through to the most brutal manifestations of injustice. It means finding ways to cultivate space for mutuality and reciprocity while rejecting that which deadens wonder, bypasses joy, forecloses laughter. It means permitting ourselves to enter into feeling with one another, knowing that this necessarily entails opening ourselves out to each other. To be against seduction is ultimately to be *for* more enriching and sustainable ways of relating, in whatever form this may take for us as individuals at different times in our lives. It is to attempt – however imperfectly – to live 'from within outward' (Lorde 1984: 58).

Postscript: Power and Politics in Feminist Fieldwork

When presenting this research at seminars and conferences I am almost invariably asked two questions. The first is usually along the lines of 'What was it like to do this research as a woman?' This is not an easy question to answer. Encompassing more than a year's fieldwork, the project comprised a complex array of relationships and a contradictory mix of emotions, all of which are related to but not determined solely by my gender. I thus find it hard to summarise my experiences succinctly or to pick out specific moments that can stand in for more general patterns. Furthermore, I have nothing to compare it with and cannot presume any other woman would have had the same experiences I did. The second question I am most often asked is whether or not I myself ever faced seduction attempts in the course of undertaking the research. I can admit a certain frustration in repeatedly being confronted with this latter question, tending as it does towards the voyeuristic and displacing attention from the substance of the arguments I am making. When posed as an auxiliary to the first, it asks me to reveal something more than I have already told. At the same time, because it is usually asked with an air of incredulity – the prospect that I may indeed have been met with such overtures appearing genuinely risible to some – it forecloses the possibility of discussing some of the more uncomfortable dynamics this project has involved.

In this postscript I discuss my experiences undertaking the research and navigating a community-industry which promises heterosexual men 'mastery' with women. Without attempting to respond directly to or answer definitely the above questions, I reflect on some of the ambiguities and ambivalences the project has generated. Informing my discussion throughout is the crucial insight that the 'experiences of the theorist are the means by which the theorist becomes a knowing subject' (Skeggs 1997: 167). I consider how my positioning as a young, white and middle-class woman has shaped the research and informed the analytic insights I have gone on to develop. I make connections to wider methodological debates, demonstrating that, although some of the issues I faced were related to

167

particularities of the research setting, they were by no means unique to this sphere. Thinking about power and politics in feminist fieldwork more broadly, I detail some of the difficulties and discomforts that have accompanied the project and ask what a commitment to feminist research in principle really commits us to in practice.

Negotiating femininity

Conducting research as a woman with and among men almost inevitably throws up the question of how to present oneself in gendered terms. Faced with this conundrum, many women researchers attempt to downplay their difference vis-à-vis their research participants, adopting masculine codes and conventions in an effort to emulate those they are investigating. In her exemplary study of masculinity and sexuality in an American high school, C. J. Pascoe (2007) describes cultivating a 'least gendered identity', distancing herself from local norms of femininity while mimicking the appearance, comportment and interactional style of the young men she was researching. Discussing this strategy, she explains: 'This appearance muted my difference and helped me to gain access to boys' worlds and conversations – if not as an honorary guy, at least as some sort of neutered observer who wouldn't be offended' (Pascoe 2007: 181).

While my research also necessitated that I position myself as someone who would not be offended, I could not do so in gender-neutral terms. Given the investment many of those who participate in this industry have in maintaining strictly delineated gender roles, I was aware that any attempt to 'de-gender' my appearance would be unlikely to garner favour. Women who work in the seduction industry are generally of a highly feminine and conventionally attractive appearance, many also working or having formerly worked as models or actresses. One of those I spoke to described this as an essential requirement of her job, noting that it applied only to women and not to men: 'As a female pickup coach I have to look attractive. It doesn't matter what the trainers – if the male trainers are not good-looking that works in their favour, like "I'm not good-looking, but look what I can get", you know, that's great. But a female coach has got to look desirable.' Explaining what this meant for her personally, she went on to say: 'I have to dress really well. Not sexy, but at least in a desirable way. It's a massive pressure, that side of it. And if you're meeting other pickup artists as well . . . you know, they're judging you. You're there basically on how good-looking you are, really.'

Though my day-to-day appearance is normatively feminine, I lack the kind of accentuated femininity women who work in the industry typically embody. While I could have adopted a more stylised aesthetic, which might have enabled me to more readily access and move around within the seduction industry, I was concerned that doing so could lead to confusion over my role as a researcher. I thus decided to dress neither 'down' nor 'up' but, instead, to undertake research appearing much the same as I would on any other day. Yet during my fieldwork I could not help but become self-conscious about my appearance. This heightened self-awareness was precipitated, in large part, by the constant scrutiny of women's bodies that took place around me. During in-field sessions, trainers and students alike openly assessed women passing in the street or sitting in cafés, offering surprisingly detailed commentary on their clothing, make-up, hair styles, and so on. I had not anticipated men being quite so thorough in their surveillance of women or so damning in their appraisals.

In our interview, one trainer outlined the numerical ranking system used by many of those who participate in the seduction industry when discussing women's appearance. Though I was aware of the existence of this system, having heard men refer to women as 'sixes' and 'sevens' in the course of other observations, I was nevertheless chilled by the casual cruelty his description contained:

> This is strictly the physical scale – we're not actually factoring in the woman's personality – this is just strictly on how the woman looks. So a one would be a very disfigured person, you know, some genetic condition or a burns victim or something. That's a one. A two is very unattractive, where you would have three or four, like, exaggerated features, like a massive nose with a big chin and big ears, to the point where some people might find it laughably unattractive. A three would be again very unattractive – they'll be seen as unattractive by pretty much everyone. Very obese women would fall into that category, even if they have a normal face. A four, again, unattractive with maybe two exaggerated features, like a pretty big nose with, like, I don't know, hairy arms or something. Then a five is neutral, you'd have a couple of unattractive features. A six is kinda cute, kinda cute. She might be like a cute Italian girl, she's pretty but has a big nose, for example. A seven, again, slight imperfections. An eight is attractive. Everyone would say she's attractive, very few imperfections. A nine is someone who would be deemed very attractive by everyone and has no visible facial imperfections. So, she'd only have details that would give her an individual look or character, but basically no major imperfections. So like the model types I guess, model types. Especially lingerie models, that would be like a nine. And then a ten doesn't exist because it assumes perfection.

It would be hard to find a more explicit example of the sexist objectification of women's bodies that has become culturally commonplace and is further codified within the seduction community. Though the trainer states that perfection is impossible, the precision with which he itemises the various ways in which women's bodies can be deemed deficient suggests that an ideal of absolute perfection nevertheless persists. Even those who endure debilitating medical conditions and have suffered devastating injuries are still available to be held up for sexual scrutiny, their personal tragedies ensuring they are relegated to the very bottom of the scale.

During fieldwork, the supposed shortcomings of my own appearance – in particular, my lack of feminine stylisation – were repeatedly brought to my attention by participants. One trainer, on granting me permission to attend an event he was hosting in a few weeks' time, added the proviso: 'You'll have to wear nicer shoes.' Glancing towards my feet and the loafers I was wearing at the time, I asked what he meant. Throwing his eyes upward and sighing incredulously, he clarified: 'You'll need to wear high heels.' Another trainer chastised me when I showed up one evening to a seminar he was running, saying: 'I didn't know it was you at first, you look totally different. Your hair, it's totally different. You've really let yourself go.' Having been invited to attend this event at the last minute, I only had time to pull on my jacket before walking out the door. Apparently, it showed, and, more importantly, I was to be made aware that it showed.[1]

As those versed in seduction theory will be quick to point out, it is true that these kinds of comments may represent attempts at 'negging', a technique which involves making ambiguous statements with negative elements, the objective being to undermine a woman's confidence. It is also true that they may have been deployed strategically by participants seeking to level perceived power imbalances, subverting any authority I might have as a researcher by calling into question my desirability as a woman. Yet as the research progressed I came to see that such comments were very often laced with resentment. After all, men who participate in this sphere go to great lengths to try to embody normative ideals of masculinity. For some, the apparent lack of effort I was making to embody corresponding feminine ideals was an affront to their efforts. Those who took to criticising my appearance, cajoling me to adopt a more stylised aesthetic, were attempting to discipline my femininity. They correctly read my lack of stylisation not as failure but as *recalcitrance*, not as an inability but as a *refusal* to embody the kind of accentuated femininity that carries value in this setting and in society more broadly. Such comments further attuned me to the investment many of these men have not in beauty per se, as a characteristic that manifests in the idiosyncrasies of a particular combination of features, but in femininity as a more concerted form of stylisation that instantiates sexual difference.

While for some trainers my appearance left much to be desired, I could still be of use to them. For one thing, having a woman at seduction training events has a kind of sanitising effect, reassuring attendees that there is nothing wrong with what they are learning – as though femaleness were somehow inimical to sexism and misogyny. To this end, some trainers invite women friends and girlfriends along to their events, and so having me along was not entirely out of the ordinary. At a number of events I attended, I became aware of students glancing in my direction, as though looking for any trace of disagreement or discomfort. Trainers themselves would occasionally call on me to corroborate their teachings, to endorse this or that statement about how women think or feel. On more than one occasion, I was asked to appear in promotional materials. One trainer with whom I had arranged an interview emailed me a few days before our meeting, telling me he was going to bring along a camera so we could film a short video together afterwards. When I replied saying this might not be appropriate – citing concerns about anonymity and partiality – he cancelled the interview. At another event, a trainer filming student testimonials suddenly swung the camera in my direction, asking what I thought of the programme. Not wanting to be seen to endorse the company, I offered an essentially descriptive commentary I hoped would be too bland to make the final cut. On yet another occasion, I found myself introduced not as a researcher but as the trainer's 'assistant', and I was later called upon to join him on stage for a 'live demonstration'.

Attempts by women researchers to distance themselves from conventional modes of femininity while undertaking fieldwork with and among men are very often caught up with a desire to avoid being sexualised by their research participants. Indeed, Pascoe's discussion of her attempts to cultivate a 'least gendered identity' features as part of an extended appendix entitled 'What if a guy hits on you?' (2007: 175–93). Despite adopting a more masculine appearance while on research, Pascoe nevertheless found herself being drawn into the sexuality of the young men she was researching, who attempted to mobilise her as a masculinising resource in much the same way they did girls of their own age. Pascoe's experience is by no means unique but, instead, illustrates a wider trend, as evidenced by the depressingly large body of literature that has accrued detailing women's experiences of sexual harassment while conducting research with and among men (Arendell 1997; Gailey and Prohaska 2011; Grenz 2005;

Lee 1997; Pascoe 2007; Presser 2005; Sharp and Kremer 2006; Stanley and Wise 1979; Willott 1998; Zurbriggen 2002).[2] Discussing this issue, Beverley Skeggs wryly observes: 'I am sure this rarely happens to male researchers' (1994: 82).

Injurious intimacies

During the period I was undertaking fieldwork, sexual overtures and harassment became a workplace hazard. Some participants attempted to sexualise our interactions by flirting obliquely. When I asked one man in our interview what kinds of women he approaches, he looked out the window of the café in which we were sitting and pointed: 'I would approach a girl like her. Sun kissed, tanned skin, brunette.' Pausing, he then looked back to me and said: 'I approach redheads as well.' With this statement, he introduced the possibility of our relationship extending beyond the research encounter, suggesting that I myself am the kind of woman he would approach on the street. Another participant described being attracted to women with foreign accents, adding: 'I would definitely say Irish accents are a big plus.' In such instances, participants implied that, while in the context of the interview our roles were more or less clearly defined, these might later be displaced or discarded in favour of a sexual relationship. In doing so they were able to signal their sexual interest in me discretely and in a manner which could be plausibly denied if I were to question this. While I did not welcome these kinds of comments, neither did they unduly concern me, because I was able to brush them aside and refocus attention on the interview with relative ease.

For other participants, the research experience was awash with sexual intrigue, furnishing an opportunity to talk to a young woman who would listen attentively and at length. One especially forthcoming participant spent a considerable time during our first meeting detailing his use of pornography and masturbation habits. I had not asked about these details of his intimate life and initially thought this volubility may have been occasioned by a sense of being on display to me as a researcher and uncertainty as to what it was I wanted to know. What was clear was that he believed that I had little understanding of what he was describing, as he tried to convey the visual frenzy of pornography by saying: 'To a man, that is . . . that is incredible visual stimulation, it's like very arousing, it's like . . . I don't know how to explain it to a girl, it's like . . . putting a huge chocolate cake in front of you.' Yet, as the interview went on, I had the sense that the confessional he had embarked upon unbidden was more for his own benefit than for mine. This was later confirmed when, at the end of the follow-up interview he requested, the participant told me: 'This interviewing by you, it's a very therapeutic process. It's almost like this process, it carries a lot more weight in terms of my overall improvement then sarging, like, ten women right now. So I'm really glad to have done this.' For this particular man, participating in the research served as a proxy for or supplement to seduction training, and an apparently effective one at that. Despite the fact that he was contributing to my project, and that I would ultimately have control over the materials these meetings produced, I was nevertheless left feeling somehow taken advantage of.

A small number of participants were more persistent in their attempts to sexualise our interactions. One man I interviewed repeatedly questioned my motivations for researching the seduction community, finding it hard to believe that I would undertake such a project for purely academic reasons and more or less asserting that I must have sexual motivations. Taken aback by his forwardness, I asked how he had come to that conclusion. Laughing at my obvious consternation, he replied: 'I mean, I don't believe that you don't want it [sex]. This is what it is, you know. This is what I believe. I just know because of the way you are. Because I've met many women like that, the way you dress and everything.' When I asked what he meant by this latter comment, he responded by saying: 'One woman, she's like in a short skirt or whatever, she's obviously dressed like – yeah, she's sucking dick. But the one over there, with the nice jumper and jeans and glasses – she's sucking it twice as much.' This latter description itemised my own attire, implicitly suggesting that I am the one 'sucking it twice as much'. He then went on to contend that, if I didn't allow myself to be seduced in the course of the research, I would be relying on what he termed 'indirect experience'. Following this, he openly propositioned me for sex, saying: 'If you want to spread your legs, that's your choice. I can tell you, you know what, I would love to have you the whole weekend.' Apparently unperturbed by my now open disdain, he invited me to go home with him then and there, saying he had deliberately arranged our meeting at a coffee shop near his apartment with the intention of taking me there afterwards. Finally unable to put up with this any longer, I ended the interview and left. This was an acutely humiliating encounter. Listening to the interview recording, my irritation is barely disguised: my tone is curt, my manner guarded, my rebukes sharp. Transcribing the interview was a frustrating and degrading experience, as I questioned my abilities as a researcher and chastised myself for failing to exercise greater control over the interaction. It vexed me to have to transcribe the tape at all, lending his words additional weight by fixing them to the page, and now reproducing them here. Yet what was perhaps most concerning about the interaction was that this man appeared to be either unaware of or indifferent to the discomfort he was causing me.

While I was able to avoid further face-to-face encounters with this participant – though he continued to contact me by email for many months after this episode – in other cases the realities of my fieldwork were such that it was difficult to avoid participants who were similarly persistent in their attempts to sexualise our relationship. To this end, the most troubling relationship of my fieldwork involved a trainer I met early on in the project at an event hosted by one of the few companies that had been responsive to my initial requests for access. The trainer made his sexual interest in me clear from the outset by continually commenting on my appearance and touching me in an excessively familiar way. While in group settings I could usually find ways to avert his overtures – by deflecting his attention back onto students or otherwise drawing others into our interactions – when we met for a one-to-one interview this was much more difficult.

To begin with, he insisted on choosing the venue, then showed up late and pretended not to see me when he did arrive. When we sat down and I took out my recorder, he told me he wanted to have a coffee before beginning, after which he wanted to go to a nearby sushi bar for something to eat. By the time we actually started the interview, we had been together for over an hour. During the interview itself, he insisted on taking multiple breaks and changing locations several times, such that our meeting was actually conducted across a number of locations in and around London's Southbank Centre. With these and other manoeuvres, the trainer was attempting what is known in seduction parlance as 'frame control', as he tried to redefine the terms of our interaction by displacing the framework I imposed as a researcher with one of his own choosing: that of a seduction script.

During the interview, I asked this participant if he had a specialism as a trainer – a question I asked all those who work in the industry, and which typically elicited detailed technical responses. Leaning in, he told me that he was an expert in methods of 'physical escalation' – using touch to progress an interaction towards sex – and instructed me to hold out my hand. I did so reluctantly, recoiling inwardly as he began to massage the flesh of my palm. Perhaps sensing my discomfort – I was straining away from him – he said: 'Just hold it. Relax. It feels nice, doesn't it?' Trying to appear nonchalant, I asked about the theory behind the technique, hoping that as he began talking again he would relinquish my hand. Instead, he leaned closer, saying: 'This is something that you'd start doing once you've extracted a girl to a situation when you could potentially have sex with her. And, from here, you could escalate to massaging here …' With this latter comment, he began moving his hand further up the inside of my arm. By now decidedly uncomfortable, I nodded quickly to indicate I understood what he meant before pulling my arm free of his grasp and abruptly changing the subject. Apparently unfazed, he settled back in his chair and the interview continued.

Later, when we had finished, the trainer insisted we go for a drink, saying I owed him that much at least. Knowing I was reliant on his good will for continued research access, I agreed, telling myself I would stay only a short while. Not long after we sat down, he told me he was taking massage classes and wanted to demonstrate what he had learned. Ignoring my protests, he got up from the table and came to stand behind me. Already tense, I stiffened further under his unwelcome touch. Again, I tried to diffuse the situation by asking questions. He was not going to be so easily put off this time and straightened my shoulders flush against the back of the chair when I tried to turn around to face him. Gripping my neck more firmly now, his fingers filling the space over my collarbones, he held my gaze in the mirror that hung on the wall in front of us. Not wanting him to see how deeply unnerving this was for me, I composed my face into what I hoped was a neutral expression, panic rising inwardly as I tried to think of a way out of this. After another few moments, I disingenuously thanked him for the massage, which was the only way I could think to end the encounter without causing offence. Shortly afterwards, I made my excuses and left, managing to get out of the pub and around the corner before the anxiety this encounter provoked bubbled over and I burst into tears.

While I was constrained in this instance by a need to maintain research access – this trainer not only worked for a company where I was already undertaking research but was well connected in the London seduction scene more generally – the seeming impossibility of expressly asking or, indeed, telling him to stop touching me was a stark reminder of how gendered social conventions limit and constrain women's agency. It forced me to confront anew how deeply ingrained women's acquiescence to and accommodation of men is to the social ontology of gender. To this end, I began to wonder how I would have handled the same situation had it occurred in another context – say, at a friend's dinner party or with a work colleague. For, while I generally think of myself as someone who is able to assert their boundaries, I had to ask myself: was my apparent inability – and it certainly felt like an *inability* rather than an *unwillingness* – to voice my objection explicitly conditioned solely by my need for research access?

Would I be able to object more forcefully to a man touching me in this manner in another kind of social situation? Or would the gendered power dynamics inherent in such interactions prevent me from doing so? These questions remain unanswered, but asking them has been important in directing my attention to the ways in which gendered power dynamics are written through the body and mind. For while this form of subjugation was disconcerting for me as a researcher – I was, after all, trying to cultivate some kind of professional identity for myself – it was not unfamiliar to me as a woman.

Already struggling to ensure sufficient research access, and knowing how crucial this would be to develop an understanding of the industry's inner workings, I could not afford to give up the relationship I had with the company this trainer worked for, and as such further meetings were largely unavoidable. During the next few months we saw each other again many times, throughout which he continued to try to sexualise our interactions, confecting reasons for us to be alone together, boasting to me about his sexual prowess, and implying to others that we were intimately involved. Fearing this trainer had the capacity to jeopardize the project as a whole if I were to challenge any of this – worried that he would tell his contacts in the industry not to grant me research access – I was forced to go along with this much of the time. Having given him my phone number when arranging the interview, he took to texting me periodically with updates about his students and business ventures. Soon after this, he began calling me, promising to facilitate meetings with other trainers but insisting that we would need to meet privately first to discuss the details. By this point, it was abundantly clear that he was using my need for research access as leverage for sex, and I stopped answering when he called. Nevertheless, the texts continued, now dispensing with any pretence of professional interest through open declarations of sexual intent. Though infrequent, these messages were unwelcome incursions into my personal life.

Being the target of such relentless sexual pursuit was an immensely draining experience and one that negatively impacted my wellbeing. I became increasingly uneasy as the fieldwork period wore on, wary not only of running into this man unexpectedly – which did happen on a number of occasions – but also of his finding some way to compromise the project so severely that it would collapse around me. Yet, when I related these experiences to friends and colleagues, I was regularly met with statements such as: 'What did you expect?' After all, I was conducting research in a setting that promises heterosexual men 'mastery' with women, and thus I should have anticipated that some would regard me as a legitimate target of their seduction attempts. In this way, my experiences of being harassed were attributed to the field in which I was conducting research rather than to the individual men who occupy this field, thereby reproducing a more general construction of sexual harassment as something that *happens* to women rather than something men *do* to women.

On being complicit

While recruiting participants and undertaking research I did not announce my feminism. In part, this reluctance to name myself as a feminist was born of an awareness of the negative associations that so often attach to this term, such that to do so would mean having to constantly negotiate all the assumptions that come with this territory, not least persistent caricatures of feminists as 'anti-male' and 'man-hating' (Calder-Dawe and Gavey 2016; Edley and Wetherell 2001). I was also conscious of the much publicised hostilities between feminists and pickup artists and did not want prospective participants to assume my analyses and arguments had been determined in advance, when in actuality this was far from being the case. I thus resigned myself to the idea that 'in certain circumstances the best that can be expected is work that is *covertly* feminist' (Acker 1994: 55). Interestingly, however, the same stereotypes that kept me from declaring my feminism led some participants to assume that I could not possibly be a feminist. Thus one trainer concluded his assessment of the deleterious effects feminism has had on society by pronouncing that the balance is now being restored by 'lovely feminine girls like you, Rachel'.

Though I was never actually asked about my political beliefs, participants continually sought out my opinions on the industry in general as well as on specific knowledge-practices. Some positioned me as a kind of moral arbiter, as when one participant asked:

> Morally, what's your view on the seduction community? I know you don't want to sort of write the conclusion before you've done it, but just as an initial . . . you know, do you see it as a bunch of guys who are on the prowl and taking advantage of women, or do you think it's a good thing and women are enjoying it just as much as the men?

This line of questioning demonstrates an awareness of the ethical ambiguities of seduction alongside a presumption that, as a woman, I would immediately recognise and could not possibly endorse sexism or misogyny. Others asked these same kinds of questions in a way that presupposed a particular answer, as when another participant asked what I thought of men using these techniques, only to answer his own question by reiterating the oft-cited claim that, ultimately, seduction is of benefit to women: 'If there are more guys doing it, do you think that'd be good or something bad? You're in the situation where more guys are approaching, so you're in the situation of getting approached more. Do you think that's good for girls? Because as a girl you have also more choice.'

Some of the trainers I interviewed seemed taken back by the lack of opprobrium in our meetings, evidently having suspected I would be more critical of the industry. Midway through our interview, one trainer praised my interview method: 'You're a very good interviewer. You've kept it very neutral. That's good.' Later, when we were wrapping up, he asked: 'So now that it's over, I actually wanted to ask you your kind of stance on it, if you have one. How do you feel about it? Because I see you're trying to keep it completely neutral.' When I asked what he had expected, he explained: 'Most people are always like . . . I say something and then they're like, "Ah, but ..." They'll try to contradict me. Do you know what I mean? They'll raise an argument, where maybe what I'm saying falls down on a logical level, or on an emotional level.' We discussed negative perceptions of the seduction community a little while longer before he returned to the issue once again: 'I mean, you haven't really answered the question. So what do you personally think of . . . or maybe you've been influenced so much by the research you're doing that you've become even more neutral in your kind of personal thinking about it?' Relieved that he had provided me with a way out of giving a more definitive answer, I agreed that this might be the case, and the conversation moved on.

Where participants themselves voiced concerns about or criticisms of the seduction community, I tried to create space for such discussions. Yet, when I invited participants to elaborate on these kinds of comments, my questions were often met with resistance. Describing the decision-making processes involved in pairing trainers with students for one-to-one coaching, one trainer highlighted concerns about the safety of his women colleagues as an important factor: 'With our female trainers, we have to make a decision – can we send this student out with a female trainer unescorted for six hours? Because at the end of the day, if anything happened to the female trainer, it's going to come back to the company.' Having attempted to raise concerns about gendered power dynamics with this trainer already, I followed up by asking whether he ever had concerns about how students relate to women more generally. I could see his eyes narrowing even as I spoke. My voice trailed off, the question hanging in the air uncomfortably between us, until he slowly said: 'How would that be an issue?' Recognising that I was in danger of damaging the rapport we had established – rapport that, at the time, I thought could sustain this kind of questioning – I did not pursue the issue further. These and other tense moments left me in no doubt that there were limits to the lines of enquiry I could pursue without jeopardising research relationships. There were a multitude of indeterminate boundaries I always seemed in danger of crossing, such that I had continually to determine in the context of individual encounters what kind of critical weight the dialogue could bear.

I had known from the outset that researching the seduction community would involve accommodating myself to certain kinds of complicities and silences. This is a well-recognised and much discussed feature of feminist scholarship, which necessarily involves 'being at risk in the face of the practices and discourses into which one inquires' (Haraway 1997: 190). In order to undertake this project at all, I had to learn how to absorb sexism and misogyny, as it was only by exposing myself to these affects and discourses that I would be able to make sense of the seduction industry as a cultural formation. My fieldwork was thus predicated upon a willingness to silence myself. I said nothing when trainers told students that all women secretly desire to be physically and psychologically dominated by powerful men. I did not object when men covertly filmed their interactions with women in my presence, or when these recordings were later screened for all-male audiences who appeared unperturbed by the fact that the women involved did not know they were being watched. I muted my horror when the trainer who facilitated a good deal of my research access punctuated a seminar with jokes about sexual violence, reeling inwardly at the punchline: 'She got raped again!' I swallowed my panic when another trainer, who had been telling me of his infatuation with Russian women, pulled out his phone and began showing me pictures of a half-dressed sleeping woman, knowing that in all likelihood that she was entirely unaware of having been photographed or the purposes to which these images were being used.

Much as I would have liked to 'talk back' (Griffin 1991) in these and other instances – to rage against the entitlement and disregard some men demonstrated towards women – I was prevented from doing so by an overarching need to maintain research access. Silencing myself in this way was difficult and often painful, as I was forced to collude in the indignities and injustices to which I bore witness. Occasionally the studied quietude I cultivated slipped and I intervened without thinking. One day, a trainer I was observing in-field told his student, a man in his thirties, to approach two girls who were browsing the stalls in Covent Garden. Seeing how young they were – they could not have been more than sixteen years old, if that – I interrupted abruptly, the words leaving my mouth before I even knew what I was saying. Keenly aware of the three men now looking at me quizzically after this sudden outburst, I stammered that the girls were too young. With a shrug of indifference the trainer looked around the crowd once more, and we moved on without further discussion.

At other times, my interventions were more deliberate, as when a participant emailed me with a new hypothesis he had devised. Detailing a number of 'unsuccessful' dates he had had – by which he meant dates that did not culminate in sex – he explained that in order to pursue any kind of relationship with a woman it is necessary to have sex on the first date, so that 'she will not really have anything left to lose and can resign herself to her attraction to you.' Reading his email, I experienced a by then familiar sinking feeling, recognising how the programmatic logics of seduction preclude genuine dialogue and enable men to bypass all but the most nominal considerations of consent. Here was a participant telling me in no uncertain terms that when a woman resisted him sexually he intended to push on regardless. I shuddered, wondering how he had come to formulate this hypothesis. Though he was not seeking my opinion or advice, I nevertheless felt compelled to warn him against adopting such a singular stance. In reply, I explained the crucial importance of ensuring sexual experiences are mutually desired, advocating express communication and detailing the variety of non-verbal cues to which partners must attend. This email did not receive a response, and it was some months before this participant wrote to me again. When he next got in touch, it was to send me a link to a discussion thread on an online forum about why people so often misunderstand seduction.

Many of the most excruciating moments of my research took place not in the field, as it were, but in my own home. Media analysis comprised a major component of this research, as I examined materials including books, blogs and video content. Sometimes these analysis sessions were planned, as when I determined to examine a particular book or set of blog posts on a given day. Very often, however, my engagement with this material was more spontaneous, as when I followed links circulated via mailing lists and ended up clicking through to other things. Importantly, such materials offer a view of seduction as it is marketed to and performed for an assumed audience of heterosexual men, without the moderating function that my presence may have had when attending live events. Watching a secretly filmed in-field video, and seeing a woman turning her head away from the pressing lips of the man pinning her against a wall outside a nightclub, I squirmed with discomfort and felt myself also leaning away in a desperate effort to help her escape. Seeing another video, in which a woman was cajoled at length into having sex in a casino bathroom – evidently unaware that she was being filmed for online display – I shouted at the screen, willing her to hear me, slamming my fist against the table in frustration at my inability to intervene in what I was seeing. Reading a boastful account of a practised seducer coaxing a clearly reluctant young woman into sex until she finally relented – every possible strategy of resistance clearly having been exhausted – I held my breath, my whole body tense, recognising this as yet another instance of the coercive dynamics that too often pass for 'just sex'. Alone, there was no need to stifle the dread with which these scenes filled me. I wept bitterly, consumed by anger and grief.

In her celebrated essay 'The scent of memory: strangers, our own, and others', Avtar Brah (1999) recounts her experiences as an Asian woman interviewing white people for a project on identity and place in west London. In evocative and illuminating prose, she recalls how the racist intonations of some of her participants served to annihilate her both discursively and emotionally: 'In some cases, my face-to-face presence during interviews seemed to be completely obliterated, as if I did not exist, while they heaped a variety of stereotypic constructions upon Asian populations' (Brah 1999: 7). Describing the implications this had for her efforts to maintain 'objectivity', Brah goes on to say: 'I could not be a disinterested listener, although I listened attentively. My intellect, feelings, and emotions had all been galvanised by my respondent's discourse. I was framed within it, whether I liked it or not' (ibid.). While the contexts of our research as well as our subject positions differ in many ways, the sense of being expunged or eradicated was something I also experienced in the course of undertaking this project. As a woman, I was personally implicated in statements made about women in general and had a direct stake in the modes of relationality being advocated here. I found myself caught up – through a combination of personal biography and identification with other women – in the sexual politics of the seduction industry. It was not simply that the particular iterations of sexism and misogyny on display here offended me, but that in a more profound way they rendered my very being untenable. At a psychological and emotional level, it seemed impossible to reconcile my own understanding of the world with that promoted within this sphere. And yet, at the same time, I was keenly aware that of course this worldview does exist and, indeed, that it does so on a larger scale than any alternative I might wish to project.

Painful though it was at times, the insights I gained from conducting this research as a woman have been crucial to ensuring this project carries with it the recognition that 'feminist knowledge has some grounding in women's *experiences*, and in how it *feels* to live in unjust gendered relationships' (Ramazanoglu and Holland 2002: 16). Yet silence in the research process begets analytic and ethical questions in fieldwork's aftermath. Writing this account, I am left to wonder how participants would have responded had I challenged sexism more openly, pushed back against misogyny, called out racism. It is possible that doing so would only have occasioned more of the same. But there is also the chance that intervening in this way might have enabled a different kind of dialogue to emerge. I am also faced with questions about my own ethical stance towards participants. Given that I did not object to expressions of sexism and racism at the time, what right do I have to critique them now in print? Does this risk reinforcing a perception of feminists as scheming and duplicitous, set upon getting one over on men in general and the seduction industry in particular? For many feminist scholars, complicity in the research process is admissible – or simply made bearable – because the research is intended to serve larger political goals (Grenz 2005). Yet it is difficult to know precisely how to go about this or what the personal costs may be. As Alison Phipps (2014) points out in a discussion of the 'impact agenda' in higher education, 'there is a price to be paid by anyone who gains a public profile – and this is especially true for women who talk about gender' (see also Jane 2012; Penny 2011).

(En)countering others

Questions of relationality have long been central to debates about feminist research methods. While striving towards greater mutuality with research participants has been championed by many as a necessary corrective to the exploitative and extractive tendencies of male-dominated and empiricist social science (Bowles and Duelli Klein 1983), this stance is not without its own problems. In a major intervention, Judith Stacey argues that the much vaunted reciprocity of feminist ethnography may expose participants to greater risks than more conventional approaches: 'The greater the intimacy, the apparent mutuality of the researcher/researched relationship, the greater is the danger' (1988: 24). For Stacey, it is important for feminist researchers to recognise that, whatever other intentions we may have, relationships with participants are fundamentally a means of producing research material: 'The lives, loves, and tragedies that fieldwork informants share with a researcher are ultimately data, grist for the ethnographic mill, a mill that has a truly grinding power' (ibid.: 23). This analysis calls on feminist researchers to confront the strategic nature of the rapport we seek to develop with research participants. In the context of this project – centring as it does on the workings of a community-industry that regards intimacy and trust not so much as relational practices as tactical manoeuvres – her critique takes on particular significance. What, after all, distinguishes the researcher who seeks to establish rapport for the purposes of research from the seducer who attempts to conjure affinity as a means to procure sex?

For some of those who participated in the research, interviews proved to be highly emotional encounters. Many found themselves talking about subjects they had seldom discussed with others, sharing deeply held hurts and closely guarded secrets. Having met just a few weeks before, a half hour into our interview one participant said: 'You actually probably know more about my life than most of my friends do. Virtually all of my friends don't know . . . all of those details.' Another broke down in tears during our meeting, saying: 'I have never, ever, told anyone – not even my best friends – the stuff I'm telling you now.' Pointing to the recorder that sat on the table between us, he went on to say:

> The guy you have on that tape is the real me. I mean, balls to bones, the real me. The guy that I have to be at work, the guy that was in that nightclub – that's a façade. You're probably the first person in twenty years who, balls to bone, knows me for me. And I don't think I would ever say any of this again to anyone I know.

These kinds of emotional outpourings underline the crushing loneliness many men experience as they attempt to navigate the dictates of a culture that scorns weakness and punishes vulnerability, especially among men. Such moments also forced me to reckon with the profound responsibility that comes with undertaking research and attempting to represent the lives of others, even and especially when there are important differences in how we see the world.

On a number of occasions I found myself drawn to identify with participants who described experiences of injustice, reading – and at times misreading – their narratives through the lens of my own life experiences and political commitments. A young black man I interviewed, who had only recently moved to London, described being shocked and disappointed by the overt racism he had already encountered here. We spoke about this for some time, my heart twisting when he said: 'If I think about it day and night, I'd just . . . I'd end up having a cardiac arrest ten years from now. So I don't. I don't want that. Like, I'm better than that. So I just don't think about it.' Grappling towards a fuller understanding of his experience, I asked how the racist encounters he had described made him feel, not realising as I did so that I was now pressing him to expose further the wounds of racism he had already acknowledged. His voice dropping low, he said: 'The first time? Bad. Really bad. But then you get over it, over time.' I responded by saying I wanted things to be different, such that no one would have to 'get over' racism. To this he said: 'Yeah, but what can you do? What can I – I don't have a machine that goes into people's minds. If you get into this fight, trying to show that you're different, you end up not living your life. You end up living your life through other people's eyes, and I don't think that's right.' Though my attempt to acknowledge the structural dimensions of racism and the collectivities needed to counter its many permutations was born of a sense of solidarity, it involved a failure to appreciate the gravity of what it means to live with the seemingly immovable force of racism in everyday life.

Elsewhere, the empathy and solidarity I felt for participants who related experiences of racism meant that I too readily assumed a shared perspective on this and related issues. One man I interviewed spoke at length about the myriad exclusions he experienced as a person of Asian heritage and Muslim faith. At one point, he described a university lecturer telling him, in what seemed to me an unambiguously racist episode, he would never amount to much and should take a job as a taxi driver or corner shopkeeper. When I followed up by asking if he felt that such experiences were the product of persistent racism in the UK, his response was emphatic: 'No, no. It's not a racist society. It's a racial stereotypes society.' He then went on to explain:

> I'll give you an example. I'll order a Coke, and someone will – I guaran-
> tee you someone will say, 'It's 'cause of your religion.' And I'll go, 'No, I
> don't drink because I choose not to drink, because I don't want to drink.'
> I say, you know, 'My religion is personal to me.' But people assume
> because of who you are and that – you know. But that's not being racist,
> that's just stereotyping.

Given the tremendous pain involved in recognising how large-scale ine-qualities manifest in our day-to-day lives, it isn't surprising that he resisted my introduction of the term 'racism' into our conversation, and in hindsight I should have been more sensitive to this. Yet as our conversation went on it became evident that his rejection of structural oppression as a framework of understanding was closely bound up with the prejudices he himself harboured towards other racialised groups, as he offered another example of supposedly harmless stereotypes: 'If I saw three black guys in hoods walking down the street, I'm going to cross over, because I'm going to assume they're muggers. Does that make me racist, or does that just make me a victim of society's stereotyping?' After a long pause, he concluded: 'It depends on how you want to see it.'

Interviewing women who work in the seduction industry raised a number of issues, ethically, politically and personally. For one thing, because there are so few women overall, maintaining the anonymity of those who participated in the research has been a continual concern. As a result I have chosen to limit the extent to which I discuss the perspectives and experiences of the three women I spoke to, a decision which brings with it yet further misgivings, not least as this may be seen as a failure to honour their contributions. My interviews with women – while not entirely different from the interviews I did with men – often involved distinct patterns of relationality. To begin with, there was usually more laughter, as we relayed shared frustrations about the view of women promoted in this sphere with a mixture of incredulity and exasperation. One woman decried the commonplace assumption among her colleagues and students alike that women enjoy endless sexual choice, citing this as a major challenge in her work:

> There's a lot of misapprehensions that men will have generally about women. Like, that ahm . . . you know, like, that women have this abundance, this *choice* in their dating life, and we just sit here looking beautiful and men have to do *all this work* to understand, and we just reject them left, right and centre. We don't care and like – it's like – it's not like that, obviously, so I consider it really important that I push against that.

Another spoke with obvious irritation about the gamified logics that underwrite many seduction knowledge-practices, most especially the idea that women will always respond favourably if the 'system' is followed:

> That pisses me off. I *hate* that. There's not a 'system' like that. It won't always work. There might be loads of times a girl will not be interested in you – she might not fancy you, she might not like your look, she might not be attracted to you. So what, someone else might? Just because you've used the 'system' doesn't mean she will. It's about being the best you can be for yourself, which doesn't mean being this clone, like everyone else, because you've all learned the same stupid 'system'. There is no such 'system' – it doesn't exist.

Talking about the absurdities of seduction enabled a sense of identification with one another and, more importantly, provided a space for women who work in the industry to vent frustrations usually kept to themselves or shared only with other women.

These relatively light-hearted exchanges often served as a prelude to sharing more serious misgivings and making more personal disclosures. All the women I spoke to were acutely aware of the much maligned status of women in the industry in general, whether or not they believed this extended to them personally. Describing the routine disparagement directed towards women in what remains an overwhelmingly male-dominated industry, one woman drew attention to the gendered dynamics that underwrite this wider pattern: 'It seems to mainly be a thing of "Why is a woman doing it?" It's like, with the men it's like "He's so stupid", or "I don't think he can get women, I think he's a fraud, I think he's not really teaching properly." With us, it's immediately, "She's a prostitute", "I heard she's a prostitute."' Another woman, who seemed to have a more positive experience overall, affirmed her exceptionality by saying: 'I feel like I'm the only girl they let into the boys' club!' This narrative quickly began to unravel, however, when just minutes later she described a recent episode of being sexually harassed while at work:

> I did an event two weeks ago and I turned around and one of the official photographers was trying to take a picture up my skirt. Like, literally, he was on the floor. And I grabbed him, I yanked him up by his collar, and I said, I told him, 'Don't you dare do that – would you do that to any of the men that are here? Would you try and pull their trou – well don't fucking do that to me.' I was like, 'Do not disrespect me.'

To this, she then added: 'It is very much a woman in a man's world. You have to have rock-solid boundaries. I have to be prepared to be intellectually challenged every single day.'

Even while acknowledging problematic gender dynamics within the seduction industry, women tended to downplay the deleterious effects this could have on them, both professionally and personally. In a particularly illuminating example of this, one woman attempted to renege on earlier comments she had made about the 'sexualised degradation' she faces from male colleagues and competitors:

> I don't want to sit there and say . . . and sound like I'm so upset about it, because I do realise that in an industry like this you're going to just have to get on with it. The same way as I expect that my colleagues will flirt with me and say things which in any other workplace would be considered inappropriate. It doesn't bother me at all. I'm pretty thick skinned about this, I have a good laugh at it. It's fine.

After a pause, she then went on: 'But some of the stuff, I think that they do go too far. It's almost like they just don't like women. I think a lot of pickup artists don't like women.' The ambivalence contained in this sequence of statements is striking, as she first acknowledges the widespread sexism that exists within the industry, then denies that it causes her any harm, only to conclude that many of the men who work in this sphere are certifiable misogynists. Certainly, it demonstrates the difficulty of enunciating critique in an avowedly postfeminist context, where acknowledging injury is so often regarded as denying one's own agency and wallowing in victimhood.

Listening to the stories women shared and seeing the patterns between them – patterns they may or may not be able to see themselves – I felt a sense of injustice on their behalf. In the context of our individual discussions, I wanted to politicise their experiences in order to move towards a recognition of sexism not as incidental but as *functional* to the workings of the seduction industry. I am well aware, however, that this reading is unlikely to be shared by any of the women I interviewed. For, despite the frustrations and humiliations that patterned their working lives and seeped into other areas, all three professed to enjoy their jobs and were clearly attached to the industry more generally. Thus, while we shared certain points of identification as women, there were also limits to this, as ultimately we have different perspectives and hold different allegiances. Undoubtedly, these relationships involve an element of the betrayal Stacey warns of, as the revelations these women made – born of fleeting intimacies – would later become ammunition for me to deploy against an industry in which they are all deeply invested.

Writing in *Journal of Contemporary Ethnography*, Orit Avishai, Lynne Gerber and Jennifer Randles (2012) argue that there is a fundamental tension between feminism as an analytic project and feminism as a political project (cf. Mahmood 2005), a tension they contend produces 'the feminist ethnographer's dilemma'. Outlining this predicament, they explain: 'The dilemma ensues when our feminist political commitments clash with our subjects' worldviews, forcing us to reconcile our perspectives with those of respondents who do not share our understanding and valuation of rights, opportunities, liberation, and constraints, but whose views we have a responsibility to interpret and represent accurately and fairly' (Avishai et al. 2012: 397). The authors contend that this dilemma is unavoidable in 'conservative field sites', where the contrast between participants' own interpretations of the social world they inhabit are liable to differ markedly from those of the researcher. On this basis, the authors conclude that, 'in order to produce valid research, feminists should be cognisant of the tension between feminism's dual agendas as a political and analytical project and how the former must cede to the latter' (ibid.: 421).

Certainly, there is something to be said for continually reminding ourselves that all knowledge is situated (Haraway 1988) and reflects a particular politics of location (Rich [1984] 1986). I also agree with Avishai and her colleagues that it is crucial to think carefully through the realities of the sites we are investigating rather than impose pre-existing frameworks of understanding onto them. However, I cannot accept the premise that feminist analytics and politics are inherently oppositional or that politics must cede to analysis when conflicts do arise. As Matthew Ezzell points out in his rejoinder to their piece, a commitment to feminism as a (clearly multifaceted) political project means that it is even more important that we strive to get the analysis right. He argues: 'Our task is not to push our political goals to the backseat in favour of analysis, but to ground our analyses in the data, making sense of the lived experiences of our participants through a critically engaged, explicit political perspective' (Ezzell 2013: 445). Seen in this light, doing justice to our political commitments means doing justice to our research participants and speaking truth to the realities of their lives. Feminist scholars cannot abdicate our responsibility to critique but, rather, must strive to ensure that the always composite portraits we produce are nevertheless as complete and as accurate as possible. After all, if we want to challenge the wider economies of power in which we all operate, it is necessary to know as much as possible, in as much detail as possible, about the foundations on which they are built.

Appendix I: Participants' Biographical Information

All interview participants were asked to provide details of their sexual orientation, ethnicity and/or nationality, age, education and occupation. All names have been changed. Ages and timescales pertain to the date of the interview.

Adam is a heterosexual white British man in his thirties. He lives in London and has been involved with the seduction community for many years. He works as a pickup trainer. Interviewed in person, 2012.

Ali is a heterosexual British Asian man in his early twenties. He lives in London and has been involved in the seduction community for less than a year, primarily attending free events. He is currently pursuing a postgraduate degree at a UK university. Interviewed in person, 2012.

Andrew is a heterosexual white British man in his thirties. He is based in London but spends most of his time abroad. He has been involved in the seduction community for many years and works as a pickup trainer. Interviewed by Skype, 2012.

Antonio is a heterosexual white European man in his late twenties. He lives in Europe and came to London for a weekend training course, having previously undertaken pickup training courses elsewhere in Europe. He is currently pursuing a postgraduate degree at a European university. Interviewed by Skype, 2012.

Anwar is a heterosexual British Pakistani man in his late thirties. He lives in London and has been involved in the seduction community for about a year, having recently undertaken a weekend training course. He holds an undergraduate degree and works in business. Interviewed in person, 2012.

Brent is a heterosexual black African man in his early twenties. He lives in London and has been involved with the seduction community for a number of years, primarily attending free events. He is currently undertaking an undergraduate degree at a UK university. Interviewed in person, 2012.

Danny is a heterosexual white British man in his late twenties. He lives in London and has been involved in the seduction community for many years. He works as a pickup trainer. Interviewed in person, 2013.

David is a heterosexual Indian man in his late thirties. He lives in London and has been involved in the seduction community for a number of years, receiving one-to-one training and attending free events. He holds an undergraduate degree and works in business. Interviewed in person, 2012.

Derek is a heterosexual white British man in his early twenties. He lives in London and has been involved in the seduction community for less than a year. He has undertaken a number of commercial training courses and plans to become a pickup trainer himself. He recently completed an undergraduate degree and works in finance. Interviewed in person, 2012.

Doug is a heterosexual white British American man in his late twenties. He lives in London and has been involved with the seduction community for a few years. Having recently undertaken a commercial training course, he is currently receiving one-to-one training. He holds a postgraduate degree and works in finance. Interviewed in person, 2012.

Elijah is a heterosexual British Filipino man in his late twenties. He lives in London and has been involved in the seduction community for a number of years, primarily attending free events. He holds an undergraduate degree and works in entertainment. Interviewed in person, 2013.

Emma is a bisexual white British woman in her twenties. She lives in London and has been involved in the seduction community for a number of years. She works as a pickup trainer. Interviewed in person, 2012.

Emmanuel is a heterosexual black African man in his early twenties. He lives in London and has been involved in the seduction community for a number of years, primarily attending free events. He holds an undergraduate degree and works in business. Interviewed in person, 2012.

Gavin is a heterosexual British Indian man in his late twenties. He lives in London and has been involved with the seduction community for many years. He has undertaken a number of commercial training courses and currently receives regular one-to-one training. He works in engineering. Interviewed in person, 2013.

George is a heterosexual Chinese man in his early thirties. He lives in the east of England and came to London for a commercial training course. He holds multiple postgraduate degrees and works in education. Interviewed in person, 2012.

Harry is a heterosexual white British man in his early twenties. He lives in South East England and comes to London regularly for seduction-related events. He is currently undertaking an undergraduate degree at a UK university. Interviewed by phone, 2013.

Jack is a heterosexual white British man in his twenties. He lives in London and has been involved in the seduction community for a number of years. He holds an undergraduate degree and works as a pickup trainer. Interviewed in person, 2012.

James is a heterosexual white Northern Irish man in his late twenties. He is divorced and lives in London. He has been involved in the seduction community for a few years and has undertaken commercial training courses. He works in retail security. Interviewed in person, 2012.

Javed is a heterosexual Indian man in his late thirties. He lives in London and has been involved in the seduction community for a number of years, primarily attending free events as well as participating in online forums. He holds multiple postgraduate degrees and works in education. Interviewed in person, 2012.

Jay is a heterosexual Chinese man in his early twenties. He has been involved in the seduction community for a few years and has undertaken a number of commercial training courses. He is currently undertaking a postgraduate degree at a UK university. Interviewed in person, 2013.

Jenny is a heterosexual white British woman in her twenties. She lives in London and works as a pickup trainer. Interviewed in person, 2012.

Kalim is a heterosexual British Asian man in his late twenties. He lives in London and has been involved with the seduction community for many years, primarily attending free events as well as participating in online forums. He holds a postgraduate degree and is currently seeking employment. Interviewed in person, 2012.

Katherine is a heterosexual white British woman in her twenties. She lives in London and works as a pickup trainer. Interviewed in person, 2013.

Mark is a heterosexual white European man in his thirties. He lives in London and has been involved in the seduction community for a number of years. He works as a pickup trainer. Interviewed in person, 2012.

Moe is a heterosexual Middle Eastern man in his early thirties. He lives in Europe and came to London for a weekend training course; previously he has undertaken pickup training courses elsewhere in Europe. He holds an undergraduate degree and works in business. Interviewed by Skype, 2012.

Rahul is a heterosexual British Indian man in his thirties. He lives in London and has been involved with the London seduction community for many years. He works as a life coach. Interviewed in person, 2013.

Ralph is a heterosexual white British man in his late forties. He is divorced and lives in London. He has been involved in the seduction community for a few years, undertaking a number of commercial training courses and attending free events. He holds a postgraduate degree and works in education. Interviewed in person, 2013.

Ravi is a heterosexual Indian man in his thirties. He lives in London and has been involved in the seduction community for a number of years, mostly attending free events and also participating in online forums. He holds a postgraduate degree and works in research. Interviewed in person, 2013.

Ryan is a heterosexual white European man in his late twenties. He lives in London and is currently separated from his wife. He has been involved in the seduction community for less than a year and recently undertook a commercial training course. He holds a postgraduate degree and works in finance. Interviewed in person, 2012.

Stefan is a heterosexual white European man in his early twenties. He lives in London and has been involved with the seduction community for a number of years, mostly attending free events and participating in online forums. He works in social care. Interviewed in person, 2012.

Tim is a heterosexual white European man in his early thirties. He lives in Europe and came to London for a weekend training course. He holds an undergraduate degree and works in education. Interviewed by Skype, 2012.

William is a heterosexual white British man in his thirties. He is based in London but spends most of his time abroad. He has been involved in the London seduction community for many years and works as a pickup trainer. Interviewed by Skype, 2013.

Appendix II: Collated Biographical Information

Gender: Twenty-nine men and three women were interviewed for this project.

Age: Interview participants range in age from their early twenties to their late forties, though over the course of my fieldwork I met men both younger and older than this. Of those who formally participated, nineteen are in their twenties and twelve in their thirties. Only one participant is over forty years of age.

Education: Participants are highly educated, with almost all holding undergraduate degrees and a full third either possessing or currently pursuing postgraduate degrees. In total, twenty hold undergraduate degrees, seven hold masters' level degrees, and three hold or are completing doctoral degrees. The majority of these degrees are in the fields of business, science and education. Two participants hold GCSE qualifications and have not attended university.

Occupation: The majority of participants in this study work in professional occupations. Specific professions (all indexed here in the plural) include secondary schoolteachers, private tutors and academic researchers; scientists and engineers; entrepreneurs and business owners; psychologists and therapists; professional carers; human resources and information technology professionals; and security personnel. The overwhelmingly professional character of participants in this study and the London seduction community more generally can be attributed, in part, to the significant costs involved in participation. Weekend training courses in London typically cost several hundred pounds, while week-long residential programmes cost thousands of pounds. Free events also presume a certain financial status, as attendees must have both the time and the income required to socialise in central London and be relatively comfortable navigating middle-class environs.

Sexual orientation: With the exception of one woman who identifies as bisexual, all those who participated in this research identify as heterosexual. Questions to men about their sexual orientation often elicited emphatic responses such as: 'Straight. *Full on straight.*' In other cases, this question caused confusion, as when one participant responded: 'I'm heterosexual. I mean straight, right, just to be clear? I'm quite certain. I'm quite certain on that. I mean, like, I'm sure.' One participant described a near exclusive attraction to transsexual women (his term), which he was struggling to overcome, saying: 'It's like a virus in the system.'

'Race' and ethnicity: The London seduction community reflects the general population of London in that it is predominantly but by no means exclusively white. At most of the events I attended, white men accounted for somewhere between half and three-quarters of attendees. British Asian and South Asian men are somewhat overrepresented, a trend that was frequently commented on during my fieldwork. Despite this overrepresentation, it is notable that the most well-known and commercially successful trainers are white. Set against the general population, relatively few black men participate in this sphere, a pattern that led some participants to conclude that black men are 'naturally' good with women. Reflecting these general characteristics, just over half of interview participants (eighteen) identify as white British or white European; eight described themselves as South Asian, British Asian or British Indian; three as East Asian; two as black African; and one as Middle Eastern.

Disability and mental health: I did not ask participants to disclose disabilities and none related having disabilities. A number of participants disclosed mental health problems such as depression. One participant stated that he has autism, while another described himself as having 'autistic tendencies'.

Involvement in the seduction community: Of those interviewed, twelve work in the seduction industry, half on a full-time and half on a part-time basis. Three of those who work in the industry are women. All other participants can be regarded as students or clients involved in the seduction community in a learning capacity. The majority of these participants have paid for training products or services of some kind and have spent anywhere between a few hundred and several thousand pounds on this over months or years.

Notes

Introduction

1 In the US context this functions somewhat differently, with trainers such as J. T. Tran claiming to use seduction techniques to thwart stereotypes of Asian-Americans as sexually timid. Though Tran frames his seduction practice as a kind of postcolonial critique – tapping into issues of 'racial castration' (Eng, 2001) – he does so while positioning white women as the ultimate prize and status symbol for Asian-American men (for discussion, see Solomon, 2011).

2 In response to one of the numerous heavily staged instructional videos featuring professional models posted to La Ruina's *YouTube* channel, a highly rated comment reads: 'Why don't you pick up girls with a hidden camera and then post it here? Too much talk and I don't even know if you are good at this' (see La Ruina, 2014).

3 Paul Gilroy's work (2013) is of particular interest, since he examines the writings of Robert Greene, the author of Machiavellian business texts such as *The 48 Laws of Power* and *The 50th Law* (co-written with the rapper and entrepreneur 50 Cent). Though it does not form part of Gilroy's analysis, which is concerned specifically with the elaboration of a 'black vernacular neoliberalism' via financial self-help texts, Greene is also the author of the similarly Machiavellian *The Art of Seduction* ([2001] 2003).

Chapter 1 The Work of Seduction

1 Despite this, Strauss remains closely involved with the industry via the seduction training company he founded, Stylelife Academy.

2 By 'opening sets', Mark is referring to the practice of approaching and initiating conversations with women. This phrasing is widely used within the seduction community.

3 Notably in this regard, a number of trainers I interviewed spontaneously mentioned – without my having asked – that many of their clients pay for sex. One estimated that at least half of the men she works with have paid for sex, while another put the figure at between half and three-quarters of his clients.

4 Derek's phrasing here cites indirectly the well-known British seduction trainer Adam Lyons, often referred to as 'AFC Adam'. In contending that he wants his future partner to know 'I could have had anybody. But I chose her', Derek closely approximates a pronouncement repeatedly made by Lyons in interviews. In an interview with *The Independent* in 2008, for example, Lyons is quoted as saying: 'I want to be able to say to the girl that I eventually end up with: "I could have had almost anybody, and I chose you"' (Walker 2008). Derek's near identical reproduction of this statement was one of a number of instances in which participants rehearsed comments made by well-known seduction trainers, demonstrating how the enormous authority accorded to these men as masculine exemplars informs the sexual aspirations and intimate ambitions of other men.

5 Such patterns raise questions about the ways in which the psychic and embodied dynamics of heterosexual desire are shaped by the vagaries of a visual culture that celebrates an exceedingly narrow definition of feminine beauty. And although it is virtually taken for granted that idealised imagery negatively shapes women's relationship with their own bodies – 'normative discontent' having become a sociological banality (McRobbie, 2009: 94–8) – there is little comparable feminist discussion about how the desires of heterosexual men are shaped by the ubiquity of these images, now displayed not simply via billboards and magazines but through highly orchestrated yet seemingly authentic performances on social media. For further discussion, see O'Neill (2016b).

6 The demand for trainers to demonstrate experiential authority functions additionally as a means to police the parameters of the seduction community as a homosocial setting. While a small number of women work in the seduction industry in London, their status as trainers is deeply contested. In our interview, Danny pronounced: 'I have my reservations on female trainers.' He went on to claim that, while bisexual women represent a partial exception, they too lack the necessary gendered subject positioning to teach seduction. Talking about a bisexual woman trainer he knows, Danny said: 'The reason for my reservations is because, yes, she picks women up, but she's going to go through different obstacles to what a man would encounter. You know what I mean, so she can *never ever* talk from the point of view of the man, what it is to go through these challenges as a male.' The demand for experiential authority thus further encompasses a demand for common gendered positioning, on the presumption that men have a certain shared experience as men. Interestingly, however, women trainers I interviewed invoked their own version of experiential authority to claim expertise. As Katherine related: 'I think there's a lot I can – me or any other female trainer – can bring into training, because we are women, and they want to learn how to speak to and meet women. So we can give them first-hand advice, which male trainers can never do. They can only

assume really.' This logic is underwritten by the further assumption that women are relatively homogeneous and predictable. Katherine went on to explain: 'As a woman, you know what you'd want a guy to say to you. So you know what works when guys hit on you and what doesn't work – that's the biggest advantage that anyone could have, I think. A guy trainer can never have that.'

7 Notably, both separately cited the 2005 film *Hitch* as a useful entry point to such discussions. In contrast to earlier filmic representations of career pickup artists – most notably Tom Cruise's turn as the maniacal Frank T. J. Mackey in the 1999 film *Magnolia* – *Hitch* provides a positive cultural reference point for real-life seducers. Because the eponymous Hitch is presented to viewers not as a 'pickup artist' but as a 'dating consultant' whose flair with women is a personal talent, the existence of the wider seduction industry is obscured. Given the context in which trainers I spoke to referenced the film, it is somewhat ironic to note that one of its main plot lines concerns Hitch's attempts to conceal his profession from his love interest.

Chapter 2 Pedagogy and Profit

1 This, however, is not to say that male heterosexuality doesn't permit a certain amount of sexual flexibility. While masculinities scholarship often assumes that homosexual sex goes against normative conventions of heterosexual masculinity, the work of Jane Ward (2015) demonstrates just how much male-to-male sexual contact takes place among avowedly heterosexual men. Her analysis is especially important in demonstrating that sexual activity among straight white men frequently serves to reaffirm these identities and shore up existing power relations among men based on gender, sexuality and 'race'.

2 In a further example of this logic, Tom Torero describes the transformative qualities of a good wardrobe:

> Despite having a very low salary and living in a small room, I was going to the most exclusive venues in London with some of the hottest girls. I'd often put on the cheap version of the high-end look the style consultant had given me – jacket, shirt, jeans, shoes – and stroll down Bond Street (the poshest shopping street in London), picking up the phone numbers of some stunning women out shopping on their platinum credit cards from Prada, Dolce Gabbana [sic] and Gucci. With a sharp look and a beautiful woman on my arm, I'd walk into posh South Kensington bars or Knighsbridge [sic] restaurants. Other punters and staff would just assume I was another banker or hedgefund manager strolling through the doors. They'd never have guessed I was a primary school teacher who'd met the girls I was with on the street, without money or power. (2012: 440)

3 The in-field training format has superseded previously employed teaching practices such as the 'HB section' ('HB' standing for 'hot babe'), where companies hired women for their students to practise with/on in a private setting. In-field formats have obvious financial benefits over the HB section, as trainers no longer need to pay women to work at these events or deal with any comments or criticisms they might have about the knowledge-practices being expounded. Moreover, because a small number of women initially hired to work in the HB section at various events have now gone on to establish rival training companies – the best known being Kezia Noble – eliminating this format also serves to limit women's formal involvement in the industry.

4 Recording in-field footage at these events serves an additional purpose. Students whose interactions are filmed are often asked to give consent for the footage to be used in any future training products produced by companies; indeed, they are often offered incentives to do so, such as free or discounted access to various training materials or events. The women who feature in the footage alongside students – who are almost inevitably unaware of having been filmed in the first place – are not asked to consent to the use of their image or provided with any incentives to do so.

5 Nevertheless, the spectre of prostitution continually haunts women's work within the seduction industry. Exemplifying this, one of the female trainers I interviewed guarded against the presumption that she or her staff exchange sex for money in response to a question I asked about the role of 'wing girls' in training regimes:

> I mean like it's completely – they don't ever do anything physical with the guys, it's not like the world's cheapest escort service [laughing]. They're actually just smart, interesting women, like the kind of women I think the guys would ideally like to date. And they can just spend an hour with the guy and they usually just go for a coffee or a drink and just chat to them and afterwards they create a feedback report for me, so I get some kind of feedback loop as to how the guy's coming across, then it allows me to more specifically tailor my training to address what's going on.

6 The acronym 'AMOG' stands for 'Alpha Male Other Guy'. In the parlance of the seduction community, the term is used to refer to a man who – by virtue of denominators such as power or wealth – has the greatest claim to masculine status in any given context.

Chapter 3 Manufacturing Consent

1 In this and other respects, *Daygame* appears to have been closely modelled on its predecessor *The Game*, as Strauss also describes grappling with a

kind of existential angst resulting from the apparently near mechanical proficiency of his seduction methods.

2 It is worth pointing out that what might be seen to constitute 'sexism' and 'misogyny' cannot be assumed in advance. In our interview Ravi spoke about Krauser, whose blog posts are discussed in the next section of this chapter, in idealised terms. He appeared to be in awe of the sexual lifestyle Krauser has cultivated: 'He gets the kind of girl that I can't even think of as of now. Maybe later in my life I can try some of them. But, ahm, yeah ... seemingly he's making the impossible possible!' Thus Ravi indicted unnamed pickup artists as 'shallow' and 'misogynist', while at the same time lauding one of the most overtly predatory and misogynist figures associated with the London seduction industry.

3 Even where the submission of one party to another is actively negotiated and expressly agreed, this does not negate the ongoing negotiation of consent. As Aleksandra Antevska and Nicola Gavey argue: 'Even for women who do want to take up a submissive sexual position, these kinds of assumptions would be highly problematic, as such desires are unlikely to constitute a carte blanche acceptance of being treated in any kind of dominating, disrespectful and degrading way' (2015: 620).

4 Mills writes: 'it presumably does not need to be emphasized that white ignorance is not the only kind of privileged, group-based ignorance. Male ignorance could be analyzed similarly and clearly has a far more ancient history and arguably a more deep-rooted ancestry in human interrelations, insofar as it goes back thousands of years' (2007: 22).

5 Indeed, some seducers seem to reconcile themselves to causing hurt, doing damage, inflicting pain. In an especially flagrant example of this – which has since become the basis of a campaign to get Amazon to stop selling his books – Roosh V (Daryush Valizadeh), in the seduction travelogue *Bang Iceland* (2011), recounts: 'While walking to my place, I realised how drunk she was. In America, having sex with her would have been rape, since she legally couldn't give her consent. It didn't help matters that I was sober, but I can't say I cared or even hesitated. I won't rationalise my actions, but having sex is what I do' (cited in Charles, 2015).

Chapter 4 Seduction and Sexual Politics

1 Notably, none of the women I interviewed invoked biological or evolutionary logics to account for the seduction community but, instead, discussed this in terms of social and cultural change. Evolutionary narratives were also less prevalent among men of colour I interviewed. While Jay, who is Chinese and has lived in the US for a number of years, was a strong proponent of evolutionary views, few of the British Asian men I spoke to mentioned biological mandates and then did so only in passing. Neither of the

two black men I interviewed made any reference to biology or evolution whatsoever. Thus, while McCaughey suggests that evolutionary rhetorics have the effect of 'forging a common, biological identity among men' (2008: 84), in the British context at least this discourse appears to be racialised, hailing some men more readily than others.

2 Continual references to *Fight Club* among men I interviewed reflect a broader preoccupation with the film in the seduction community. Exemplifying this are the many seduction-based communal living arrangements named after the film's Project Mayhem. In *The Game* (2005), Strauss documents the formation of Project Hollywood, while in the UK a group known as Rock Solid Game rented a house in Hampstead which they referred to as Château RSG (Krauser 2017). The founder of the American company Real Social Dynamics, Eoin Cooke, uses the pseudonym Tyler Durden in an apparent homage to Pitt's character.

3 Even those who professed to support the idea of women being more proactive had highly circumscribed views about what this might actually entail. Emma described encouraging women to make themselves 'more approachable': 'I say give him the opportunity to be the man. You know, ask a stupid question or something, ask for his opinion, ask for him to help you with something – let him step into that masculine role, to help you be the woman.' In keeping with the basic precepts of seduction, Emma claims that, by adhering to defined gender roles, women and men can achieve relational harmony. That such conformity may restrict women and men alike, causing emotional attenuation for both parties, is not considered.

4 Gilligan's words appear as chapter prefaces alongside those of other prominent feminist scholars, including Gloria Steinem and Catherine MacKinnon. Asked in interviews with the press as to why he chose to include such quotes, Strauss claimed that he felt the book needed more women's voices. Given the dramatically counterposed purposes to which he puts their arguments, this seems at best misleading and at worst deeply cynical. For example, Strauss prefaces a chapter entitled 'Blasting last-minute resistance' with a quote from Catherine MacKinnon: 'What is sexual is what gives a man an erection . . . if there is no inequality, no violation, no dominance, no force, there is no sexual arousal' (1989, cited in Strauss 2005: 378). Using the quote in this way, Strauss appears to suggest that MacKinnon endorses the idea that inequality, violation and dominance are necessary preconditions to male sexual arousal, when in actuality she is problematising precisely this assumption.

5 Furthermore, given the centrality of mothering to feminist object-relations theory, this perspective also lends itself to the claim – already discussed in the previous section of this chapter – that it is the overbearing influence of mothers that produces male neuroses: 'if mothering is to blame for male domination then, in the final analysis, men are blameless' (Brittan 1989: 195 cited in McMahon 1993: 687).

6 This is an especially salient point given that some professional seducers exploit this dynamic by delivering attractive women to nightclubs in exchange for a fee. In *Daygame* (2012), for example, Tom Torero details the arrangement he has with management at a venue in Mayfair, which sees him paid a fee for every woman he brings to the club on a given night.

Conclusion

1 This same dynamic can be seen to play out elsewhere, most obviously in the tragicomic rituals of contemporary exercise, offered up as a solution to the problems that arise from increasingly sedentary lifestyles among certain populations. Mark Greif (2015: 3) observes: 'Nothing can make you believe we harbour nostalgia for factory work but a modern gym . . . with the gym we import vestiges of the leftover equipment of industry to our leisure. We leave the office, and put the conveyor belt under our feet, and run as if chased by devils.'
2 Discussing the preoccupation with 'sex difference' in areas such as psychology, Raewyn Connell notes: 'In fact the main finding, from about eighty years of research, is the massive psychological *similarity* between women and men . . . If it were not for the bias of both writers and readers, we might long ago have been talking about this as "sex similarity" research' (2002: 62).
3 For discussion of this case in relation to the wider climate of amped-up misogyny, see Karla Mantilla's *Gendertrolling: How Misogyny Went Viral* (2015: 60–2).
4 In her essay 'Cockblocked by redistribution: a pickup artist in Denmark' (2013), Katie J. M. Baker points to this issue when she surmises – based on the testimony of seducers themselves – that seduction techniques are less effective in Denmark than in other Western societies on account of the country's strong welfare system and anti-individualist culture.

Postscript

1 A similar dynamic is elucidated by Sandra Lee Bartky (1990) in her writings on the phenomenology of oppression. Bartky discusses how, in the context of street harassment, men compel women to see themselves through men's eyes. She recounts an episode of catcalling to which she herself was subject: 'While it is true that for these men I am nothing but, let us say, a "nice piece of ass", there is more involved in this encounter than their fragmented perception of me. They could, after all, have enjoyed me in silence . . . But I must be *made* to know that I am a "nice piece of ass": I must be made to see myself as they see me' (1990: 23).
2 While the frequency with which women experience sexual harassment while undertaking research should disabuse us of the notion that dressing

a certain way will ward off unwanted sexual advances, it is nevertheless important to recognise that adopting less feminine modes of dress may confer less tangible benefits. Relating her own experiences, Deborah Lee describes:

> I realised that what is most important about changing one's appearance is not that it will be a fail-safe way to deflect a man from sexual interest, but that making the changes functions as a psychological prop for the woman interviewer . . . I felt that I had at least gone some way to minimising the potential for trouble and the threat of sanction if trouble did arise. (1997: 558–9)

References

Acker, Sandra (1994) *Gendered Education: Sociological Reflections on Women, Teaching and Feminism*. Buckingham: Open University Press.

Ahmed, Sara (2002) 'Racialized bodies', in *Real Bodies: A Sociological Introduction*, ed. Mary Evans and Ellie Lee. Basingstoke: Palgrave, pp. 46–63.

—— (2007a) 'A phenomenology of whiteness', *Feminist Theory* 8(2): 149–68.

—— (2007b) 'The promise of happiness', *New Formations* no. 63: 121–37.

—— (2010a) 'Feminist killjoys (and other willful subjects)', *The Scholar and Feminist Online* 8, http://sfonline.barnard.edu/polyphonic/ahmed_01.htm.

—— (2010b) *The Promise of Happiness*. Durham, NC: Duke University Press.

Allan, Jonathan A. (2015) 'Phallic affect, or why men's rights activists have feelings', *Men and Masculinities* 19(1): 22–41.

Allen, Louisa (2007) '"Sensitive and real macho all at the same time": young heterosexual men and romance', *Men and Masculinities* 10(2): 137–52.

Anderson, Paul Thomas (1999) *Magnolia*. New Line Cinema [film].

Ansari, Aziz (2015–) *Master of None*. Netflix [TV series].

Antevska, Aleksandra, and Nicola Gavey (2015) '"Out of sight and out of mind": detachment and men's consumption of male sexual dominance and female submission in pornography', *Men and Masculinities* 18(5): 605–29.

Arendell, Terry (1997) 'Reflections on the researcher–researched relationship: a woman interviewing men', *Qualitative Sociology* 20(3): 341–68.

Attwood, Feona, Jamie Hakim and Alison Winch (2017) 'Mediated intimacies: bodies, technologies and relationships', *Journal of Gender Studies* 26(3): 249–53.

Avishai, Orit, Lynne Gerber and Jennifer Randles (2012) 'The feminist ethnographer's dilemma: reconciling progressive research agendas with fieldwork realities', *Journal of Contemporary Ethnography* 42(4): 394–426.

Baker, Joanne (2010) 'Claiming volition and evading victimhood: post-feminist obligations for young women', *Feminism & Psychology* 20(2): 186–204.

Baker, Katie J. M. (2013) 'Cockblocked by redistribution: a pick-up artist in Denmark', *Dissent* 60(4): 8–11.

Baker, Robin (1996) *Sperm Wars: The Science of Sex*. New York: HarperCollins.

Banerjee, Sikata (2012) *Muscular Nationalism: Gender, Violence, and Empire in India and Ireland, 1914–2004*. New York: New York University Press.

Banet-Weiser, Sarah (2015) Popular misogyny: a Zeitgeist, *Culture Digitally*, http://culturedigitally.org/2015/01/popular-misogyny-a-zeitgeist/.

Banks, Tyra (2009) 'The secret code of men', in *The Tyra Banks Show*. Warner Brothers Television Distribution [US talk show].

Barker, Meg-John (2013a) 'Consent is a grey area? A comparison of understandings of consent in *Fifty Shades of Grey* and on the BDSM blogosphere', *Sexualities* 16(8): 896–914.

—— (2013b) *Rewriting the Rules: An Integrative Guide to Love, Sex and Relationships*. Hove, East Sussex: Routledge.

Barker, Meg-John, and Justin Hancock (2017a) *Enjoy Sex (How, When and if You Want to): A Practical and Inclusive Guide*. London: Icon.

—— (2017b) http://megjohnandjustin.com.

Barker, Meg-John, Rosalind Gill and Laura Harvey (2018) *Mediated Intimacy: Sex Advice in Media Culture*. Cambridge: Polity.

Barre, Yad (2016) 'A letter from Yad Barre, founder of Day Game Blueprint', *Daygame Blueprint*, http://daygameblueprint.com/about.

Bartky, Sandra Lee (1990) *Femininity and Domination: Studies in the Phenomenology of Oppression*. London: Routledge.

Bay-Cheng, Laina Y., and Rebecca K. Eliseo-Arras (2008) 'The making of unwanted sex: gendered and neoliberal norms in college women's unwanted sexual experiences', *Journal of Sex Research* 45(4): 386–97.

Beasley, Chris (2013) 'Mind the gap? Masculinity studies and contemporary gender/sexuality thinking', *Australian Feminist Studies* 28(75): 108–24.

Beasley, Christine (2008) 'Rethinking hegemonic masculinity in a globalizing world', *Men and Masculinities* 11(1): 86–103.

Beck, Ulrich, and Elisabeth Beck-Gernsheim (1995) *The Normal Chaos of Love*. Cambridge: Polity.

Behrendt, Greg, and Liz Tuccillo (2004) *He's Just Not That into You*. New York: Simon & Schuster.

Berggren, Kalle (2014) 'Sticky masculinity: post-structuralism, phenomenology and subjectivity in critical studies on men', *Men and Masculinities* 17(3): 231–52.

Berlant, Lauren (2011) *Cruel Optimism*. Durham, NC: Duke University Press.

Bernstein, Elizabeth (2001) 'The meaning of the purchase: desire, demand and the commerce of sex', *Ethnography* 2(3): 389–420.

—— (2010) *Temporarily Yours: Intimacy, Authenticity, and the Commerce of Sex*. Chicago: University of Chicago Press.

Billig, Michael, Susan Condor, Derek Edwards, Mike Gane, David Middleton and Alan Radley (1988) *Ideological Dilemmas: A Social Psychology of Everyday Thinking*. London: Sage.

Bowles, Gloria, and Renate Duelli Klein (1983) *Theories of Women's Studies*. London: Routledge.

Bradshaw, Peter (2012) 'A brief history of pozzing and negging', *The Guardian*, 21 January, www.theguardian.com/commentisfree/2015/jan/21/negging-loathsome-trend.

Brah, Avtar (1999) 'The scent of memory: strangers, our own, and others', *Feminist Review* 61: 4–26.

Brennan, Siofra (2017) '"British women are entitled and overweight": seduction expert who's dated 200 Russian ladies says men should look to Eastern Europe to find a beautiful, intelligent wife', *Daily Mail*, 2 August, www.dailymail.co.uk/femail/article-4752706/Seduction-expert-says-men-date-Russian-women.html.

Brew, Alex (2011) 'Not for the faint-hearted', *Middlesex University*, www.mdx.ac.uk/__data/assets/pdf_file/0007/59380/NOT-FOR-THE-FAINT-HEARTED-PAMPHLET-1.pdf.

Bridges, Tristan (2013) 'A very "gay" straight? Hybrid masculinities, sexual aesthetics, and the changing relationship between masculinity and homophobia', *Gender & Society* 28(1): 58–82.

Bridges, Tristan, and C. J. Pascoe (2014) 'Hybrid masculinities: new directions in the sociology of men and masculinities', *Sociology Compass* 8(3): 246–58.

Brittan, Arthur (1989) *Masculinity and Power*. Oxford: Blackwell.

Bröckling, Ulrich (2015) *The Entrepreneurial Self*. London: Sage.

Brown, Wendy (2005) 'Neoliberalism and the end of liberal democracy', in Brown, *Edgework: Critical Essays on Knowledge and Politics*. Princeton, NJ: Princeton University Press, pp. 37–59.

—— (2015) *Undoing the Demos: Neoliberalism's Stealth Revolution*. London: Zone Books.

Brown-Bowers, Amy, Maria Gurevich, Alexander T. Vasilovsky, Stephanie Cosma and Sarde Matti (2015) 'Managed not missing: young women's discourses of sexual desire within a postfeminist heterosexual marketplace', *Psychology of Women Quarterly* 39(3): 320–36.

Buchbinder, David (1998) *Performance Anxieties: Re-producing Masculinity*. St Leonards, NSW: Allen & Unwin.

Burkett, Melissa, and Karine Hamilton (2012) 'Postfeminist sexual agency: young women's negotiations of sexual consent', *Sexualities* 15(7): 815–33.

Buss, David M. ([1994] 2003) *The Evolution of Desire: Strategies of Human Mating*. New York: Basic Books.

Buss, David Michael, and David P. Schmitt (2011) 'Evolutionary psychology and feminism', *Sex Roles* 64(9–10): 768–87.

Butler, Jess (2013) 'For white girls only? Postfeminism and the politics of inclusion', *Feminist Formations* 25(1): 35–58.

Butler, Judith ([1990] 2011) *Gender Trouble: Feminism and the Subversion of Identity*. Abingdon: Routledge.

Calder-Dawe, Octavia, and Nicola Gavey (2016) 'Jekyll and Hyde revisited: young people's constructions of feminism, feminists and the practice of "reasonable feminism"', *Feminism & Psychology* 26(4): 487–507.

Cameron, Deborah (2009) 'Sex/gender, language and the new biologism', *Applied Linguistics* 31(2): 173–92.

—— (2015) 'Evolution, language and the battle of the sexes', *Australian Feminist Studies* 30(86): 351–8.

Cendrowski, Mark (2007–) *The Big Bang Theory*. Warner Brothers Television [TV series].

Charles, Caroline (2015) 'Petition: Amazon – stop selling Roosh V (Daryush Valizadeh) rape books', www.change.org/p/amazon-com-amazon-stop-selling-rooshv-daryush-valizadeh-rape-books?just_created=true.

Chung, Donna (2005) 'Violence, control, romance and gender equality: young women and heterosexual relationships', *Women's Studies International Forum* 28(6): 445–55.

Coleman, Rebecca (2010) 'Dieting temporalities: interaction, agency and the measure of online weight watching', *Time & Society* 19(2): 265–85.

Connell, R. W. (2000) *The Men and the Boys*. Berkeley: University of California Press.

Connell, Raewyn (2002) *Gender*. Cambridge: Polity.

Connell, Raewyn, and James W. Messerschmidt (2005) 'Hegemonic masculinity: rethinking the concept', *Gender & Society* 19(6): 829–59.

Connell, Raewyn, and Julian Wood (2005) 'Globalization and business masculinities', *Men and Masculinities* 7(4): 347–64.

Cornwall, Andrea, and Nancy Lindisfarne (1994) 'Dislocating masculinity: gender, power and anthropology', in *Dislocating Masculinity: Comparative Ethnographies*, ed. Cornwall and Lindisfarne. London: Routledge, pp. 11–47.

Cornwall, Andrea, Frank G. Karioris and Nancy Lindisfarne (2016) *Masculinities under Neoliberalism*. London: Zed Books.

Couldry, Nick, and Jo Littler (2008) 'The work of work: reality TV and the negotiation of neoliberal labour in *The Apprentice*', in *Rethinking Documentary: New Perspectives and Practices*, ed. Thomas Austin and Wilma de Jong. Maidenhead: Open University Press, pp. 258–67.

Dabiri, Emma (2013) 'Who stole all the black women from Britain?' *Media Diversified*, 5 November, https://mediadiversified.org/2013/11/05/who-stole-all-the-black-women-from-britain/.

Davis, Alexander K., Laura E. Rogers and Bethany Bryson (2014) 'Own it! Constructions of masculinity and heterosexuality on reality makeover television', *Cultural Sociology* 8(3): 258–74.

Daygame (2015) 'Frequently asked questions', www.daygame.com/faq/.

——— (2016) 'Learn how to get a stunning girlfriend', www.daygame.com/home/.

de Beauvoir, Simone ([1949] 1997) *The Second Sex*, trans. H. M. Parshley. London: Vintage.

de Boise, Sam (2017) 'The personal is political … just not always progressive: affective interruptions and their promise for CSMM', *Norma: International Journal for Maculinity Studies*, 12 May: 1–17.

de Boise, Sam, and Jeff Hearn (2017) 'Are men getting more emotional? Critical sociological perspectives on men, masculinities and emotions', *Sociological Review* 65(4): 779–96.

Dempster, Steve (2011) 'I drink, therefore I'm man: gender discourses, alcohol and the construction of British undergraduate masculinities', *Gender and Education* 23(5): 635–53.

Denes, Amanda (2011) 'Biology as consent: problematizing the scientific approach to seducing women's bodies', *Women's Studies International Forum* 34(5): 411–19.

Donaghue, Ngaire (2015) 'The "facts" of life?', *Australian Feminist Studies* 30(86): 359–65.

Dosekun, Simidele (2015) 'For Western girls only? Post-feminism as transnational culture', *Feminist Media Studies* 15(6): 960–75.

Downing, Lisa (2013) 'Safewording! Kinkphobia and gender normativity in *Fifty Shades of Grey*', *Psychology and Sexuality* 4(1): 92–102.

du Gay, Paul (1991) 'Enterprise culture and the ideology of excellence', *New Formations* no. 13: 45–61.

Duffy, Brooke Erin (2015) 'The romance of work: gender and aspirational labour in the digital culture industries', *International Journal of Cultural Studies* 9(4): 441–57.

Duncombe, Jean, and Dennis Marsden (1993) 'Love and intimacy: the gender division of emotion and "emotion work"', *Sociology* 27(2): 221–41.

Eck, Beth A. (2014) 'Compromising positions: unmarried men, heterosexuality, and two-phase masculinity', *Men and Masculinities* 17(2): 147–72.

Edley, Nigel, and Margaret Wetherell (2001) 'Jekyll and Hyde: men's constructions of feminism and feminists', *Feminism & Psychology* 11(4): 439–57.

Edwards, Tim (2011) *Fashion in Focus: Concepts, Practices and Politics*. Abingdon: Routledge.

Elias, Ana Sofia, Rosalind Gill and Christina Scharff (2016) *Aesthetic Labour: Rethinking Beauty Politics in Neoliberalism*. Basingstoke: Palgrave.

Eng, David (2001) *Racial Castration: Managing Masculinity in Asian America*. Durham, NC: Duke University Press.

Evans, Adrienne, Sarah Riley and Avi Shankar (2010) 'Technologies of sexiness: theorizing women's engagement in the sexualization of culture', *Feminism & Psychology* 20(1): 114–31.

Ezzell, Matthew (2013) 'Getting the story right: a response to "the feminist ethnographer's dilemma"', *Journal of Contemporary Ethnography* 42(4): 439–50.

Fahs, Breanne (2011) *Performing Sex: The Making and Unmaking of Women's Erotic Lives*. Albany: State University of New York Press.

Faludi, Susan (1999) *Stiffed: The Betrayal of the American Man*. New York: Putnam.

Fanon, Frantz (1986) *Black Skin, White Masks*, trans. Charles Lam Markmann. London: Pluto Press.

Farrar, John (2007) *The Rules of Seduction*. Channel 4 [TV documentary].

Farris, Sara, and Catherine Rottenberg (2017) 'Introduction: righting feminism', *New Formations* no. 91: 5–15.

Farvid, Panteá, and Virginia Braun (2013a) 'Casual sex as "not a natural act" and other regimes of truth about heterosexuality', *Feminism & Psychology* 23(3): 359–78.

—— (2013b) 'The "sassy woman" and the "performing man": heterosexual casual sex advice and the (re)constitution of gendered subjectivities', *Feminist Media Studies* 14(1): 118–34.

Fein, Ellen, and Sherrie Schneider (1995) *The Rules: Time-Tested Secrets for Capturing the Heart of Mr Right*. New York: Warner Books.

Ficarra, Glenn, and John Requa (2011) *Crazy, Stupid, Love*. Warner Brothers [film].

Fincher, David (1999) *Fight Club*. 20th Century Fox [film].

Fisher, Andy (2005) *Jimmy Kimmel Live!* Buena Vista Television [TV series].

Fisher, Mark (2009) *Capitalist Realism: Is There No Alternative?* London: Zero Books.

Flood, Michael (2008) 'Men, sex, and homosociality: how bonds between men shape their sexual relations with women', *Men and Masculinities* 10(3): 339–59.

—— (2013) 'Male and female sluts', *Australian Feminist Studies* 28(75): 95–107.

Forrester, Katrina (2017) 'Libidinal politics', *Harper's*, February, https://harpers.org/archive/2017/02/trump-a-resisters-guide/5/.

Foucault, Michel (1972) *The Archaeology of Knowledge*. London: Tavistock.

—— ([1980] 1984) 'Truth and power', in *The Foucault Reader*, ed. Paul Rabinow. New York: Pantheon, pp. 51–75.

—— ([1985] 1990) *The History of Sexuality*, Vol. 2: *The Use of Pleasure*, trans. Robert Hurley. New York: Vintage.

Frank, Katherine (1998) 'The production of identity and the negotiation of intimacy in a "gentleman's club"', *Sexualities* 1(2): 175–201.

—— (2003) '"Just trying to relax": masculinity, masculinizing practices, and strip club regulars', *Journal of Sex Research* 40(1): 61–75.

Frankel, David (2003) 'Pick-a-little, talk-a-little', in *Sex and the City*. Warner Brothers Television [TV series].

Fraser, Nancy (2009) 'Feminism, capitalism and the cunning of history', *New Left Review* 56: 97–117.

Freeman, Hadley (2014) 'Women, beware this PUA army of sleazebags, saddos and weirdos', *The Guardian*, 12 November, www.theguardian.com/commentisfree/2014/nov/12/pua-pick-up-artists-julien-blanc-dapper-laughs.

Frosh, Stephen, Ann Phoenix and Rob Pattman (2001) *Young Masculinities: Understanding Boys in Contemporary Society*. Basingstoke: Palgrave.

Fryman, Pamela (2005–14) *How I Met Your Mother*. 20th Century Fox Television [TV series].

Futrelle, David (2017) *We Hunted the Mammoth: The New Misogyny, Tracked and Mocked*, http://wehuntedthemammoth.com/author/manboobz/.

Gailey, Jeannine A., and Ariane Prohaska (2011) 'Power and gender negotiations during interviews with men about sex and sexually degrading practices', *Qualitative Research* 11(4): 365–80.

García-Favaro, Laura, and Rosalind Gill (2015) '"Emasculation nation has arrived": sexism rearticulated in online responses to lose the lads' mags campaign', *Feminist Media Studies* 16(3): 379–97.

Gardiner, Judith Kegan (2002) *Masculinity Studies and Feminist Theory: New Directions*. New York: Columbia University Press.

Gavey, Nicola (1992) 'Technologies and effects of heterosexual coercion', *Feminism & Psychology* 2(3): 325–51.

—— (2005) *Just Sex? The Cultural Scaffolding of Rape*. New York: Routledge.

—— (2011) 'Feminist poststructuralism and discourse analysis revisited', *Psychology of Women Quarterly* 35(1): 183–8.

Gavey, Nicola, Kathryn McPhillips and Virginia Braun (1999) 'Interruptus coitus: heterosexuals accounting for intercourse', *Sexualities* 2(1): 35–68.

Gebrial, Dalia (2017) 'Decolonising desire: the politics of love', *Verso*, 13 February, www.versobooks.com/blogs/3094-decolonising-desire-the-politics-of-love.

Gibson, Megan (2014) 'Is this the most hated man in the world?', *Time*, 12 November, http://time.com/3578387/julien-blanc-feminism-real-social-dynamics/.

Giddens, Anthony (1992) *The Transformation of Intimacy: Sexuality, Love and Eroticism in Modern Societies*. Cambridge: Polity.

Gilbert, Jeremy (2013) 'What kind of thing is "neoliberalism"?', *New Formations* no. 80–81: 7–22.

Gill, Rosalind (2003) 'Power and the production of subjects: a genealogy of the new man and the new lad', *Sociological Review* 51(1): 34–56.

—— (2007a) 'Critical respect: the difficulties and dilemmas of agency and "choice" for feminism: a reply to Duits and van Zoonen', *European Journal of Women's Studies* 14(1): 69–80.

—— (2007b) *Gender and the Media*. Cambridge: Polity.

—— (2007c) 'Postfeminist media culture: elements of a sensibility', *European Journal of Cultural Studies* 10(2): 147–66.

—— (2008a) 'Culture and subjectivity in neoliberal and postfeminist times', *Subjectivity* 25(1): 432–45.

—— (2008b) 'Empowerment/sexism: figuring female sexual agency in contemporary advertising', *Feminism & Psychology* 18(1): 35–60.

—— (2009) 'Mediated intimacy and postfeminism: a discourse analytic examination of sex and relationships advice in a women's magazine', *Discourse & Communication* 3(4): 345–69.

—— (2014) 'Powerful women, vulnerable men and postfeminist masculinity in men's popular fiction', *Gender and Language* 8(2): 185–204.

Gilmore, James H., and Joseph B. Pine (1997) 'The four faces of mass customization', *Harvard Business Review*, January–February, https://hbr.org/1997/01/the-four-faces-of-mass-customization.

Gilroy, Paul (2013) '"... We got to get over before we go under ...": fragments for a history of black vernacular neoliberalism', *New Formations* no. 80–81: 23–38.

Ging, Debbie (2017) 'Alphas, betas, and incels: theorizing the masculinities of the manosphere', *Men and Masculinities*, 10 May, online first.

Graeber, David (2014) 'What's the point if we can't have fun?', *The Baffler* no. 24, https://thebaffler.com/salvos/whats-the-point-if-we-cant-have-fun.

Gray, John (1992) *Men are from Mars, Women are from Venus*. London: HarperCollins.

Greene, Robert ([2001] 2003) *The Art of Seduction*. Concise edn, London: Profile Books.

Gregg, Melissa (2011) *Work's Intimacy*. Cambridge: Polity.

—— (2013) 'Spousebusting: intimacy, adultery and surveillance technology', *Surveillance & Society* 11(3): 301–10.

Greif, Mark (2015) *Against Everything*. London: Verso.

Grenz, Sabine (2005) 'Intersections of sex and power in research on prostitution: a female researcher interviewing male heterosexual clients', *Signs* 30(4): 2091–113.

Griffin, Christine (1991) 'The researcher talks back: dealing with power relations in studies of young people's entry into the job market', in *Experiencing Fieldwork: An Inside View of Qualitative Research*, ed. William B. Shaffir and Robert Adam Stebbins. London: Sage, pp. 109–19.

Griffin, Penny (2013) 'Gendering global finance: crisis, masculinity, and responsibility', *Men and Masculinities* 16(1): 9–34.

Gwynne, Joel, and Nadine Muller (2013) *Postfeminism and Contemporary Hollywood Cinema*. Basingstoke: Palgrave Macmillan.

Halberstam, Jack (1998) *Female Masculinity*. Durham, NC: Duke University Press.

Hall, Jeffrey A., and Melanie Canterberry (2011) 'Sexism and assertive court-ship strategies', *Sex Roles* 65(11–12): 840–53.

Hall, Matthew, and Jeff Hearn (2017) *Revenge Pornography: Gender, Sexualities and Motivations*. Abingdon: Routledge.

Hall, Stuart (2011) 'The neo-liberal revolution', *Cultural Studies* 25(6): 705–28.

Hamad, Hannah (2014) *Postfeminism and Paternity in Contemporary US Film: Framing Fatherhood*. Abingdon: Routledge.

Haraway, Donna (1988) 'Situated knowledges: the science question in feminism and the privilege of partial perspective', *Feminist Studies* 14(3): 575–99.

―― (1997) *Modest_Witness@Second_Millenium. FemaleMan©_Meets_OncoMouse* TM: *Feminism and Technoscience*. London: Routledge.

Harvey, David (2005) *A Brief History of Neoliberalism*. London: Verso.

Hawkes, Gail (1996) *A Sociology of Sex and Sexuality*. Buckingham: Open University Press.

Heaphy, Brian (2007) *Late Modernity and Social Change: Reconstructing Social and Personal Life*. Abingdon: Routledge.

Hearn, Alison (2008) '"Meat, mask, burden": probing the contours of the branded "self"', *Journal of Consumer Culture* 8(2): 197–217.

―― (2014) 'Producing "reality": branded content, branded selves, precarious futures', in *A Companion to Reality Television*, ed. Laurie Oultlette. Oxford: Wiley Blackwell.

Heckert, Jamie, and Richard Cleminson (2011) *Anarchism and Sexuality: Ethics, Relationships and Power*. Abingdon: Routledge.

Hendriks, Eric C. (2012) 'Ascetic hedonism: self and sexual conquest in the seduction community', *Cultural Analysis* 11: 1–16.

Hesford, Victoria (2005) 'Feminism and its ghosts: the spectre of the feminist-as-lesbian', *Feminist Theory* 6(3): 227–50.

Hlavka, Heather R. (2014) 'Normalizing sexual violence: young women account for harassment and abuse', *Gender & Society* 28(3): 337–58.

Hochschild, Arlie Russell (1979) 'Emotion work, feeling rules, and social struc-tures', *American Journal of Sociology* 85(3): 551–75.

―― (1983) *The Managed Heart: Commercialization of Human Feeling*. Berkeley: University of California Press.

―― (2012) *The Outsourced Self: Intimate Life in Market Times*. New York: Metropolitan Books.

Hoefinger, Heidi (2011) 'Professional girlfriends', *Cultural Studies* 25(2): 244–66.

Holland, Janet, Caroline Ramazanoglu and Sue Sharpe (2004) *The Male in the Head: Young People, Heterosexuality and Power*. London: Tufnell Press.

Hollway, Wendy (1984) 'Women's power in heterosexual sex', *Women's Studies International Forum* 7(1): 63–68.

hooks, bell (1992) *Black Looks: Race and Representation*. Boston: South End Press.

Howe, Adrian (2012) 'Book review: *The Aftermath of Feminism: Gender, Culture and Social Change*', *Theoretical Criminology* 16(1): 109–13.

Illouz, Eva (2012) *Why Love Hurts: A Sociological Explanation*. Cambridge: Polity.

—— (2013) *Cold Intimacies: The Making of Emotional Capitalism*. Cambridge: Polity.

—— (2014) *Hard-Core Romance: Fifty Shades of Grey, Best-Sellers, and Society*. Chicago: University of Chicago Press.

Jackson, Stevi (1996) 'The social construction of female sexuality', in *Feminism and Sexuality: A Reader*, ed. Stevi Jackson and Sue Scott. Edinburgh: Edinburgh University Press, pp. 62–73.

Jackson, Stevi, and Sue Scott (1997) 'Gut reactions to matters of the heart: reflections on rationality, irrationality and sexuality', *Sociological Review* 45(4): 552–75.

James, E. L. (2012) *Fifty Shades of Grey*. London: Arrow Books.

Jamieson, Lynn (1999) 'Intimacy transformed? A critical look at the "pure relationship"', *Sociology* 33(3): 477–94.

Jane, Emma A. (2012) '"Your a ugly, whorish, slut": understanding e-bile', *Feminist Media Studies* 14(4): 531–46.

Jeffreys, Sheila (2005) *Beauty and Misogyny: Harmful Cultural Practices in the West*. London: Routledge.

Jensen, Tracey, and Imogen Tyler (2012) 'Austerity parenting: new economies of parent-citizenship', *Studies in the Maternal* 4(2).

Kalra, Virinder S. (2009) 'Between emasculation and hypermasculinity: theorizing British South Asian masculinities', *South Asian Popular Culture* 7(2): 113–25.

Karioris, Frank G. (2014) 'Towards an intersectional approach to patriarchy: male homosociality in an American context', *IDS Bulletin* 45(1): 104–10.

Kelan, Elisabeth K. (2009) 'Gender fatigue: the ideological dilemma of gender neutrality and discrimination in organizations', *Canadian Journal of Administrative Sciences* 26: 197–210.

Keller, Jessalynn, Kaitlynn Mendes and Jessica Ringrose (2016) 'Speaking unspeakable things: documenting digital feminist responses to rape culture', *Journal of Gender Studies*, July, online first.

Kelly, Liz, Sheila Burton and Linda Regan (1994) 'Researching women or studying women's oppression?', in *Researching Women's Lives from a Feminist Perspective*, ed. Mary Maynard and June Purvis. Abingdon: Taylor & Francis.

Kenny (2012) 'Greatest PUA fights of all time', https://kennyspuathoughts.com/2012/07/28/greatest-pua-beefs-of-all-timebetween-instructors/.

Kimmel, Michael (2005) *The Gender of Desire: Essays on Male Sexuality*. Albany: State University of New York Press.

—— (2013) *Angry White Men*. New York: Nation Books.

Kitzinger, Celia (1994) 'Experiential authority and heterosexuality', in *Changing*

Our Lives: Doing Women's Studies, ed. Gabriele Griffin. London: Pluto Press, pp. 135–44.

Koffman, Ofra, and Rosalind Gill (2013) '"The revolution will be led by a 12-year-old girl": girl power and global biopolitics', *Feminist Review* 105(1): 83–102.

Krauser, Nick (2014a) 'Players outrank scientists in the art of seduction', *Krauser PUA*, 21 October, https://krauserpua.com/2014/10/21/players-outrank-scientists-in-the-art-of-seduction/.

—— (2014b) 'Tom Torero fakes an infield kiss close', *Krauser PUA*, 12 December, https://krauserpua.com/2014/12/12/tom-torero-fakes-an-infield-kiss-close./

—— (2015) 'Belgrade diaries 2015 – part two', *Krauser PUA*, 27 July, https://krauserpua.com/2015/07/27/belgrade-diaries-2015-part-two/.

—— (2017) *A Deplorable Cad*. Raleigh, NC: Lulu [self-published].

Kwapis, Ken (2009) *He's Just Not That into You*. New Line Cinema [film].

La Ruina, Richard (2007) *The Natural Art of Seduction: Secrets of Success with Women*. London: Pennant Books.

—— (2013) *The Natural: How to Effortlessly Attract the Women You Want*. Croydon: Vermilion.

—— (2014) *Night Game Masterclass Part 1: Body Language, Non-verbal Opening, & Dance Floor Game*, YouTube, www.youtube.com/watch?v=9mVFtDiMyLY.

Lair, Daniel J. (2011) 'Surviving the corporate jungle: *The Apprentice* as equipment for living in the contemporary work world', *Western Journal of Communication* 75(1): 75–94.

Lamont, Ellen (2014) 'The limited construction of an egalitarian masculinity: college-educated men's dating and relationship narratives', *Men and Masculinities* 18(3): 271–92.

Lee, Deborah (1997) 'Interviewing men: vulnerabilities and dilemmas', *Women's Studies International Forum* 20(4): 553–64.

Leong, Nancy (2013) 'Racial capitalism', *Harvard Law Review* 126(8): 2151–226.

Littler, Jo (2013) 'Meritocracy as plutocracy: the marketising of "equality" under neoliberalism', *New Formations* no. 80–81: 52–72.

Lorde, Audre (1984) 'Uses of the erotic: the erotic as power', in Lorde, *Sister Outsider*. Freedom, CA: Crossing Press, pp. 53–9.

Mac an Ghaill, Máirtín (2000) 'Rethinking (male) gendered sexualities: what about the British heteros?', *Journal of Men's Studies* 8(2): 195–212.

McCaughey, Martha (2008) *The Caveman Mystique: Pop-Darwinism and the Debates over Sex, Violence, and Science*. New York: Routledge.

McClelland, Sara I. (2014) 'Intimate justice', in *Encyclopedia of Critical Psychology*, ed. T. Teo. London: Springer Reference, pp. 1010–13.

McDowell, Linda (2014) 'The sexual contract, youth, masculinity and the uncertain promise of waged work in austerity Britain', *Australian Feminist Studies* 29(79): 31–49.

McGraw, Phil (2008) 'Male egos: out of control', in *Dr Phil*. King World Productions [TV talk show].

McKinnon, Susan (2005) *Neo-Liberal Genetics: The Myths and Moral Tales of Evolutionary Psychology*. Chicago: Prickly Paradigm Press.

McMahon, Anthony (1999) *Taking Care of Men: Sexual Politics in the Public Mind*. Cambridge: Cambridge University Press.

McNair, Brian (1996) *Mediated Sex: Pornography and Postmodern Culture*. London: Arnold.

McNay, Lois (2009) 'Self as enterprise: dilemmas of control and resistance in Foucault's *The Birth of Biopolitics*', *Theory, Culture & Society* 26(6): 55–77.

Macpherson, Linda (2009) 'The UK photographer's rights guide', www.sirimo.co.uk/wp-content/uploads/2009/05/ukphotographersrights-v2.pdf.

McRobbie, Angela (2009) *The Aftermath of Feminism: Gender, Culture and Social Change*. London: Sage.

—— (2015) 'Notes on the perfect', *Australian Feminist Studies* 30(83): 3–20.

Maddison, Stephen (2013) 'Beyond the entrepreneurial voyeur? Sex, porn and cultural politics', *New Formations* no. 80–81: 102–18.

Mahmood, Saba (2005) *Politics of Piety: The Islamic Revival and the Feminist Subject*. Princeton, NJ: Princeton University Press.

Mantilla, Karla (2015) *Gendertrolling: How Misogyny Went Viral*. Santa Barbara, CA: Praeger.

Mellström, Ulf (2017) 'A restoration of classic patriarchy?', *Norma* 12(1): 1–4.

Messerschmidt, James W. (2012) 'Engendering gendered knowledge: assessing the academic appropriation of hegemonic masculinity', *Men and Masculinities* 15(1): 56–76.

Mills, Charles W. (1997) *The Racial Contract*. Ithaca, NY: Cornell University Press.

—— (2007) 'White ignorance', in *Race and Epistemologies of Ignorance*, ed. Shannon Sullivan and Nancy Tuana. Albany: State University of New York Press, pp. 13–38.

Mooney-Somers, Julie, and Jane M. Ussher (2010) 'Sex as commodity: single and partnered men's subjectification as heterosexual men', *Men and Masculinities* 12(3): 353–73.

Moore, Andy, and Yad Barre (2016) 'Daygame blueprint', http://daygame-blueprint.com/product/daygame-blueprint.

Mortimer, David (2000) *Louis Theroux's Weird Weekends*, Series 3, BBC 3 [TV documentary series].

Mystery [von Markovik, Erik] (2007) *The Mystery Method: How to Get Beautiful Women into Bed*. New York: St Martin's Press.

Negra, Diane, and Yvonne Tasker (2013) 'Neoliberal frames and genres of inequality: recession-era chick flicks and male-centred corporate melodrama', *European Journal of Cultural Studies* 16(3): 344–61.

—— (2014) *Gendering the Recession: Media and Culture in an Age of Austerity*. Durham, NC: Duke University Press.

North, Anna (2012) 'Do Pickup Artist Techniques Lead To Sexual Assault?', *Buzzfeed*, 30 July, www.buzzfeed.com/annanorth/do-pickup-artist-techniques-lead-to-sexual-assault?utm_term=.afqDLNJ2Y#.qp35rWBnM.

O'Connell Davidson, Julia (1995) 'British sex tourists in Thailand', in *(Hetero) sexual Politics*, ed. Mary Maynard and June Purvis. London: Taylor & Francis.

Oesch, Nathan, and Igor Miklousic (2012) 'The dating mind: evolutionary psychology and the emerging science of human courtship', *Evolutionary Psychology* 10(5): 899–909.

O'Malley, Harris (2014) 'Can you be an ethical pickup artist?', *The Good Men Project*, 17 August, https://goodmenproject.com/featured-content/ask-dr-nerdlove-can-ethical-pickup-artist-hesaid/.

O'Neill, Rachel (2015) 'Whither critical masculinity studies? Notes on inclusive masculinity theory, postfeminism, and sexual politics', *Men and Masculinities* 18(1): 100–20.

—— (2016a) 'Reply to Borkowska', *Men and Masculinities* 19(5): 550–4.

—— (2016b) 'The aesthetics of sexual discontent: notes from the London "seduction community", in *Aesthetic Labour: Beauty Politics in Neoliberalism*, ed. Ana Sofia Elias, Rosalind Gill and Christina Scharff. London: Palgrave Macmillan, pp. 333–49.

ONS (2016) *Annual Survey of Hours and Earnings: 2016 Provisional Results*. London: Office for National Statistics.

Pascoe, C. J. (2007) *Dude, You're a Fag: Masculinity and Sexuality in High School*. Berkeley: University of California Press.

Pateman, Carole (1988) *The Sexual Contract*. Cambridge: Polity.

Patton, Wendy, and Mary Mannison (1998) 'Beyond learning to endure: women's acknowledgement of coercive sexuality', *Women's Studies International Forum* 21(1): 31–40.

Penny, Laurie (2011) 'A woman's opinion is the mini-skirt of the internet', *The Independent*, 4 November.

Pereira, Maria do Mar (2012) '"Feminist theory is proper knowledge, but …": the status of feminist scholarship in the academy', *Feminist Theory* 13(3): 283–303.

Phadke, Shilpa, Sameera Khan and Shilpa Ranade (2011) *Why Loiter? Women and Risk on Mumbai Streets*. New Delhi: Penguin.

Phipps, Alison (2014) 'The dark side of the impact agenda', *Times Higher Education*, 4 December, www.timeshighereducation.com/comment/opinion/the-dark-side-of-the-impact-agenda/2017299.article.

Phipps, Alison, and Isabel Young (2014) 'Neoliberalisation and "lad cultures" in higher education', *Sociology* 49(2): 305–22.

Pine, Joseph B., and James H. Gilmore (1998) 'Welcome to the experience economy', *Harvard Business Review*, July–August, https://hbr. org/1998/07/welcome-to-the-experience-economy.

Pleasants, Robert K. (2011) 'Men learning feminism: protecting privileges through discourses of resistance', *Men and Masculinities* 14(2): 230–50.

Plummer, Ken (1995) *Telling Sexual Stories: Power, Change and Social Worlds.* London: Routledge.

Potts, Annie (1998) 'The science/fiction of sex: John Gray's Mars and Venus in the bedroom', *Sexualities* 1(2): 153–73.

Powell, Anastasia, and Nicola Henry (2017) *Sexual Violence in a Digital Age.* Basingstoke: Palgrave.

Power, Nina (2009) *One Dimensional Woman.* Winchester: Zero Books.

Presser, Lois (2005) 'Negotiating power and narrative in research: implications for feminist methodology', *Signs* 30(4): 2067–90.

PUA Training (2017a) 'Stealth attraction', www.puatraining.com/stealthat traction.

—— (2017b) 'Terms and conditions', www.puatraining.com/terms.

Ramazanoglu, Caroline, and Janet Holland (2002) *Feminist Methodology: Challenges and Choices.* London: Sage.

Redclift, Victoria (2014) 'New racisms, new racial subjects? The neo-liberal moment and the racial landscape of contemporary Britain', *Ethnic and Racial Studies* 37(4): 577–88.

Rich, Adrienne (1973) *Diving into the Wreck: Poems 1971–72.* London: W. W. Norton.

—— (1980) 'Compulsory heterosexuality and lesbian existence', *Signs* 5(4): 631–60.

—— ([1984] 1986) 'Notes toward a politics of location', in *Blood, Bread and Poetry: Selected Prose 1979–1985*, ed. Rich. London: Little, Brown, pp. 210–31.

Richardson, Diane (2010) 'Youth masculinities: compelling male heterosexuality', *British Journal of Sociology* 61(4): 737–56.

Ridley, Matt (1993) *The Red Queen: Sex and the Evolution of Human Nature.* London: Penguin.

Ringrose, Jessica, and Valerie Walkerdine (2008) 'Regulating the abject', *Feminist Media Studies* 8(3): 227–46.

Ringrose, Jessica, Laura Harvey, Rosalind Gill and Sonia Livingstone (2013) 'Teen girls, sexual double standards and "sexting": gendered value in digital image exchange', *Feminist Theory* 14(3): 305–23.

Rivers-Moore, Megan (2012) 'Almighty gringos: masculinity and value in sex tourism', *Sexualities* 15(7): 850–70.

Robinson, Sally (2011) 'Feminized men and inauthentic women: *Fight Club* and the limits of anti-consumerist critique', *Genders* no. 53, www.colorado. edu/gendersarchive1998-2013/2011/05/01/feminized-men-and-inau-thentic-women-fight-club-and-limits-anti-consumerist-critique.

Rogers, Anna (2005) 'Chaos to control: men's magazines and the mastering of intimacy', *Men and Masculinities* 8(2): 175–94.

Roosh V. ([2007] 2010) *Bang: The Most Infamous Pickup Book in the World*. United States: CreateSpace.

—— (2011) *Don't Bang Denmark: How to Sleep with Danish Women in Denmark (if You Must)*. United States: CreateSpace.

—— (2012) *Bang Ukraine: How to Sleep with Ukrainian Women in Ukraine*. United States: CreateSpace.

Rose, Daniel (2008) *The Sex God Method*. Raleigh, NC: Lulu [self-published].

Rose, Nikolas (1998) *Inventing Ourselves: Psychology, Power, and Personhood*. Cambridge: Cambridge University Press.

Roth, R. D. (2007–8) *The Pickup Artist*. Vh1 [reality TV show].

Rottenberg, Catherine (2014) 'The rise of neoliberal feminism', *Cultural Studies* 28(3): 418–37.

Rubin, Gayle (1984) 'Thinking sex: notes for a radical theory of the politics of sexuality', in *Pleasure and Danger: Exploring Female Sexuality*, ed. Carole Vance. New York: Routledge.

Rutherford, Jonathan (1992) *Men's Silences: Predicaments in Masculinity*. London: Routledge.

Salter, Michael, and Thomas Crofts (2015) 'Responding to revenge porn: challenges to legal impunity', in *New Views on Pornography: Sexuality, Politics and the Law*, ed. Lynn Comella and Shira Tarrant. Westport, CT: Praeger, pp. 233–56.

Samra, Gumrit (2017) *Attract Any Woman Anywhere*. Amazon/Lion Gent Productions [documentary film].

Scharff, Christina (2013) *Repudiating Feminism: Young Women in a Neoliberal World*. Farnham: Ashgate.

Schrock, Douglas, and Michael Schwalbe (2009) 'Men, masculinity, and manhood acts', *Annual Review of Sociology* 35: 277–95.

Schwalbe, Michael (1992) 'Male supremacy and the narrowing of the moral self', *Berkeley Journal of Sociology* 37: 29–54.

Seal, David Wyatt, and Anke A. Ehrhardt (2003) 'Masculinity and urban men: perceived scripts for courtship, romantic, and sexual interactions with women', *Culture, Health & Sexuality* 5(4): 295–319.

Segal, Lynne ([1990] 2007) *Slow Motion: Changing Masculinities, Changing Men*. London: Virago Press.

Seidler, Victor Jeleniewski (2011) 'Review symposium: Angela McRobbie: *The Aftermath of Feminism: Gender, Culture and Social Change*', *Sociology* 45(4): 705–6.

Sharp, Gwen, and Emily Kremer (2006) 'The safety dance: confronting harassment, intimidation, and violence in the field', *Sociological Methodology* 36: 317–27.

Sieg, Ellen (2007) '"What you want, or what you get?" Young women talking about the gap between desired and lived heterosexual relationships in the 21st century', *Women's Studies International Forum* 30(2): 175–86.

Skeggs, Beverley (1994) 'Situating the production of feminist ethnography', in *Researching Women's Lives from a Feminist Perspective*, ed. Mary Maynard and June Pervis. London: Taylor & Francis, pp. 72–92.

—— (1997) *Formations of Class and Gender: Becoming Respectable*. London: Sage.

Smith, Erika W. (2016) 'Judge sentences professional pickup artist to prison for gang rape, says PUA school "is about being a rapist"', *Bust*, 9 May, http://bust.com/feminism/18751-pickup-artist-rapist-prison.html.

Smith, S. E. (2012) 'Are pickup artists contributing to rape culture?', *xoJane*, 31 July, www.xojane.com/issues/are-pickup-artists-contributing-rape-culture.

Solomon, Akiba (2011) 'Wesley Yang confuses Asian masculinity with white male supremacy', *Colorlines*, 16 May, www.colorlines.com/articles/wesley-yang-confuses-asian-masculinity-white-male-supremacy.

Sonnet, Esther (1999) 'Erotic fiction by women for women: the pleasures of post-feminist heterosexuality', *Sexualities* 2(2): 167–87.

Spencer, Rachel (2016) 'The former model charging men £4,000 a week to teach them how to chat up women (and her tips on who to avoid when YOU go on Tinder', *Mail Online*, 30 September, www.dailymail.co.uk/femail/article-3814209/The-former-model-charging-men-4-000-WEEK-teach-chat-women.html.

Stacey, Judith (1988) 'Can there be a feminist ethnography?', *Women's Studies International Forum* 11(1): 21–7.

Stanley, Liz, and Sue Wise (1979) 'Feminist research, feminist consciousness and experiences of sexism', *Women's Studies International Quarterly* 2(3): 359–74.

Strauss, Neil (2005) *The Game: Penetrating the Secret Society of Pickup Artists*. Edinburgh: Canongate.

Stuart, Avelie, and Ngaire Donaghue (2011) 'Choosing to conform: the discursive complexities of choice in relation to feminine beauty practices', *Feminism & Psychology* 22(1): 98–121.

Sullivan, Shannon, and Nancy Tuana (2007) *Race and Epistemologies of Ignorance*. Albany: State University of New York Press.

Tasker, Yvonne, and Diane Negra (2007) *Interrogating Postfeminism: Gender and the Politics of Popular Culture*. Durham, NC: Duke University Press.

Tennant, Andy (2005) *Hitch*. Columbia Pictures [film].

Terry, Gareth (2012) '"I'm putting a lid on that desire": celibacy, choice and control', *Sexualities* 15(7): 871–89.

Terry, Gareth, and Virginia Braun (2009) '"When I was a bastard": constructions of maturity in men's accounts of masculinity', *Journal of Gender Studies* 18(2): 165–78.

Thorn, Clarisse (2012) *Confessions of a Pickup Artist Chaser: Long Interviews with Hideous Men*. USA: Smashwords [self-published].

Tibbett, Carl (2014) 'White Christmas', in *Black Mirror*. Endemol UK [TV series].

Toback, James (1987) *The Pick-Up Artist*. 20th Century Fox [film].

Torero, Tom (2012) *Daygame*. Raleigh, NC: Lulu [self-published].

—— (2014) *Bar-to-Bedroom: Full Date Infield!*, *YouTube*, previously at www.youtube.com/watch?v=IhWEQf76758.

—— (2017) *Stealth Seduction*. Raleigh, NC: Lulu [self-published].

Tufall, Waqas (2015) 'Rotherham, Rochdale, and the racialised threat of the "Muslim grooming gang"', *International Journal for Crime, Justice and Social Democracy* 4(3): 30–43.

Tyler, Melissa (2004) 'Managing between the sheets: lifestyle magazines and the management of sexuality in everyday life', *Sexualities* 7(1): 81–106.

Walker, Tim (2008) 'The art of the pick-up', *The Independent*, 14 September.

Ward, Jane (2015) *Not Gay: Sex between Straight White Men*. New York: New York Univerity Press.

Washko, Angela (2015) 'Banged', http://angelawashko.com/section/409417_BANGED.html.

Watt, Nicholas, and Rowena Mason (2014) 'Home Office minister calls for "pickup artist" Julien Blanc to be denied UK visa', *The Guardian*, 14 November, www.theguardian.com/politics/2014/nov/14/home-office-minister-julien-blanc-visa.

Weber, Barbara (2009) *Makeover TV: Selfhood, Citizenship and Celebrity*. Durham, NC: Duke University Press.

Weiner, Matthew (2007–15) *Mad Men*. Lionsgate Television [TV series].

Wetherell, Margaret (1998) 'Positioning and interpretative repertoires: conversation analysis and post-structuralism in dialogue', *Discourse & Society* 9(3): 387–412.

Wetherell, Margaret, and Nigel Edley (1999) 'Negotiating hegemonic masculinity: imaginary positions and psycho-discursive practices', *Feminism & Psychology* 9(3): 335–56.

Whitehead, Stephen (2002) *Men and Masculinities: Key Themes and New Directions*. Cambridge: Polity.

Wiegman, Robyn (2001) 'Object lessons: men, masculinity and the sign women', *Signs* 26(2): 355–88.

Williams, Raymond (1977) 'Structures of feeling', in Williams, *Marxism and Literature*. Oxford: Oxford University Press, pp. 128–35.

Willott, Sara (1998) 'An outsider within: a feminist doing research with men', in *Standpoints and Differences: Essays in the Practice of Feminist Psychology*, ed. Karen Henwood, Christine Griffin and Ann Phoenix. London: Sage, pp. 174–90.

Willott, Sara, and Christine Griffin (1997) '"Wham bam, am I a man?"

Unemployed men talk about masculinities', *Feminism & Psychology* 7(1): 107–28.

Winch, Alison (2012) 'The girlfriend gaze', *Soundings* no. 52: 21–32.

—— (2014) *Girlfriends and Postfeminist Sisterhood*. Basingstoke: Palgrave Macmillan.

Wolf, Naomi (1990) *The Beauty Myth*. London: Vintage.

Woolf, Nicki (2012) '"Negging": the anatomy of a dating trend', *New Statesman*, 25 May, www.newstatesman.com/blogs/voices/2012/05/negging-latest-dating-trend.

Zadrozny, Brandy (2016) 'Pickup artists preyed on drunk women, brought them home, and raped them', *Daily Beast*, 21 September, www.thedaily beast.com/pickup-artists-preyed-on-drunk-women-brought-them-home-and-raped-them.

Zheng, Tiantian (2009) *Red Lights: The Lives of Sex Workers in Postsocialist China*. Minneapolis: University of Minnesota Press.

Zurbriggen, Eileen L. (2002) 'Sexual objectification by research participants: recent experiences and strategies for coping', *Feminism & Psychology* 12(2): 261–8.

Index